BROOKINGS PAPERS ON
EDUCATION
POLICY

2004

Diane Ravitch
Editor

Sponsored by
the Brown Center on
Education Policy

BROOKINGS INSTITUTION PRESS
Washington, D.C.

Copyright © 2004
THE BROOKINGS INSTITUTION
1775 Massachusetts Avenue, N.W., Washington, DC 20036

Library of Congress Catalog Card No. 98-664027
ISSN 1096-2719
ISBN 0-8157-7369-2

BROOKINGS PAPERS ON
EDUCATION POLICY
2004

₿ THE BROOKINGS INSTITUTION

THE BROOKINGS INSTITUTION is an independent organization devoted to nonpartisan research, education, and publication in economics, government, foreign policy, and the social sciences generally. Its principal purposes are to aid in the development of sound public policies and to promote public understanding of issues of national importance.

The Institution was founded on December 8, 1927, to merge the activities of the Institute for Government Research, founded in 1916, the Institute of Economics, founded in 1922, and the Robert Brookings Graduate School of Economics and Government, founded in 1924.

The general administration of the institution is the responsibility of a Board of Trustees charged with safeguarding the independence of the staff and fostering the most favorable conditions for scientific research and publication. The immediate direction of the policies, program, and staff of the institution is vested in the president, assisted by an advisory committee of the officers and staff.

In publishing a study, the institution presents it as a competent treatment of a subject worthy of public consideration. The interpretations and conclusions in such publications are those of the author or authors and do not necessarily reflect the views of the other staff members, officers, or trustees of the Brookings Institution.

BROOKINGS PAPERS ON EDUCATION POLICY contains the edited versions of the papers and comments that were presented at the fifth annual Brookings conference on education policy, held in May 2003. The conference gives federal, state, and local policymakers an independent, nonpartisan forum to analyze policies intended to improve student performance. Each year Brookings convenes some of the best-informed analysts from various disciplines to review the current situation in education and to consider proposals for reform. This year's issue addresses the question of why school systems in the United States do not have the steady supply of well-prepared and effective teachers it needs. The conference and journal were funded by the Herman and George R. Brown Chair in Educational Studies at Brookings. Additional support from the Miriam K. Carliner Endowment for Economic Studies and from the John M. Olin Foundation is gratefully acknowledged.

The papers in this volume have been modified to reflect some of the insights contributed by the discussions at the conference. In all cases the papers are the result of the authors' thinking and do not imply agreement by those attending the conference. Nor do the materials presented here necessarily represent the views of the staff members, officers, or trustees of the Brookings Institution.

Subscription Rates

Individuals $29.95
Institutions $43.95

For information on subscriptions, standing orders, and individual copies, contact Brookings Institution Press, 1775 Massachusetts Avenue, N.W., Washington, DC 20036. Call 202/797-6258 or 800/275-1447. E-mail bibooks@brookings.edu. Visit Brookings online at www.brookings.edu.

Brookings periodicals are available online through Online Computer Library Center (contact the OCLC subscriptions department at 800/848-5878, ext. 6251) and Project Muse (http://muse.jhu.edu).

Conference Participants	Ellynne Bannon, *House Education and Workforce Committee*
	Joan Baratz-Snowden, *American Federation of Teachers*
	Sheila Byrd, *American Diploma Project (ACHIEVE)*
	Kevin Carey, *The Education Trust*
	Nesa Chappelle, *National Education Association*
	Arthur Cole, *U.S. Department of Education*
	Lynda Edwards, *U.S. Department of Education*
	Emerson Elliott, *National Council for Accreditation of Teacher Education*
	Larry Feinberg, *National Assessment Governing Board*
	Karen Foreman, *George Washington University*
	Leslie Fritz, *National Education Association*
	William Galston, *University of Maryland*
	Sarah Hall, *Senate Committee on Health, Education, Labor, and Pensions*
	Janet Hansen, *Committee on Economic Development*
	Lisa Haverty, *Carnegie Learning*
	Anne Heald, *Economic Policy Institute*
	Bess Heller, Education Week
	Rick Hess, *American Enterprise Institute*
	Sharon Horn, *U.S. Department of Education*
	Ginny Hudson, *George Washington University*
	Richard Kahlenberg, *The Century Foundation*
	Andrew Kelly, *American Enterprise Institute*
	Eugenia Kemble, *American Federation of Teachers*
	Anne Lewis, *education journalist*
	Bruno Manno, *Annie E. Casey Foundation*
	Robert Maranto, *Villanova University*
	Jean Miller, *Council of Chief State School Officers*
	Patty Mitchell, *Learning First Alliance*
	Jane Oates, *Senate Committee on Health, Education, Labor, and Pensions*
	Michael Petrilli, *U.S. Department of Education*
	Anne Pfitzner, *Office of Senator Joseph Lieberman*
	David Salisbury, *The Cato Institute*
	Alvin Sanoff, *Columbia University Teachers' College*
	Fredreka Schouten, *Gannett News*
	Kelly Scott, *Senate Committee on Health, Education, Labor, and Pensions*
	Doris Sligh, *U.S. Department of Education*
	Robert Spillane, *U.S. Overseas Schools*
	Victoria Van Cleef, *The New Teacher Project*
	Kate Walsh, *National Council on Teacher Quality*
	Greg White, *American Psychological Association*
	Elizabeth Whitehorn, *U.S. Department of Education*
	Ben Wildavsky, U.S. News and World Report
	Judy Wurtzel, *Learning First Alliance*

Introduction

DIANE RAVITCH

The 2003 conference of the Brown Center on Education Policy of the Brookings Institution addressed the question of why the United States does not have the teachers it needs. While the media typically focus on a looming teacher shortage, the discussants went beyond the issue of quantity to ponder why it is that American schools always seem to be scrambling to find enough well-prepared and effective teachers. What can be done about a perennial teacher shortage for certain fields, especially mathematics and the sciences? Why are so many teachers assigned to teach subjects in which they have neither a major nor a minor? Is it more important for a future teacher to gain pedagogical knowledge or content knowledge? Why do so many urban schools have disproportionate numbers of teachers who are uncertified and inexperienced? Why are so many poor and minority children assigned to classes taught by rookie teachers? What can states and districts do to change the situation? These and many other issues related to teacher education, teacher preparation, teacher assignment, and teacher compensation were thoroughly debated by participants from a wide variety of disciplines and perspectives.

The papers and discussions in this volume examine the controversies that have been raging in policy circles for many years. As one would expect, no firm conclusions were reached by the end of the conference. Where so much dissension exists, the only meeting that might produce firm conclusions would be one in which the participants represent only a narrow range of the political spectrum. That was not the case. While the participants did not issue any ringing policy manifestos, their clear and cool analysis moves the issues closer to the formulation of good policies and worthy experiments by shedding light on important problems.

One of the distinguishing features of the annual Brown Center meetings, as compared with the usual conference on education, is the heavy represen-

1

tation of economists. This is intentional and reflects the Brookings Institution's long-standing commitment to a hard-headed, unsentimental economic analysis of policy issues. This strong element of economic analysis, I believe, has given the Brookings education conference a distinctive voice in the field of education, separating it from the run-of-the-mill forums that all too often seem to be afflicted with self-pleading and defensiveness (hardly surprising when many teacher educators are education researchers or work in the same institutions).

In their essay, Eric A. Hanushek and Steven G. Rivkin ask how the supply of high-quality teachers can be improved. Hanushek and Rivkin together have been responsible for much of the current research into the economic analysis of teacher quality. They review the state of research as it pertains to the relative value of teacher education, teacher experience, teacher testing, and teacher certification. Given the inadequacy of data now available, they conclude that value-added assessment of student achievement is likely the best measure of teacher quality. Using such data, they find that some teachers are able to bring about dramatic gains in achievement for their students. "A string of good teachers," they suggest, "can overcome the deficits of home environment ... and can push students with good preparation even further." But how does a state or district get good teachers? Most attempt to do so by tightening entry into teaching, but Hanushek and Rivkin argue that this is not the best way to identify good teachers. Nor would it be useful to raise all salaries, because both good and not-so-good teachers would benefit equally from such a move. They recommend that the best way to improve student performance is to focus relentlessly on student performance. The best quality teachers, they find, are those who succeed in improving student performance. The discussants, Richard Rothstein and Michael Podgursky, differ diametrically in their assessment of Hanushek and Rivkin's paper.

Richard M. Ingersoll reviews the causes of out-of-field teaching, a remarkably widespread phenomenon in American schools. Ingersoll, a leading researcher of this issue, has carried out numerous analyses for the U.S. Department of Education. An out-of-field teacher is someone teaching an academic subject who has neither a major nor a minor in that subject. Ingersoll finds that about a third of all high school mathematics teachers are out of field, as are about a quarter of secondary English teachers, one-fifth of secondary science teachers, and one-fifth of secondary social studies teachers. He counts education degrees such as math education, science education, and social studies education, as well as speech and communications, as if they were academic degrees. His estimates would be far higher for out-of-field teaching if education degrees were excluded. When he looks at a specific academic field, such as physics or history, more than half of those teaching the subject are without either a major or minor in the subject. Ingersoll attributes the extent of this problem not to poorly prepared teachers, but to administrative practices related to hiring and assigning by principals. Caroline M. Hoxby and Adam F. Scrupski are the discussants for this paper.

The schools of education have long been a punching bag for critics of education. David F. Labaree takes an unusual tack in responding to the critics. He says that the education schools cannot be held responsible for the faults of the education system because they are too weak to have had much influence. Labaree analyzes the goals of two different groups of progressive educators: The pedagogical progressives were led by John Dewey; the administrative progressives, by Edward Lee Thorndike. Labaree holds that the administrative progressives set the tone for American public schools over the past century. But while the administrative progressives gained control of the direction of the schools, the pedagogical progressives won the battle for the hearts and minds of education faculty. Thus the paradox described by Labaree. E. D. Hirsch and Barbara Beatty come to distinctly different conclusions about Labaree's central argument.

Sandra Stotsky (with Lisa Haverty) describes the dramatic overhaul of state-mandated requirements for teachers in Massachusetts. She is uniquely positioned to describe the changes because she was the official responsible for preparing and implementing them. Massachusetts embarked on a major reform of its public school system in 1993–94 with the goal of improving student achievement. The centerpiece was a new system of tests and accountability, along with a substantial increase in funding. Massachusetts also established new licensing requirements for teachers, teacher testing, bonuses for new teachers, a career ladder program, new routes into teaching, and a variety of other programs, all geared to improving the supply of well-educated teachers and increasing the knowledge of the current teaching force. Massachusetts's program is likely the most comprehensive state effort in the nation to increase the supply and quality of its teaching force. While the audience at Brookings seemed impressed by the sweeping changes in the Bay State, the response of the discussants, Margaret Raymond and John T. Wenders, ranged from dubious to scornful.

Marguerite Roza and Paul T. Hill describe the inequities within school districts that prove harmful to schools with the poorest, lowest-performing students. The authors review budgets in four school districts—Baltimore City schools, Baltimore County schools, Cincinnati public schools, and Seattle public schools. They examine the true dollar cost of personnel in specific schools, including teachers and administrators. They find significant differences in spending patterns between schools serving the poorest children and other district schools. These differences are masked, they determine, by the practice of teacher salary cost averaging. They quantify the uneven distribution of personnel and dollars across districts and show which schools are at the losing end of this equation. Their discussants are Susan Sclafani and Sheree Speakman, both of whom have extensive experience with district-level budgeting.

Kati Haycock discusses the problem of "the elephant in the living room"; that is, the maldistribution of teacher quality among schools serving children who are mainly low-income and minority and the schools serving their better-off, nonminority peers. Haycock assembles a large amount of data to show that poor kids usually are in classrooms staffed by the least experienced teachers. Their teachers are less likely to be certified, more likely to have failed a licensing exam, less likely to have an academic major in the field they teach, and less likely to have attended a high-quality undergraduate institution. All of these factors add up to a heavy burden for the most vulnerable children, Haycock concludes. She reviews a number of recent efforts to redress these inequities and adds her own suggestions. Her discussants are Hamilton Lankford and Lynn Olson.

At the Brookings conference, a panel of front-line educators discussed the obstacles facing those who wanted to enter the teaching profession in big-city districts. Vicki Bernstein, who has managed the New York City Teaching Fellows Program, explained how the district often lost promising new teachers. Michelle Rhee of the New Teacher Project added to the description of the problems—some of them self-created—that make it harder to bring willing teachers into urban schools. The respondents to their presentations were C. Emily Feistritzer and Lewis C. Solmon.

If there were a dividing line in the discussion amongst the conference participants, it would be between those who believe that the state must raise the quality of the teacher force by regulating entry into the profession and those who saw such regulation as an unnecessary bottleneck that reduces supply without increasing quality. If there were a point of agreement (though not by unanimous consent), it would be in opposition to a single salary scale based on education and experience instead of performance. A number of participants suggested that school districts should pay more to teachers who are most successful and to teachers in shortage areas. Raising salaries across the board, they said, would neither reward effectiveness nor attract a greater or better supply of people to hard-to-staff schools and hard-to-staff subject areas. However, one participant, a seasoned school superintendent, warned that merit pay was easier to describe than to implement, because of political pressures.

On one point there was no dissension. The quality of teachers in the nation's schools matters very much. For some children, the quality of their teacher is the difference between success and failure. A nation with the goal of "no child left behind" will have to find effective strategies to ensure that every child has good teachers and that every teacher has working conditions in which to do his or her job well.

How to Improve the Supply of High-Quality Teachers

ERIC A. HANUSHEK *and*
STEVEN G. RIVKIN

When considering schools, one must pay attention to teachers. After all, teachers are the largest single budget item of schools, and many believe that they are the most important determinant of school quality. Yet research does not find a systematic link between teacher characteristics and student outcomes, leading to doubts about many current policy thrusts that are keyed to measurable attributes of teachers and their background.

The relevant research follows four distinct lines that relate in varying ways to teacher quality. At the most aggregate level and possibly the most influential, a variety of studies have traced changes over time in the salaries of teachers relative to those in other occupations. Going beyond that, a second level of studies relates pay and other characteristics of teaching jobs to the characteristics of teachers in different schools and districts and teacher turnover. A third line of research, following naturally from these, relates teacher characteristics to student performance. The failure to find a strong relationship between the contributions of teachers to student achievement and other outcomes, on the one hand, and teacher education, experience, and salaries, on the other, is inconsistent with the popular view of teachers as a key determinant of the quality of education. Finally, the fourth line of research appears to have solved this conundrum by demonstrating both the large impact of teachers on student learning and the lack of explanatory power of traditional quality measures.

The central focus of this paper is to relate these various bodies of research to a set of teacher quality policy initiatives. These proposals can be divided into three broad areas that are not mutually exclusive. First, because salaries

7

of teachers have fallen relative to other jobs, some argue that an obvious move is simply to restore teacher salaries to their previous position in the earnings distribution to attract better teachers into the profession. Second, states should adopt more stringent qualifications for teachers such as mandatory master's degrees to improve quality. Salary increases are often, but by no means always, recommended along with more stringent qualifications to offset any possible negative impacts on teacher supply. Finally, an alternative set of policy proposals has taken a different tack. These typically advocate less strict instead of stricter requirements in combination with incentives for higher teacher performance and improved school personnel practices.

Research on Teacher Quality

While the evidence related to teacher quality is widely scattered, common themes do emerge. A key distinction is whether or not the investigations are related directly to student outcomes or simply rely upon a presumed relationship.

Aggregate Salary Trends

A starting point in the consideration of teacher quality is the evolution of teacher salaries over time. Figure 1 traces the wages of teachers age twenty to twenty-nine compared with those of other young college graduates between 1940 and 2000. The calculations, done separately by gender, give the proportion of nonteachers with a bachelor's degree or more who earn less than the average teacher.[1]

Over the entire time period since World War II, salaries of young female and male teachers have fallen relative to those for other occupations. However, we have shown that substantial gender differences are evident in the time path of relative salaries.[2] For males, relative salaries fell between 1940 and 1960 but have remained roughly constant afterward. For females, relative salaries started out high—above the median for college-educated females—but then continuously fell. The changes are easiest to see for young teachers and college graduates, for whom the adjustment has been larger, but they also hold for teachers of all ages. In other words, the growth in late-career salaries has not offset the decline in salaries for younger teachers.

Figure 1. Percent College Educated Earning Less Than Average Teacher, by Gender, Age Twenty to Twenty-Nine, 1940–2000

Percent

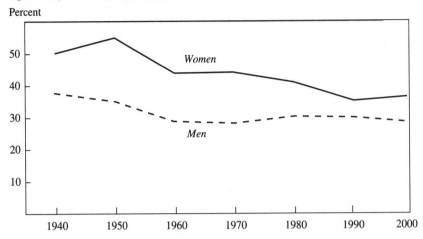

Source: Eric A. Hanushek and Steven G. Rivkin, "Understanding the Twentieth Century Growth in U. S. School Spending," *Journal of Human Resources*, vol. 32, no. 1 (1997), pp. 35–68, updated to 2000.

Others have attempted to go deeper into the structure of teacher supply responses. Frederick Flyer and Sherwin Rosen describe a more formal model of changing female opportunities and its impact on the teaching profession.[3] Darius Lakdawalla extends this to concentrate on the role of productivity changes in competing industries.[4] Technological change, expanded opportunities for women, growth in international trade, and other factors that have increased the demand for highly skilled workers have placed upward pressure on teacher salaries.

The decline in the relative earnings of teachers has likely led to a fall in average teacher quality over this period, though Dale Ballou and Michael Podgursky discuss why the shorter-term implications of a change in relative earnings are less clear-cut.[5] However, the extent of that quality decline is unclear and depends in large part on the correlation between teaching skill and the skills rewarded in the nonteacher labor market. In a simple unidimensional skill framework in which nonpecuniary factors play no role, the substantial decline in relative salary would be expected to lead to a large fall in teacher quality. However, a more complex and realistic framework in which the skill set of teachers differs from that of other professionals suggests the possibility of a more muted response to the salary changes. For example, if teaching places greater emphasis on a set of communication and interpersonal relation skills than the general labor market, the salaries relative to all college graduates may not provide a particularly good index of teacher quality.

The Supply of Teachers and Teacher Characteristics

A substantial body of research examines the effects of salary and nonpecuniary factors on the flows into and out of teaching and implicitly the supply of teachers with particular characteristics. Joseph A. Kershaw and Roland N. McKean in one of the first such studies considered how the uniform pay structure in teaching led to shortages in specific areas, such as mathematics and science, where teachers had better outside earnings opportunities.[6] This 1962 study underscored the well-recognized fact that various differences among teachers were important and that policies and institutions had differential effects on teachers with different characteristics.

This research, extended in a variety of dimensions, has a common form:

$$TC = f(P, B, WC), \tag{1}$$

where TC is a specific teacher characteristic, P is pay, B is benefits, and WC is working conditions.

This general form has been considered in a wide variety of circumstances, including entry into teaching, mobility of teachers across schools and districts, and exit from teaching. Four general types of teacher characteristics have received considerable attention: (1) experience, (2) measured achievement or skill, (3) specialty or subject area, and (4) credentials and certification.

The analysis of experience comes in two separate lines of research. First, from consideration of teacher mobility, a general finding is that teachers with more seniority tend to make moves related to the characteristics of the students—such as race, income, or achievement.[7] These movements may be conditioned by district policies, but the underlying analyses identify how attributes of schools affect the characteristics of teachers who are attracted to them.[8] Moreover, Eric A. Hanushek, John F. Kain, and Steve G. Rivkin demonstrate that nonpecuniary factors may have a stronger influence than salaries in determining the location of teachers with differing seniority.[9] Because teachers, particular women teachers, are unresponsive to salary differences, it would take very large bonuses to neutralize the larger teacher turnout found in the most disadvantaged schools. Second, a large number of studies of exit from teaching find that salaries and outside opportunities have differing impacts on teachers depending on experience.[10] These studies also find varying responses to salaries and other conditions, including suggestions that opportunity costs are much less important than the complementarity of family considerations and school working conditions.[11]

In a different dimension, salaries and other attributes of teaching careers have been seen to influence the average skill level of teachers as measured by achievement scores. The majority of this work has considered entry into the teaching profession.[12] These studies also suggest that the stringency of requirements for teacher certification influences training and career choices.

The consideration of preparation has focused on the varying opportunity costs of teachers with different specialties. For example, following on Kershaw and McKean's analysis, Russell W. Rumberger examines how salaries affect the supply of science and math teachers.[13]

Finally, considerable attention (although limited analysis) has been devoted to the possibility that school characteristics affect the ability of schools to hire fully credentialed teachers. In general this analysis simply reports gross correlations of lower proportions of uncertified teachers in central city and lower socioeconomic status schools. Nonetheless, these casual observations almost surely do describe the reality—even if they do not fully identify the underlying impacts of individual, district, and state policy choices on the outcomes.

Two important conclusions flow from this literature. First, much of the policy discussion about teacher quality relates to these studies. They indicate how various policies and other factors influence the characteristics of teachers. Second, the importance of these findings depends crucially on the relevance of the identified characteristics for determining student performance and other outcomes; that is, the relationship with effectiveness of teaching.

Teacher Characteristics and Student Achievement

A general approach to the identification of the determinants of teacher quality is to estimate the relationship between student achievement and other outcomes, on the one hand, and specific measures of teacher quality, on the other. While important issues surround how best to conduct this analysis, this approach fits naturally into most policy discussions.

BASIC STRUCTURE. A large number of investigations of student achievement have focused on how various teacher characteristics influence outcomes. These studies take a variety of forms.

A basic framework for the study of teacher effects begins with a model of achievement such as

$$O_g = f(F^{(g)}, P^{(g)}, C^{(g)}, T^{(g)}, S^{(g)}, \alpha), \tag{2}$$

where O_g is the outcome for a student in grade g; F, P, C, T, and S represent vectors of family, peer, community, teacher, and school inputs, respectively; α is ability; and the superscript g indicates all of the inputs are cumulative from birth through grade g. Simply put, student achievement at any time represents the cumulative outcome of a wide variety of inputs.

This model, which is frequently referred to as an educational production function, has been applied often. Its history is generally traced back to the Coleman Report, an early study conducted under the auspices of the U.S. government.[14] Since 1966, more than four hundred such studies have been published in journals and books. Empirical research pursuing this type of analysis typically collects data on the relevant inputs into performance from either administrative records or surveys.

However, empirical studies clearly do not analyze this complete model, because complete school and family histories are rarely available. Instead, virtually all work considers the influence of contemporaneous school and teacher inputs and a limited number of family characteristics. This is a serious drawback, because the omission of current and historically important factors that are correlated with the contemporaneous inputs raises a number of questions about how to interpret the results. Perhaps most important is the extent to which any observed association between a school or teacher variable and a student outcome captures a causal relationship. For example, if children in higher-income families attend schools with smaller classes on average than children in lower-income families, the finding that smaller classes raise achievement may be driven in part by a failure to fully account for the direct effect of family income on student performance.

An alternative approach attempts to isolate the effects of inputs over a specified period of time. One form of such a value-added model analyzes achievement growth between grade g^* and grade g:

$$O_g - O_{g^*} = f'(F^{(g-g^*)}, P^{(g-g^*)}, C^{(g-g^*)}, T^{(g-g^*)}, S^{(g-g^*)}, \alpha). \tag{3}$$

The lagged test score O_{g*} may also be included on the right-hand side under somewhat different assumptions and estimation complications. The precise estimation approach, and the resulting interpretation of any results, depends fundamentally on a series of assumptions about the structure of achievement and the underlying data generation process.[15] Regardless of the specifics, the fundamental purpose of this approach is the identification of the effects of specific inputs during the specified grades. Generally, when the effects of teachers and schools are approximately additive, the prior achievement measure will summarize the historical inputs.

Though the use of such value-added models mitigates problems resulting from the lack of historical information, an important remaining limitation of virtually all education production function studies is the use of a small number of observed characteristics to capture school and teacher quality. While this fits into general econometric schemes, it proves to be very restrictive, because most studies use administrative or survey data that typically contain a limited number of characteristics. The most commonly available characteristics, teacher education and experience, are important variables to consider, because they almost always enter into the determination of teacher pay. Thus it is plausible to think that they should be directly related to productivity. And, because of their administrative uses, these data are frequently available for researchers. Yet they explain little of the variation in teacher effectiveness, and even more detailed information about college quality, scores on standardized examinations, or other information leaves much unexplained. Moreover, whenever separate surveys are designed to provide a richer set of characteristics, the specific items are seldom replicated in other surveys, thus providing little ability to ascertain the generalizability of any factor.

The specific estimation of such models takes many forms. A vast majority of studies investigate student achievement as measured by some form of standardized test, although the investigations cover a range of grade levels, types of schools, areas of the United States and other countries, and other outcomes including years of schooling and future earnings. It is not possible to describe all of the studies, but a summary provides clear evidence on the relationship of key teacher characteristics and achievement.

TEACHER EXPERIENCE AND EDUCATION. The most frequently studied aspects of teachers include their education and experience levels, the items that generally enter into pay determination. The simplest summary of their impact on student achievement from available analyses comes from aggre-

Table 1. Distribution of Estimated Effect of Key Teacher Resources on Student Performance

Resources	Number of estimates	Statistically significant		Statistically insignificant
		Positive	Negative	
All estimates				
Teacher education	170	9%	5%	86%
Teacher experience	206	29	5	66
High-quality estimates[a]				
Teacher education	34	0	9	91
Teacher experience	37	41	3	56

Source: Eric A. Hanushek, "Assessing the Effects of School Resources on Student Performance: An Update," *Educational Evaluation and Policy Analysis*, vol. 19, no. 2 (1997), pp. 141–64; and Eric A. Hanushek, "The Failure of Input-Based Schooling Policies," *Economic Journal*, vol. 113 (2003), pp. F64–F98.

a. High-quality estimates come from value-added estimation (equation 3), where the sample is drawn for individual students from a single state.

gating the results across studies. Table 1 describes the estimated parameters from studies through 1994 in the United States.[16]

Perhaps most remarkable is the finding that a master's degree has no systematic relationship to teacher quality as measured by student outcomes. This immediately raises a number of issues for policy, because advanced degrees invariably lead to higher teacher salaries and because advanced degrees are required for full certification in a number of states. More than half of current teachers in the United States have a master's degree or more.

Teacher experience has a more positive relationship with student achievement, but still the overall picture is not that strong. While a majority of the studies find a positive effect, only a minority of all estimates provide statistically significant results.

The interpretation of these results is, however, complicated by concerns about the underlying estimation. The major concern about the quality of the underlying studies involves estimation bias arising from missing data. Many of the studies previously tabulated look at the level of student performance and not at a value-added version. When looking at the level of achievement, the data requirements are huge—encompassing the student's entire past history as relevant to education. Virtually none of the level studies meets such a requirement, but instead virtually all concentrate only on contemporaneous measures of teachers and schools. To the extent that past school inputs are correlated with current ones, which they almost necessarily will be, one is left with biased estimates of the parameters of interest.

A second concern is neglect of state policy variations that might be correlated with the measures of teacher quality. Even though most policy is made by separate states, variations in state policies are seldom captured in the modeling. States, for example, determine the requirements to be a certified teacher, set the rules of collective bargaining on teacher contracts, and determine the financial structure including providing varying amounts of support for local schools depending upon their circumstances and tax base. States also specify the specific curriculum and outcome standards, establish testing requirements, and regulate a wide range of matters of educational process including various class-size requirements, the rules for placement into special education classes, and disciplinary procedures. Because these policies vary widely across states, omission of them from the modeling is likely to lead to substantial bias in the estimation of the impact of teacher characteristics and other school inputs. Analyses conducted within a single state—where the policy environment is constant—eliminate the largest sources of such bias.[17]

The magnitudes of these problems can be examined by concentrating on the subset of studies that use a value-added approach and information from a single state. Specifically, value-added studies largely eliminate issues of missing historical information. Further, studies drawing their data from within single states lessen any biases from omitted measures of the state policy environment. Table 1 displays the results for high-quality studies; that is, the pay parameters for just the value-added studies conducted within a single state.

The results for the high-quality set of studies underscore the ineffectiveness of further teacher education. The estimates from the thirty-four value-added estimates within individual states are evenly split between positive and negative point estimates, but none of the positive estimates is statistically significant.

The distribution of estimates for teacher experience is largely unaffected by going to the high-quality studies. If anything, the thirty-seven value-added estimates within individual states suggest more strongly that experience has an impact, although still only 41 percent of the estimates are statistically significant.

The stability of the experience estimates across different samples and estimation forms is especially interesting. David Greenberg and John McCall as well as Richard J. Murnane found that experienced teachers frequently have an option to move across districts and to choose the school within the district in which they are teaching, and they tend to take advantage of this.[18] Hanushek, Kain, and Rivkin further show that teachers switching schools or districts tend to move systematically to places where student achievement is higher.[19] This movement suggests the possibility of a simultaneous equations bias—that higher student achievement causes more experienced teachers or at least that causation runs both ways. However, the value-added models condition on the initial achievement level of students, avoiding the largest complication that schools with high-achieving students might simply be attracting experienced teachers.

The summary table aggregates the estimates of experience across all studies relying on the crude division between positive and negative effects. No consideration is given to the magnitude of estimated effects. More important, because various analyses consider different functional forms, some of the variation in results could result from different estimation approaches and from data samples that are more or less concentrated in different parts of the distribution. For example, Richard J. Murnane and Barbara R. Phillips investigate the impact of experience with spline functions and find nonlinearities, although the estimates differ sharply across data samples.[20] Steve G. Rivkin, Eric A. Hanushek, and John F. Kain also pursue a nonparametric investigation of experience and find that experience effects are concentrated in the first few years of teaching.[21] Holding constant overall teacher quality, teachers in their first and to a somewhat lesser extent their second year tend to perform significantly worse in the classroom.

An alternative interpretation of teacher experience is that it is not that teaching skills improve over time but that teacher experience is an index of selection into teaching. Because a large number of teachers exit from teaching within the first few years, those with more experience are those who remain in teaching for that period of time—and those with few years of experience are a mixture of teachers who will stay for a long time and greater proportions of those who will leave early. Rivkin, Hanushek, and Kain investigate this within their rich longitudinal data set by separating experience effects for teachers who subsequently leave from those who continue teaching.[22] They find that the dominant effect is learning to teach better in the first few years. Following the initial period, however, little additional improvement is evident at least in terms of measured achievement.

TEACHER SALARY. Instead of concentrating on the prior characteristics of teachers that enter into salary decisions, whether or not salary directly relates to student performance can be analyzed. The interpretation is nonetheless frequently muddled. The majority of analyses relate the salary

Table 2. Distribution of Estimated Effect of Teacher Salaries on Student Performance

Resources	Number of estimates	Statistically significant		Statistically insignificant
		Positive	*Negative*	
All estimates				
Teacher salary	118	20%	7%	73%
Teacher test scores	41	37	10	53
High-quality estimates[a]				
Teacher salary	17	18	0	82
Teacher test scores	9	22	11	67

Source: Eric A. Hanushek, "Assessing the Effects of School Resources on Student Performance: An Update," *Educational Evaluation and Policy Analysis*, vol. 19, no. 2 (1997), pp. 141–64; and Eric A. Hanushek, "The Failure of Input-Based Schooling Policies," *Economic Journal*, vol. 113 (2003), pp. F64–F98.

a. High-quality estimates come from value-added estimation (equation 3), where the sample is drawn for individual students from a single state.

levels of teachers to the achievement of students. Yet the salary level for any individual teacher is a composite of pay for specific characteristics (experience, education, and other attributes) and, whenever the analysis crosses individual school districts, differences in the salary schedule. In other words, it has elements of movements along the salary schedule and shifts in the entire schedule.

The econometric evidence, presented in table 2, again shows no strong indication that salaries are a good measure of teacher quality. Overall the studies show that salaries are more likely to be positively related to student achievement than negatively. Nonetheless, only a minority is statistically significant.

Many of the studies of teacher salaries are subject to quality problems—lack of historical information and missing measures of state policy. The state policy concerns are especially important because states intervene in wage determination in a variety of ways that also are likely to influence school outcomes. Table 2 also provides information on the more refined set of value-added, single-state estimates. For this very small set of estimates, most are statistically insignificant. The estimates that are significant all come from a set of studies considering just single districts, so they provide estimates only about moves along the schedule and not what might happen with shifts in the entire schedule.

The analysis of salaries as a measure of teacher quality introduces another range of issues. A variety of analyses have highlighted the possibility that nominal salaries in part reflect compensating differentials—for cost-of-living differences, for the desirability of particular schools and their working conditions, or for such other things as urban crime.[23] Most of the studies considering compensating differentials do not directly associate job-related characteristics and salaries to student outcomes, but instead stop at showing that salaries vary with such characteristics. (An exception is found in the work of Susanna Loeb and Marianne E. Page, who argue on the basis of state panel data that compensating differentials have masked the effects of salaries in many prior studies of educational outcomes.)[24] Nonetheless the main thrust is important both for the interpretation of existing studies and for the design of new analyses of the relationship between teacher quality and pay.

TEACHER TESTS. One measured characteristic—teacher scores on achievement tests—has received considerable attention, because it has more frequently been correlated with student outcomes than teacher experience and education or teacher salary. Table 2 displays the results of these studies.

Several points are important. First, while the evidence is stronger than that for other explicit teacher characteristics, it is far from overwhelming. Second, the tests employed in these various analyses differ in focus and content, so the evidence mixes together a variety of things. At the very least, it is difficult to transfer this evidence to any policy discussions that call for testing teachers—because that would require a specific kind of test that may or may not relate to the evidence. Third, even when significant, teacher tests capture just a small portion of the overall variation in teacher effectiveness.

TEACHER CERTIFICATION. The most pervasive policy action of states aimed at teacher quality is setting certification requirements. While states vary in what is required for certification, the underlying theme is an attempt to set minimum requirements in an effort to ensure that no students are subjected to bad teaching. The problem is that, though certification requirements may prevent some poorly prepared teachers from entering the profession, they may also exclude others who would be effective in the classroom. Not only may some potentially good teachers be unable to pass the examinations, but the certification requirements also may discourage others from even attempting to enter the teaching profession.[25] The nature of this trade-off depends in large part on the objectives and skills of administrators who make teacher personnel decisions.[26]

The literature provides mixed evidence on the effects of certification on teacher quality. Extensive literature has been accumulating on the importance of teacher certification and credentials, although it has proved controversial. Much of the work is based on specifications that are susceptible to substantial biases from other determinants of achievement, though a few recent papers provide more persuasive empirical specifications. Andrew J. Wayne and Peter Youngs document the limitations of most studies on certification while reviewing some of the components of certification.[27] A heated debate has taken place on the nature of certification itself.[28]

The overall weight of the evidence suggests that existing credentialing systems do not distinguish well between good and bad teachers. Because many people teach even though they do not have standard credentials, teachers with and without certification can be compared—and little evidence shows that existing hurdles provide much information about performance in the classroom.

Total Teacher Effects

An alternative approach to the examination of teacher quality concentrates on pure outcome-based measures of teacher effectiveness. The general idea is to investigate total teacher effects by looking at differences in growth rates of student achievement across teachers. A good teacher would be one who consistently obtained high learning growth from students, while a poor teacher would be one who consistently produced low learning growth. In its simplest form, we could think of separating teacher effects from other inputs as in

$$O_g - O_{g*} = f'(F^{(g-g*)}, P^{(g-g*)}, C^{(g-g*)}, T^{(g-g*)}, S^{(g-g*)}, \alpha) + t_j, \qquad (4)$$

where t_j is the influence of having teacher j [conditional upon the other inputs, $f'(\cdot)$]. This formulation places some structure on the achievement process, but it avoids the need to explicitly measure the characteristics related to good teaching.

This approach is appealing for several reasons. First, it does not require the choice of specific teacher characteristics, a choice that data limitations often constrain. Second, and related to the first, it does not require knowledge of how different characteristics might interact in producing achievement. (Most prior work on specific characteristics assumes that the different observed characteristics enter linearly and additively in determining classroom effectiveness.) Third, it gives a benchmark for the importance of variations in teacher quality against which any consideration of specific skills or types of policy interventions can be compared.

This estimation, frequently referred to as analysis of teacher value-added, is closely related to the work of William L. Sanders and Sandra P. Horn.[29] While the estimation approaches differ, the objective is the same—extracting what individual teachers add to student learning.

A variety of studies have pursued this general approach over the past three decades.[30] Careful consideration of such work reveals the difficulties that must be overcome to estimate the variation of overall teacher effects.[31] For example, teacher effects, school effects, and classroom peer effects are not separately identified if the estimates come from a single cross section of teachers. Hanushek, however, demonstrates the consistency of individual teacher effects across grades and school years, thus indicating that the estimated differences relate directly to teacher quality and not the specific mix of students and the interaction of teacher and students.[32] Rivkin, Hanushek, and Kain go even further and remove separate school and grade fixed effects and observe the consistency of teacher effects across different cohorts, thus isolating the impact of teachers.[33]

The magnitude of estimated differences in teacher quality is impressive. Hanushek shows that teachers near the top of the quality distribution can get an entire year's worth of additional learning out of their students compared with those near the bottom.[34] That is, a good teacher will get a gain of 1.5 grade level equivalents while a bad teacher will get 0.5 year for a single academic year.

A second set of estimates comes from recent work on students in Texas by Rivkin, Hanushek, and Kain.[35] The analysis follows several entire cohorts of students and permits multiple observations of different classes with a given teacher. The authors look at just the variations in performance from differences in teacher quality within a typical school because of the difficulties involved in separating differences in teacher quality from other factors that differ among schools. The variation in teacher quality is large. Moving from an average teacher to one at the 85th percentile of teacher quality (that is, moving up 1.0 standard deviation in teacher quality) implies that the teacher's students would move up more than 4 percentile rankings in the given year. This is roughly equivalent to the effects of a ten-student (roughly 50 percent) decrease in class size. (For a variety of reasons, these are lower-bound estimates of variations in teacher quality. Any variations in quality across schools would add to this. Moreover, the estimates rely on a series of conservative assumptions, which all tend to lead to understatement of the systematic teacher differences.)

Another indication of magnitude is found in Tennessee's Project STAR (Student/Teacher Achievement Ratio) results. The average difference in performance of students in small kindergartens has been the focus of all attention, but the results differed widely by classroom. In only forty out of seventy-nine schools did the kindergarten performance in the small classroom exceed that in the regular classrooms (with and without aides). The most straightforward interpretation of this heterogeneity is that variations in teacher quality are important relative to the effects of smaller classes.[36]

These estimates of teacher quality can also be related to the popular argument that family background is overwhelmingly important and that schools cannot be expected to make up for bad preparation from home. The Rivkin, Hanushek, and Kain estimates of teacher performance suggest that having five years of good teachers in a row (1.0 standard deviation above average, or at the 85th quality percentile) could overcome the average seventh-grade mathematics achievement gap between lower-income kids (those on the free or reduced-price lunch program) and those from higher-income families.[37] In other words, high-quality teachers can make up for the typical deficits seen in the preparation of kids from disadvantaged backgrounds.

These family background deficits do not seem to be disappearing, however, because the current school system does not ensure any streaks of such high-quality teachers—particularly for disadvantaged students. In fact, the typical student now is as likely to get a run of bad teachers—with the symmetric achievement losses—as a run of good teachers. A crucial question for policy is the extent to which schools use additional resources or better working conditions to attract higher-quality teachers. Given the lack of simple measures of quality, this question is difficult to answer. However, recent work focusing on a single metropolitan area and measuring teacher quality by the contribution to student learning suggests that, while a statistically significant relationship exists between a suburban district's salary and the quality of teacher hired, the magnitude is small.[38] This is consistent both with the notion that sorting teachers based on characteristics and even an interview is difficult and with the belief that school personnel practices fail to hire, develop, and retain high-quality teachers.

Policy Implications

The review of work on teacher quality provides a number of insights into current policy proposals.

First, attention to teacher quality is warranted, because it is an important determinant of student outcomes. A string of good teachers can overcome the deficits of home environment. Moreover, a string of good teachers can push students with good preparation even further.

Second, legislating "good teachers" is extraordinarily difficult, if not impossible. The currently available data provide little reason to believe that enough is known about good teachers to set appropriate training and hiring standards. The idea behind most certification requirements is to guarantee that nobody gets a terrible teacher. In other words, the general idea is that a floor on quality can be set. But doing this requires knowledge of characteristics that systematically affect performance. The prior evidence does not indicate that this can be done with any certainty.

Third, the current screens used to make judgments on teacher quality are imprecise. Credentials, degrees, and teacher test scores are not consistently or strongly correlated with teaching skill. Thus cracking down on these—such as requirements that only fully certified teachers can enter the classroom—may have little impact on student performance, even if it can be achieved.

Some supporters of the current credentialing movement would nonetheless not concede that basic point. In fact, improving the teaching force is motivation for a variety of policies to tighten up credentials; that is, to make the standards higher and more rigorous. For example, some propose ensuring that all certified teachers have a master's degree. But, because past evidence shows that many of the master's degrees currently obtained are not useful, these proposals offer no strong expectation that quality would improve. The trick for those advocating tightened certification requirements is coming up with standards that are meaningfully correlated with teaching quality, even in the absence of strong evidence.

Fourth, the currently proposed screens are likely to be costly. Most of the current proposals call for tightening up on the entry requirements of teachers. This tightening up would come from increased course requirements in undergraduate school, from new requirements for master's degrees, and from heightened test score requirements for entry into teacher training or for certification. Each of these makes entry into teaching relatively more costly than today. Other things equal, this would reduce the supply of potential teachers and exacerbate any current problems of teacher supply. Salary increases could offset any reduction in supply. The magnitude of the needed increase would depend on the responsiveness of prospective teachers to salary changes—something about which only rudimentary knowledge is now available.

Fifth, while teacher salaries have slipped relative to other opportunities for college graduates, simply raising all salaries would be expensive and inefficient. Specifically, overall increases in salaries for teachers would have their largest potential impacts on attracting a new group of people into the profession and on retaining existing teachers who would otherwise leave the profession. But as Ballou and Podgursky point out, there is no reason to believe that this will necessarily increase the quality of teachers in the short term.[39] Retaining teachers would be beneficial if high-quality teachers were the ones retained—but the existing data on teacher labor markets do not indicate that this would be the case. Recent work by Eric A. Hanushek and others finds that the average effectiveness of those who exit a large urban district is below the average of those who remain, raising doubts that reducing turnover given the current composition of entering teachers should receive high priority.[40]

Higher salaries would tend to increase the pool of potential teachers, but the impact of that on overall teacher quality depends on the ability of principals and human resource teams in districts to choose the best teachers. Existing evidence from Ballou and Podgursky, while not definitive, suggests that schools are not effective at choosing the best teachers.[41]

A central feature of the strengthened regulation and higher salary approach with few exceptions is the lack of focus on the performance of teachers in the classroom and a de-emphasis on having administrators make personnel decisions. The alternative policy approach is to focus much more on student performance while freeing up the supply of potential teachers. Instead of tightening up on the requirements to enter teaching, the idea is to loosen up on requirements and focus much more on potential and actual effectiveness in the classroom.

A variety of experiments with alternative routes to teaching do not involve traditional certification. The existing evidence on their success or failure is limited, but one careful study of the performance of the Teach for America program by Margaret E. Raymond, Stephen Fletcher, and Javier A. Luque shows generally positive results.[42]

The simple position taken here is: If one is concerned about student performance, one should gear policy to student performance. Existing evidence on schools highlights the substantial variation in teacher quality that exists today, even among teachers with similar education and experience. This variation appears to result from several factors: differences in skill and effort; inadequate personnel practices (particularly the retention process but also the hiring process) in many schools and districts; and differences in the number and quality of teachers willing to work by subject and working conditions. The final source of variation may justify substantial differences and flexibility in pay schedules, and more should be learned about the consequences of differentiated pay. However, the variation in skill and effort raises the most difficult set of issues for policymakers, because regulations—including but not limited to certification requirements—are not likely to get at the crux of the issue.

Perhaps the largest problem with the current organization of schools is that nobody's job or career is closely related to student performance. This is not to say that teachers or other school personnel are currently misbehaving. We believe that most teachers and administrators are very hard working and that the vast majority are trying to do the best they can. It is simply a statement that they are responding to the incentives that they currently face, and these incentives do not weight student achievement heavily.

Specifically, policy advice that the evidence strongly suggests is that principals and superintendents must make decisions about teachers based on the evaluation of potential and actual effectiveness in raising student performance rather than a set of prior attributes. While room for improvement in hiring certainly exists, it will always be an imperfect process. The other aspects of personnel management, including mentoring and support, tenure review, and the management of experienced teachers, leave tremendous room for improvement.[43] Such proposals are similar to those developed in more detail in the volume edited by Marci Kanstoroom and Chester E. Finn Jr.[44] They also encapsulate the current experiments being fostered in the Teacher Advancement Program of the Milken Family Foundation.[45]

Existing research demonstrates that principals do know who the better teachers are.[46] While the evidence is not as complete as one might like, the ability to identify teachers at the top and bottom of the quality distribution almost certainly goes further than this, particularly if good tests of student achievement are administered regularly. Unfortunately, little use is made of any such information in the current system, and educators have little experience with the range of possible approaches.

Some evidence has accumulated about merit pay plans, which has not suggested that merit pay as applied to schools has been effective.[47] There is reason to believe that these experiments are, however, too limited.[48] The historical experiments in merit pay have been extensive in number but limited in the magnitude and character of the incentive scheme.[49]

The measurement of teacher or administrator performance from test score data is a complicated and often opaque process, and test scores are only one out of a number of important student outcomes. Nonetheless much more needs to be learned about the effective use of test scores specifically and outcome information more generally in the evaluation of teacher and administrator performance.

One of the obvious implications is that principals and superintendents must be held accountable for the impact of their hiring, retention, and other management decisions on student achievement. Such structures are not common in education, so little is available to build upon in the actual structuring of such a notion. Moreover, making such active decisions is often difficult and uncomfortable, and the path of least resistance is to grant tenure to virtually all teachers and to refrain from intervening except in extreme cases.

A variety of institutional structures may provide appropriate incentives, and schools across the nation are experimenting with many organizational arrangements including charter schools, school report cards, merit schools, school vouchers, and public school choice. The best way to structure incentives is currently unknown, and describing and evaluating alternative incentive schemes is beyond the scope of this paper.[50] The absence of much variety in incentive systems that have been implemented implies that very little experience or evidence has accumulated. Nonetheless, the experiments now under way offer some hope for learning.

Comment by Richard Rothstein

Two important themes in Eric A. Hanushek and Steven G. Rivkin's paper deserve further examination. First, the authors argue that excellent teachers can make a huge difference in raising student achievement. If disadvantaged students could have a string of excellent teachers, these students' achievement would rise to the level of middle-class students, eliminating the test score gap. Second, they say that identifying excellent teachers for hire and retention is extraordinarily difficult. Econometric analysis has found little correlation between students' achievement and their teachers' characteristics, such as certification, teachers' test scores, their verbal ability, or their education beyond a bachelor's degree. Because using any of these imperfect characteristics as screens for teacher hiring narrows the pool of potential teachers, schools should be permitted to hire any college graduates whom administrators believe are likely to raise student achievement. And schools should retain only those teachers who do raise student achievement.

The Role of Teacher Quality in Closing the Achievement Gap

No dispute can be raised about the important impact of teachers on student achievement. But presenting the impact as this paper does ("a string of good teachers can overcome the deficits of home environment") can be misleading and dangerous from a policy perspective.

Hanushek and Rivkin base their conclusion on analyses they have performed using student test score data from Texas, showing that low-income students can get middle-class test scores if they have five consecutive years of teachers who are "at the 85th percentile of teacher quality"; that is, more effective than 85 percent of all teachers, or a standard deviation above the mean of effectiveness. This is similar to analyses by William L. Sanders, using data from Tennessee, finding that students gain 50 percentile points from having three consecutive years of teachers who are more effective than 80 percent of all teachers.[51] Sanders calls this consequence of good teaching "awesome." His work has been widely cited to support the claim that good teaching can overcome learning impediments stemming from low socioeconomic status.

Neither Hanushek and Rivkin nor Sanders claims to identify the characteristics of such good teachers other than by a circular description—good teachers can raise student achievement, and teachers are defined as good if they raise student achievement. Yet even if good teachers could be defined more usefully (I understand that Sanders is attempting to do this in Tennessee), it might do little to eliminate the socioeconomic test score gap.

Partly it is a matter of logic. Researchers have known at least since the publication of the Coleman Report in 1966 (and subsequent reanalyses of the data) that both schools and families contribute to student achievement. Most researchers conclude that families contribute considerably more than schools but that does not negate the proposition that, in theory, stronger schools could overcome negative family influences.

Yet Hanushek and Rivkin (along with many others who cite their work) employ their findings to minimize the importance of family and social factors in student achievement. For while they are correct that stronger schools could offset, at least in part, negative family influences, stronger families could also overcome weak schools. Hanushek and Rivkin show that low-income children who have five years of 85th percentile teachers can achieve at middle-class levels. Presumably, low-income children who have 50th percentile teachers but who are the beneficiaries of social policies that raise their family characteristics by a standard deviation would also achieve at middle-class levels.

(Because families have been a more important influence than schools, the achievement gain realized by a standard deviation improvement in teachers could probably also be realized by less than a standard deviation improvement in family characteristics.)

So from a logical viewpoint, improvement in either families or schools (or in a combination of both) could be levers to close the achievement gap. It is curious, therefore, that Hanushek and Rivkin, and Sanders, identify schools alone as the appropriate lever. Why do they suggest, and permit their work to be interpreted as finding, that the achievement gap is primarily a problem of faulty schools and their poor-quality teachers?

In an earlier paper, Hanushek wrote that he frames the issue in this way simply because it is more practical: "While family inputs to education are indeed extremely important, the differential impacts of schools and teachers receive more attention when viewed from a policy viewpoint. This reflects simply that the characteristics of schools are generally more easily manipulated than what goes on in the family."[52]

If this practical conclusion is warranted, then focusing attention on schools alone makes sense. But the practical conclusion is flawed, not in the least because, after so many years of failing to close the achievement gap almost exclusively with school reform, an acknowledgment should be made that characteristics of schools are harder to manipulate than they appear.

Hanushek and Rivkin's illustration of the importance of teacher quality, invoking the provision of an 85th percentile teacher to low-achieving students, is misleading. This policy—providing high-quality teachers to low-achieving students—is not readily achievable if only schools set their goals correctly and were held accountable. Unsophisticated readers will not appreciate what a huge and unattainable improvement a full standard deviation (providing students with 85th percentile teachers) represents. In no

arena can policy reasonably aim for a full standard deviation of gain. Especially in the case of schools, where, as Hanushek and Rivkin note, they
cannot identify the characteristics of good teachers (they know they are
good only because their results are good), it is inconceivable that any policy could raise teacher quality by a full standard deviation. Even if the
recommendation of eliminating hiring screens were adopted, it is hard to
imagine that school principals and district offices could become so bril-
liantly insightful in their evaluation of candidates to be able to identify and
hire only those who are as effective as the top 15 percent of the current
pool.

As in any policy area, a more reasonable goal might be to begin by trying to improve teacher quality by a tenth of a standard deviation (teachers
who are more effective than about 54 percent of all teachers) or even two-
tenths (more effective than about 58 percent). Once one accepts that
improving teacher quality substantially (but considerably less than a full
standard deviation) will not overcome the deficits of home environment,
then it follows that other policies are also needed.

The full policy implications of Hanushek and Rivkin's claim need only
be elaborated to see how fanciful are the policy possibilities that flow from
their paper. To eliminate the achievement gap by means they favor (identifying and then assigning 85th percentile—or higher—teachers to
low-income children) would also require ensuring that middle-class children
be taught by only 50th percentile—or lower—teachers. If all teachers could
be improved so that their skills are comparable to those of 85th percentile
teachers today, then presumably the achievement of middle-class children
would also rise, maintaining the gap but at a higher level. (Possibly, the gap
would narrow because excellent teachers could make more of a difference
for low-income than for middle-class children, but the gap would still per-
sist. Nobody claims that better teachers could make no difference for
middle-class children.) What kind of policy environment would be required
to permit schools to give poor children only superb teachers and middle-
class children only mediocre ones? It is hard to imagine. But a more modest
goal would be within the realm of possibility. Salary differentials might
work to entice, say, 54th or even 58th percentile teachers to schools with disadvantaged children.

Even in this case, however, the Hanushek and Rivkin policy assumes
that high-quality teachers can readily be identified. One barrier to the identification of such teachers is the enormity of data required to ensure that

teachers who appear to achieve good results are not simply the beneficiaries of sampling error. Even where multiyear standardized test data seem to exist, the amount of consistent data for teachers and students needed to reliably assess a teacher without such error is unrealistically great. (Hanushek and Rivkin derive their conclusion about teacher effects from a database covering five years.) In attempting to identify excellent teachers, Sanders must compensate for missing data for many students of some teachers. He tries to handle the problem by substituting average results for missing data. A consequence of this choice (no better choice is available) is that good teachers appear less exemplary and poor teachers appear to be better if they teach in schools with more transient student populations.[53]

An additional impediment to the identification of 85th percentile teachers, given no attention in the papers of Hanushek and Rivkin, or in the work of Sanders, is the lack of knowledge regarding whether any substantial intersubject correlation exists in teaching effectiveness. That a string of 85th percentile teachers can raise low-income children to middle-class achievement levels has been detected only in the case of math, even though these data all come from multisubject elementary school teachers. The same teachers who achieve great results in math may not also achieve them in reading. Or in social studies. Or in art, or in music, or in social skills.

An elementary school administrator seeking to hire a good teacher must seek candidates capable of delivering a balanced curriculum. Even in the unlikely event that principals had good quantitative evidence on teacher effectiveness, they would still have to determine whether a candidate who would likely be at the 85th percentile of effectiveness in math and the 55th percentile in reading was superior to a candidate who would likely be at the 70th percentile of effectiveness in both.

To date, no publications have dealt with this problem of intersubject correlations in teacher value-added, although Dale Ballou has observed that "discrepancies will . . . arise across subjects." Ballou adds that

> for reasons probably due to the home environment, more of the variation in student reading performance is independent of school quality than is the case in math performance. As a result, it is harder to detect particularly strong (or weak) performance by reading instructors than by math teachers.[54]

But in elementary schools, reading instructors and math teachers are the same people. For this reason, as well as from conversations I have had with scholars who have worked with Sanders's data, I conclude that the intersubject correlations for teaching effectiveness are likely to be small. Hanushek and Rivkin do not investigate this problem.

Was Hanushek correct when he asserted that teacher quality is "more easily manipulated than what goes on in the family"? Surely a full standard deviation improvement in family characteristics is not conceivable. But more modest goals might be reasonable and more easily achievable (or as easily achievable) as teacher quality improvement.

For example, mobility is one of the most serious impediments to higher achievement of disadvantaged children in urban areas. Even an 85th percentile teacher cannot do much for children who enroll in one school after another for relatively brief periods. Because of the need to constantly regroup classes, review material for newcomers, and take time to identify the individual learning problems of newly arrived pupils, even stable students' achievement suffers in schools characterized by high mobility.

Mobility has many causes, but one is the lack of affordable housing in urban areas where real estate values have skyrocketed relative to working-class wages. Housing policy is not something that education researchers think much about, but realistic programs to stabilize low-income housing might have a big impact on student achievement, perhaps comparable to a tenth of a standard deviation improvement in teacher quality.

Many such social policies, some of which are relatively easy to implement, belie the notion that "schools are generally more easily manipulated" than student characteristics. Health problems that are unknown in middle-class children exist in epidemic proportions in low-income communities and contribute to low achievement. Untreated dental cavities, uncorrected vision problems, lead poisoning, environmentally provoked asthma are all easily addressed by policies that are more proven than policies to improve teacher quality. But these health problems will not be addressed if researchers and policymakers continue to focus exclusively on school reform as the way to close the test score gap. School reform (and improvement in teacher quality in particular) is certainly needed, but it cannot do the job alone and may not be the most easily manipulable lever.

One advantage of directing attention to social reforms that might enhance student achievement is that the policy environment in which the gap could be narrowed in this way is more politically realistic. It is not feasible to think the gap could be abolished by assigning only superb teachers to low-income schools and only mediocre teachers to middle-class schools. If the characteristics of superb teachers could be identified, parents of children in all schools would demand them. But no such dynamic operates in social policy. If, for example, dental clinics were placed in low-income schools and student achievement then improved (because children without toothaches can concentrate more on their studies), middle-class communities would not then demand that the achievement gap be maintained by providing improved dental care to middle-class children whose care was already adequate.

Nobody would oppose improving teacher quality across the board, simply because the gap would be maintained as middle-class children also benefited from the improvement. Equity and quality improvement are separable challenges. But if closing the gap is the objective, then a focus on policies to improve family characteristics may be more productive than an exclusive focus on teachers and schools.

Identifying and Hiring Excellent Teachers

At the end of their paper, Hanushek and Rivkin note that "the measurement of teacher or administrator performance from test score data is a complicated and often opaque process, and test scores are only one out of a number of important student outcomes." Regrettably, they do not develop this point. Were they to do so, they might look on professional educators' attachment to the certification process with more sympathy.

Taking seriously the notion that "test scores are only one out of a number of important student outcomes" makes it hard to imagine the alternative to certification put forward not only by Hanushek and Rivkin but, as they note, also by Dale Ballou and Michael Podgursky and by Chester E. Finn Jr. and Marci Kanstoroom. If teachers are to be hired and then retained irrespective of certification but on the basis of their students' achievement, a satisfactory method must be devised for measuring this achievement. None now exists. Basic skills achievement in reading and math can be and is measured, but many equally important outcomes, such as good citizenship (not the same as knowledge of history facts), collaborative behavior habits (more highly valued than academic skills by most employers), good judgment (New York courts, for example, say the aim of schools should be to develop intelligent voters and jurors), self-discipline, ethical values, artistic sensibility, a love of learning, and so on, are not now measured. No techniques have been developed for measuring these outcomes, so no alternative is left but to hire teachers who have the characteristics that administrators believe are likely to generate balanced outcomes, without quantitative evidence to support this belief.

While advocates of eliminating teacher hiring screens typically acknowledge, as Hanushek and Rivkin do, that satisfactory standardized test scores in reading and math are only one of a number of important goals of schools, the implications of this point have not been developed for their recommendations for teacher hiring. One suspects, perhaps unfairly, that this is because their recommendations lend themselves only to test scores, which are easily quantifiable and observable.

If, however, teachers must continue to be hired based on their possession of characteristics deemed likely to generate a balanced set of outcomes, what is the best way to identify whether candidates possess these characteristics? Should principals or other administrators make this judgment based on interviews and college transcripts, or should they rely, in addition, on certification that ensures that the candidate has completed a training program in an accredited teacher-training institution?

Chester E. Finn Jr. has invoked an analogy that is useful for resolving this question.[55] He acknowledges that some professions, medicine in particular, hire only those who have completed professional training programs and whose skills are certified. Few people would advocate hiring college graduates without such certification as physicians, retaining them in the profession only if their patients had a satisfactory survival rate.

But journalism, Finn says, is a different matter. Prospective reporters can, if they wish, attend a professional journalism school before seeking employment. If editors consider this training useful, candidates who have invested in professional training will have enhanced their chances of being hired. But editors are not precluded from hiring candidates without such training and many reporters are hired without professional degrees. Editors retain reporters based on the quality of their production, not on their possession of prehire credentials.

Teaching, Finn says, is more of an art like journalism and less of a science like medicine. Principals should have the same freedom to hire teachers without certification and retain them based on their output, as editors have freedom to hire reporters.

Analogies can go only so far, but this is a useful one. Yet Finn errs when he places education so heavily in the tradition of journalism and so little in the tradition of medicine. In truth, teaching is somewhat like medicine and somewhat like journalism. Medicine is less a science and more of an art than

Finn acknowledges. Teaching is less scientific but still requires substantial specialized knowledge about curriculum, pedagogy, and child and adolescent development. This specialized knowledge is especially critical when good teaching is defined as the production of a balanced set of outcomes, not test scores alone. And it is even more critical when good teachers are being especially recruited to instruct low-income children who come to school less prepared to learn.

I have recently interviewed principals and superintendents around the country about their teacher hiring practices. These administrators were not chosen randomly; I selected those who have better records of minority and majority student achievement and who have reputations of being unusually insightful and effective. These were administrators who, based on student test scores and reputation, were probably more likely than others to have large numbers of teachers who were in the top quintile of teacher effectiveness. I asked the administrators what qualities they seek in prospective teachers and whether they would prefer to choose from a candidate pool that included college graduates who had not received a teacher education degree and certification.

Almost invariably the administrators insisted that they would not willingly abandon the teacher certification process. They wanted to be assured that prospective teachers had a deep knowledge of the science of teaching as well as competence in subject matter. They wanted to know that candidates had extensive student fieldwork experience, not only a full semester of internship (student teaching) but frequent classroom observations, case studies, and practice lessons that characterize the better teacher education programs. Teaching, these reputedly excellent administrators almost uniformly insisted, has become too complex to be undertaken by those whose only qualifications were enthusiasm and academic proficiency.

Consider one principal with whom I met, in a relatively high-poverty elementary school in a Seattle suburb near the headquarters of the Microsoft Corporation. Because Microsoft gives its employees released time to contribute to their communities, this principal has had many volunteers in her school who were employed by the corporation, and she has observed them carefully. Some, especially in the high-tech downturn, wanted to teach full time. But, the principal insisted, both she and the volunteers recognized that they needed professional education training before they were ready to teach. Regardless of their good intentions and what the principal described as their "big hearts," she would not entrust children to these college graduates unless they returned with a much greater base of knowledge about the science of education.

On the whole, these administrators estimated that, if freed to hire candidates without traditional training and certification, they might choose up to 10 percent of new hires from such an unconventional pool, but no more, and with some trepidation.

This does not mean that the current teacher education and certification process is satisfactory. Many of the principals I interviewed said they have learned from experience to hire only graduates from some teacher education programs, and not others. This makes teaching distinct from medicine. The accreditation process for medical colleges is today sufficiently satisfactory that a doctor who graduated from any domestic accredited college would be certified. The same cannot be said for colleges of education.

But the solution is not to abolish certification requirements. Instead it is to upgrade teacher-training institutions so that they do, in every case, graduate only those prospective teachers in whom the care of children could be entrusted. The National Council for the Accreditation of Teacher Education (NCATE) has recently revised its standards in ways that are reasonably likely to improve the proficiency of prospective teachers. The new NCATE standards require that graduating teachers be evaluated not only by the courses they have taken but also by the quality of student work produced in classes where they have interned and given demonstration lessons. The standards require professors to engage in extensive observation and criticism of student teachers' classroom practice.

It is too soon to say if the NCATE standards will succeed in raising the quality of new teachers. But no reasonable alternative exists to pursuing such reforms. If a cub reporter blunders, no great harm is done. Editors can print a correction and, if the blunders are serious, dismiss the novice. But the harm done by putting children in the care of unqualified teachers for a year or more cannot similarly be corrected. In this respect, teaching is a lot more like medicine, and journalism-like proposals for reform ignore the enormity of a teacher's responsibility.

Beyond improvement in teacher education, more attention should also be paid to the identification and selection of high-quality principals. Because good principals can identify good teachers—not only by quantifiable measures such as teacher or student test scores but also by the application of judgment about teachers' ability to balance a wide range of curricular and child development goals—then hiring and retaining good teachers also requires hiring and retaining principals who exercise good judgment about teachers. This, in turn, requires doing a good job of identifying and selecting superintendents who exercise similarly good judgment about principals. In the selection of superintendents and principals as well as of teachers, reliance on quantitative measures such as student test scores can be only a part, perhaps only a small part, of the process.

Comment by Michael Podgursky

Eric A. Hanushek and Steven G. Rivkin provide a good review of the status of recent research on teachers and student achievement, no small part of which has been produced by the authors themselves. They highlight an anomaly that has emerged in this research. On the one hand, measurable teacher characteristics such as teacher credentials or experience seem to have little detectable effect on student achievement. Even when the effects of measurable teacher characteristics pass conventional thresholds of statistical significance, the effect sizes are small. On the other hand, a growing body of research based on large longitudinal student achievement data files in states or large school districts suggests substantial differences in classroom effectiveness of teachers. In studies in which these individual teacher effects can be recovered from the estimates and correlated with measurable teacher characteristics, the association between the two is extremely weak. For example, a 2003 paper by Daniel Aronson, Lisa Barrow, and William Sander reports that over 90 percent of the variation in these teacher effects are unexplained by any combination of measured teacher characteristics of the teachers themselves, for example, experience, certification, master's degree, or college attended.[56]

Given such findings, Hanushek and Rivkin are understandably skeptical about proposals to focus educational resources on traditional teacher credentials. They advance the reasonable argument that if the goal of public policy is to raise student achievement, then the focus of policy ought to be on student achievement and not on teacher credentials that have little or no demonstrated link to student achievement.

From an economic point of view, Hanushek and Rivkin's position is uncontroversial and surely represents the consensus of economists who are familiar with research in this area. However, it also highlights a major divide between economists and much of the education policy community on the question of teacher quality and licensing. Well-intentioned school reformers, aware of the research showing large teacher effects, are eager to tighten up regulation in the labor market as a means to improve teacher quality. Economists by training are wary of occupational licensing and are concerned that the costs of more restrictive licensing are likely to exceed the benefits.

Take the case of teacher exams. Hanushek and Rivkin point out that the evidence linking licensing exam scores and student achievement gains at best suggests only a modest relationship. Thus, even if such a policy had no cost, the benefit of raising cut scores for passing licensing exams in terms of student achievement gains would be very small. However, raising cut scores does have a cost, a point often overlooked in education policy discussions. The cost of such a policy is that it reduces the applicant pool. Local school administrators have other, and typically superior, information on the quality of applicants (for example, direct observation of classroom performance). If teacher quality is idiosyncratic, as the research suggests, then state regulators should give local school administrators leeway to audition as many candidates as possible. Restricting the pool of candidates whom a district can consider imposes a cost on the district. Moreover, this cost falls disproportionately on poor school districts that already have fewer applicants per vacancy than their suburban counterparts. Raising licensing bars risks forcing these districts to hire any certified applicant who walks through the door.

Relative Pay Trends for Female Teachers

Hanushek and Rivkin reproduce in figure 1 a chart they have presented elsewhere showing the decline in the pay of female teachers relative to other female college graduates. This leads them to the rather pessimistic conclusion that, in the long run, the relative quality of female teachers must fall as well.

Simply comparing mean annual earnings of female teachers with nonteachers may paint an overly gloomy portrait. First, as the authors note, the mix of teaching jobs held by female nonteacher college graduates has changed dramatically over the long time period covered in their chart. In 1960, 58 percent of female college graduates who were not teachers were employed as secretaries or in other jobs classified as "clerical" by the U.S. Bureau of the Census, and only 13 percent were in managerial jobs. By

1990 the clerical share had fallen to 30 percent while the managerial share rose to 35 percent, along with the shares of lawyers, doctors, and other previously male-dominated professions. No doubt 2000 census data will reveal a continuation of that trend. Thus, while relative pay was changing, so was the nature of the nonteaching jobs. As the share of managers and other professions increases, so, in all likelihood, do annual hours of work, job stress, travel, and other less attractive job characteristics, for which the higher pay compensates. If the disamenities of the nonteaching jobs have increased over time, then the relative decline in teacher pay has been overstated, particularly for college-educated women with young children.

In addition, the analysis takes no account of the massive increase in the supply of female college graduates over this period. Between 1960 and 2000, the number of bachelor's degrees awarded annually grew by 109 percent for males, but by 413 percent for females. There are now 178,000 more bachelor's degrees awarded annually to women than to men. Among adults age twenty-five or older, the share of men with a bachelor's degree rose threefold, from 9.7 to 27.8 percent over this period, while for women the share grew nearly fivefold, from 5.8 to 23.6 percent.

Teaching is a job that is attractive to women, particularly women with children, and the supply of college-educated women has increased far faster than the demand for teachers. Between 1960 and 2000 the number of public school teaching jobs increased by 110 percent while the number of women with bachelor's degrees grew by 630 percent. So while other employment opportunities have opened up for women, a far larger supply of high- and low-ability women with college degrees is available for all occupations—including teaching. The current experience with alternative certification programs in many states suggests that many high-ability female college graduates are willing to become teachers at the current level of wages and benefits, if entry barriers in the form of preservice seat time in education school pedagogy courses are relaxed. In any event, an analysis of long-term historical trends in the teaching labor market must consider not only relative pay, but also the large increase in the supply of female college graduates.

Only High-Quality Teacher Studies Count

The education research community recognizes that in evaluating the effect of teachers on student achievement a rigorous study design requires either random assignment of students to teachers or prior controls for student achievement and student socioeconomic status (SES). A 2003 survey of the research on teacher quality sets just such a standard.[57] The reason for this is clear. If the contribution of a teacher to student learning is to be estimated on the basis of a spring test score, then the level of achievement of students when they first enter the classroom in the fall must be taken into account. Even within the same school building, teacher A may have been assigned some particularly difficult students whereas teacher B may have a group with above-average achievement for the school. Even if these two teachers produce identical gains in student achievement, an examination of spring test scores alone would suggest that teacher A was less productive simply based on the students he or she was assigned in the fall.

The ideal way to evaluate teacher productivity would be to randomly assign students to teachers and then test them in the spring (although, even with random assignment, data on prior student achievement would be highly desirable). Random assignment is the scientific gold standard for policy evaluation research. Unfortunately, at present no studies of teachers meet this standard, although several are under way. In coming years a body of research on teachers will emerge that uses randomized study designs, thanks in no small part to standards set by the new Institute for Education Sciences.

However, as Hanushek and Rivkin and other researchers have shown, much can be learned from rigorous analysis of nonexperimental data, particularly from the massive longitudinal student data files being developed in states and school districts that test students annually. These longitudinal databases permit the estimation of value-added models discussed by the authors.

I think it is important that the authors broke out high-quality, value-added estimates in their survey of the literature. In my opinion, studies of teacher effects that do not provide random assignment of students to teachers or prior controls for student achievement and student socioeconomic status should be off the table in terms of research syntheses. The problem is that family background has a powerful effect on student achievement and SES controls in most data sets (for example, free and reduced-price lunch status) are very poor proxies for home educational resources. If teachers in low SES schools tend to have particular characteristics (for example, substandard certification or fewer master's degrees), then evaluations that fail to control for prior student achievement and SES are going to be overestimating the effect of these teacher characteristics on student achievement. Because all such studies are biased in the same direction, meta-analyzing fifty or five hundred of them moves educational researchers no closer to discerning the true effect. Only high-quality studies deserve attention.

Families versus Teachers

The authors claim that, based on the current longitudinal research, a string of good teachers can offset the effect of poverty for a low-income student.

> The [Steven G.] Rivkin, [Eric A.] Hanushek, and [John F.] Kain estimates of teacher performance suggest that having five years of good teachers in a row (1.0 standard deviation above average, or at the 85th quality percentile) could overcome the average seventh-grade mathematics achievement gap between lower-income kids ... and those from higher-income families.

The education policy community has an understandable desire to seize upon research that holds out the promise that good schools and teachers can compensate for unequal family resources. However, these types of calculations are likely to overstate what can realistically be expected from policy. For example, the statistical methodology in Rivkin, Hanushek, and Kain does not permit identification of the effectiveness of any particular teacher, nor does it permit any direct analysis of the stability of these teacher effects over time. My reading of this emerging literature is that some time may pass before such an experiment can be run. One problem is that it is not known ex ante which teachers, if any, are consistently in the 85th percentile and above for five consecutive years. As this type of research matures, educational researchers may be in a position to identify consistently high-performing teachers and run such an experiment (which would then run for five years). However, at this point, the efficacy of such an intervention remains speculative.

Notes

1. Salaries for teachers include all earnings, regardless of source. Thus any summer or school-year earnings outside of teaching are included. No adjustments are made, however, for any differences in the length of the school day or in the days worked during the year. Nor is any calculation of employer-paid fringe benefits made. A clear discussion of the importance of each of these along with interpretation of the overall salary differences can be found in Michael

Podgursky, "Fringe Benefits," *Education Next,* vol. 3, no. 3 (2003), pp. 71–76. For the time series comparisons, these omitted elements of compensation would be most relevant if there have been relative changes in the importance of them between teachers and nonteachers over time. Little data currently are available on any such changes.

2. See Eric A. Hanushek and Steven G. Rivkin, "Understanding the Twentieth-Century Growth in U.S. School Spending," *Journal of Human Resources,* vol. 32, no. 1 (1997), pp. 35–68.

3. Fredrick Flyer and Sherwin Rosen, "The New Economics of Teachers and Education," *Journal of Labor Economics,* vol. 15, no. 1, part 2 (1997), pp. 104–39.

4. Darius Lakdawalla, "The Declining Quality of Teachers," Working Paper W8263 (Cambridge, Mass.: National Bureau of Economic Research, 2001); and Darius Lakdawalla, "Quantity over Quality," *Education Next,* vol. 2, no. 3 (2002), pp. 67–72.

5. Dale Ballou and Michael Podgursky, *Teacher Pay and Teacher Quality* (Kalamazoo, Mich.: W. E. Upjohn Institute for Employment Research, 1997).

6. Joseph A. Kershaw and Roland N. McKean, *Teacher Shortages and Salary Schedules* (McGraw-Hill, 1962).

7. See David Greenberg and John McCall, "Teacher Mobility and Allocation," *Journal of Human Resources,* vol. 9, no. 4 (1974), pp. 480–502; Richard J. Murnane, "Teacher Mobility Revisited," *Journal of Human Resources,* vol. 16, no. 1 (1981), pp. 3–19; Eric A. Hanushek, John F. Kain, and Steve G. Rivkin, "Why Public Schools Lose Teachers," *Journal of Human Resources* (forthcoming Spring 2004); Hamilton Lankford, Susanna Loeb, and James Wyckoff, "Teacher Sorting and the Plight of Urban Schools: A Descriptive Analysis," *Educational Evaluation and Policy Analysis,* vol. 24, no. 1 (2002), pp. 37–62; and Don Boyd and others, "Do High-Stakes Tests Affect Teachers' Exit and Transfer Decisions? The Case of the Fourth-Grade Test in New York State," mimeo (Stanford Graduate School of Education, 2002).

8. Murnane, "Teacher Mobility Revisited."

9. Hanushek, Kain, and Rivkin, "Why Public Schools Lose Teachers"; and Eric A. Hanushek, John F. Kain, and Steven G. Rivkin, "The Revolving Door, " *Education Next,* vol. 4, no. 1 (2004), pp. 77–82.

10. See, for example, Richard J. Murnane and Randall Olsen, "The Effects of Salaries and Opportunity Costs on Length of Stay in Teaching: Evidence from Michigan," *Review of Economics and Statistics,* vol. 71, no. 2 (1989), pp. 347–52; Richard J. Murnane and Randall Olsen, "The Effects of Salaries and Opportunity Costs on Length of Stay in Teaching: Evidence from North Carolina," *Journal of Human Resources,* vol. 25, no. 1 (1990), pp. 106–24; Peter J. Dolton and Wilbert van der Klaauw, "Leaving Teaching in the UK: A Duration Analysis," *Economic Journal,* vol. 105 (1995), pp. 431–44; Peter J. Dolton and Wilbert van der Klaauw, "The Turnover of Teachers: A Competing Risks Explanation," *Review of Economics and Statistics,* vol. 81, no. 3 (1999), pp. 543–52; Dominic J. Brewer, "Career Paths and Quit Decisions: Evidence from Teaching," *Journal of Labor Economics,* vol. 14, no. 2 (1996), pp. 313–39; Todd R. Stinebrickner, "Estimation of a Duration Model in the Presence of Missing Data," *Review of Economics and Statistics,* vol. 81, no. 3 (1999), pp. 529–42; Todd R. Stinebrickner, "Compensation Policies and Teacher Decisions," *International Economic Review,* vol. 42, no. 3 (2001), pp. 751–79; Todd R. Stinebrickner, "A Dynamic Model of Teacher Labor Supply," *Journal of Labor Economics,* vol. 19, no. 1 (2001), pp. 196–230; R. Mark Gritz and Neil D. Theobald, "The Effects of School District Spending Priorities on Length of Stay in Teaching," *Journal of Human Resources,* vol. 31, no. 3 (1996), pp. 477–512; Richard J. Murnane and others, *Who Will Teach?* (Harvard University Press, 1991); and Benjamin Scafidi, David Sjoquist, and Todd R Stinebrickner, "Where Do Teachers Go?" mimeo (Georgia State University, 2002).

Note that these conclusions are frequently implicit from an analysis of hazard functions for exiting teaching.

11. Scafidi, Sjoquist, and Stinebrickner, "Where Do Teachers Go?"

12. See, for example, Murnane and others, *Who Will Teach?*; and Eric A. Hanushek and Richard R. Pace, "Who Chooses to Teach (and Why)?" *Economics of Education Review,* vol. 14, no. 2 (1995), pp. 101–17.

13. Kershaw and McKean, *Teacher Shortages and Salary Schedules*; and Russell W. Rumberger, "The Impact of Salary Differentials on Teacher Shortages and Turnover: The Case of Mathematics and Science Teachers," *Economics of Education Review,* vol. 6, no. 4 (1987), pp. 389–99.

14. James S. Coleman and others, *Equality of Educational Opportunity* (Government Printing Office, 1966).

15. See Eric A. Hanushek, "Conceptual and Empirical Issues in the Estimation of Educational Production Functions," *Journal of Human Resources,* vol. 14, no. 3 (1979), pp. 351–88; Steven G. Rivkin, Eric A. Hanushek, and John F. Kain, "Teachers, Schools, and Academic Achievement," Working Paper W6691 (Cambridge, Mass.: National Bureau of Economic Research, 2000, revised); and Petra E. Todd and Kenneth I. Wolpin, "On the Specification and Estimation of the Production Function for Cognitive Achievement," *Economic Journal,* vol. 113, no. 485 (2003).

16. While more studies have appeared since then, they are small in number relative to the stock in 1994, and they show no discernibly different pattern of results from those in table 1. For a description of the studies, a discussion of inclusion criteria, and the bibliography of included work, see Eric A. Hanushek, "Assessing the Effects of School Resources on Student Performance: An Update," *Educational Evaluation and Policy Analysis,* vol. 19, no. 2 (1997), pp. 141–64; and Eric A. Hanushek, "The Failure of Input-Based Schooling Policies," *Economic Journal,* vol. 113 (2003), pp. F64–F98.

17. In some other estimation, say, related to overall spending or class sizes, aggregation of data becomes an additional issue, but this is relatively unimportant for the teacher characteristics considered here, because those analyses have uniformly been conducted at lower levels of aggregation (the school district down to the classroom). See Eric A. Hanushek, Steven G. Rivkin, and Lori L. Taylor, "Aggregation and the Estimated Effects of School Resources," *Review of Economics and Statistics,* vol. 78, no. 4 (1996), pp. 611–27.

18. Greenberg and McCall, "Teacher Mobility and Allocation"; and Murnane, "Teacher Mobility Revisited."

19. Hanushek, Kain, and Rivkin, "Why Public Schools Lose Teachers."

20. Richard J. Murnane and Barbara R. Phillips, "Learning by Doing, Vintage, and Selection: Three Pieces of the Puzzle Relating Teaching Experience and Teaching Performance," *Economics of Education Review,* vol. 1 no. 4 (1981), pp. 453–65.

21. Rivkin, Hanushek, and Kain, "Teachers, Schools, and Academic Achievement."

22. Rivkin, Hanushek, and Kain, "Teachers, Schools, and Academic Achievement."

23. See, for example, Joseph R. Antos and Sherwin Rosen, "Discrimination in the Market for Teachers," *Journal of Econometrics,* vol. 2 (1975), pp. 123–50; Arik M. Levinson, "Reexamining Teacher Preferences and Compensating Wages," *Economics of Education Review,* vol. 7, no. 3 (1988), pp. 357–64; Randall W. Eberts and Joe A. Stone, "Wages, Benefits, and Working Conditions: An Analysis of Compensating Differentials," *Southern Economic Journal,* vol. 52, no. 1 (1985), pp. 74–79; Lawrence W. Kenny, "Compensating Differentials in Teachers' Salaries," *Journal of Urban Economics,* vol. 7 (1980), pp. 198–207; Eric J. Toder, "The Supply of Public School Teachers to an Urban Metropolitan Area: A Possible Source of Discrimination in Education," *Review of Economics and Statistics,* vol. 54, no. 4 (1972), pp.

439–43; Eric A. Hanushek and Javier A. Luque, "Smaller Classes, Lower Salaries? The Effects of Class Size on Teacher Labor Markets," in Sabrina W. M. Laine and James G. Ward, eds., *Using What We Know: A Review of the Research on Implementing Class-Size Reduction Initiatives for State and Local Policymakers* (Oak Brook, Ill.: North Central Regional Educational Laboratory, 2000); Jay Chambers and William J. Fowler Jr., *Public School Teacher Cost Differences across the United States* (Washington: National Center for Education Statistics, 1995); William J. Fowler Jr. and David H. Monk, *A Primer on Making Cost Adjustments in Education* (Washington: National Center for Education Statistics, 2001); and Hanushek, Kain, and Rivkin, "Why Public Schools Lose Teachers."

24. Their study, relying on interstate variations in school completion and teacher pay, faces an analytical trade-off between using aggregate state data subject to potential missing policy information and providing some control for state amenity differences. Susanna Loeb and Marianne E. Page, "Examining the Link between Teacher Wages and Student Outcomes: The Importance of Alternative Labor Market Opportunities and Nonpecuniary Variation," *Review of Economics and Statistics,* vol. 82, no. 3 (2000), pp. 393–408.

25. See, for example, Murnane and others, *Who Will Teach?*

26. We thank Dale Ballou for providing a clear description of this trade-off.

27. Andrew J. Wayne and Peter Youngs, "Teacher Characteristics and Student Achievement Gains: A Review," *Review of Educational Research,* vol. 73, no. 1 (2003), pp. 89–122.

28. Elements of the debate over the effectiveness of teacher certification can be traced through National Commission on Teaching and America's Future, *What Matters Most: Teaching for America's Future* (New York: 1996); Abell Foundation, *Teacher Certification Reconsidered: Stumbling for Quality* (Baltimore, Md.: 2001); Kate Walsh, "Positive Spin: The Evidence for Traditional Teacher Certification, Reexamined," *Education Next,* vol. 2, no. 1 (2002), pp. 79–84; Dan D. Goldhaber and Dominic J. Brewer, "Does Teacher Certification Matter? High School Teacher Certification Status and Student Achievement," *Educational Evaluation and Policy Analysis,* vol. 22, no. 2 (2000), pp. 129–45; Dan D. Goldhaber and Dominic J. Brewer, "Evaluating the Evidence on Teacher Certification: A Rejoinder," *Educational Evaluation and Policy Analysis,* vol. 23, no. 1 (2001), pp. 79–86; and Linda Darling-Hammond, Barnett Berry, and Amy Thoreson, "Does Teacher Certification Matter? Evaluating the Evidence," *Educational Evaluation and Policy Analysis,* vol. 23, no. 1 (2001), pp. 57–77. Goldhaber and Brewer, in "Does Teacher Certification Matter? High School Teacher Certification Status and Student Achievement," find, for example, that teachers with subject matter certification in mathematics perform better than other teachers, while teachers with emergency certification perform no worse than teachers with standard certification, although Darling-Hammond, Berry, and Thoreson, in "Does Teacher Certification Matter? Evaluating the Evidence," dispute the interpretation. Christopher Jepsen and Steve G. Rivkin, "What Is the Trade-off between Smaller Classes and Teacher Quality?" Working Paper W9205 (Cambridge, Mass.: National Bureau of Economic Research, 2002), find very small certification effects on teacher value added to mathematics and reading achievement once the nonlinearities in the return to experience are adequately controlled.

29. Their work has directly entered into school decisionmaking through Tennessee law. See William L. Sanders and Sandra P. Horn, "The Tennessee Value-Added Assessment System (TVAA): Mixed Model Methodology in Educational Assessment," in Anthony J. Shinkfield and Daniel L. Stufflebeam, eds., *Teacher Evaluation: Guide to Effective Practice* (Boston: Kluwer Academic Publishers, 1995), pp. 337–76; and William L. Sanders and Sandra P. Horn, "Research Findings from the Tennessee Value-Added Assessment System (TVASS) Database: Implications for Educational Evaluation and Research," *Journal of Personnel Evaluation in Education,* vol. 12 (1998), pp. 247–56.

30. See Eric A. Hanushek, "Teacher Characteristics and Gains in Student Achievement: Estimation Using Micro Data," *American Economic Review,* vol. 60, no. 2 (1971), pp. 280–88; Eric A. Hanushek, "The Trade-off between Child Quantity and Quality," *Journal of Political Economy,* vol. 100, no. 1 (February 1992), pp. 84–117; David J. Armor and others, *Analysis of the School Preferred Reading Program in Selected Los Angeles Minority Schools* (Santa Monica, Calif.: RAND Corporation, 1976); Richard J. Murnane, *Impact of School Resources on the Learning of Inner-City Children* (Cambridge, Mass.: Ballinger, 1975); Richard J. Murnane and Barbara Phillips, "What Do Effective Teachers of Inner-City Children Have in Common?" *Social Science Research,* vol. 10, no. 1 (1981), pp. 83–100; and Rivkin, Hanushek, and Kain, "Teachers, Schools, and Academic Achievement."

31. A similar study for developing countries (specifically Brazil) contains consistent findings. See Ralph W. Harbison and Eric A. Hanushek, *Educational Performance of the Poor: Lessons from Rural Northeast Brazil* (New York: Oxford University Press, 1992).

32. Hanushek, "The Trade-off between Child Quantity and Quality."

33. Rivkin, Hanushek, and Kain, "Teachers, Schools, and Academic Achievement."

34. These estimates consider value-added models with family and parental models. The sample includes only low-income minority students, whose average achievement in primary school is below the national average. The comparisons are between teachers at the 5th percentile and those at the 95th percentile. Hanushek, "The Trade-off between Child Quantity and Quality."

35. Rivkin, Hanushek, and Kain, "Teachers, Schools, and Academic Achievement."

36. A discussion of the experiment and overall results can be found in Elizabeth Word and others, *Student/Teacher Achievement Ratio (STAR), Tennessee's K–3 Class-Size Study: Final Summary Report, 1985–1990* (Nashville, Tenn.: Tennessee State Department of Education, 1990). Eric A. Hanushek, in "Some Findings from an Independent Investigation of the Tennessee STAR Experiment and from Other Investigations of Class-Size Effects," *Educational Evaluation and Policy Analysis,* vol. 21, no. 2 (1999), pp. 143–63, analyzes the basic experimental results and identifies the variation across classrooms.

37. Rivkin, Hanuschek, and Kain, "Teachers, Schools, and Academic Achievement."

38. Eric A. Hanushek and others, "The Market for Teacher Quality," paper presented at the annual meeting of the American Economic Association, Washington, D.C., 2003.

39. Ballou and Podgursky, *Teacher Pay and Teacher Quality.*

40. Hanushek and others, "The Market for Teacher Quality."

41. Dale Ballou, "Do Public Schools Hire the Best Applicants?" *Quarterly Journal of Economics,* vol. 111, no. 1 (1996), pp. 97–133; and Ballou and Podgursky, *Teacher Pay and Teacher Quality.*

42. See Margaret E. Raymond, Stephen Fletcher, and Javier A. Luque, *Teach for America: An Evaluation of Teacher Differences and Student Outcomes in Houston, Texas* (Stanford University: CREDO, 2001); and Margaret E. Raymond and Stephen Fletcher, "Teach for America," *Education Next,* vol. 2, no. 1 (2002), pp. 62–68.

43. The issues of hiring and retaining district administrators are similar to those for teachers. Little evidence exists that the current requirements for administrator certification are closely related to the effectiveness of administrators. One relevant study is Ronald G. Ehrenberg, Randy A. Ehrenberg, and Richard P. Chaykowski, "Are School Superintendents Rewarded for Performance?" in David H. Monk and Julie Underwood, eds., *Microlevel School Finance: Issues and Implications for Policy* (Cambridge, Mass.: Ballinger, 1988). A recent policy statement also makes recommendations for administrator policy that parallel the lines of thought about teachers that are contained here. See Broad Foundation and Thomas B. Fordham Institute, *Better Leaders for America's Schools: A Manifesto* (Washington: 2003).

44. Marci Kanstoroom and Chester E. Finn Jr., eds., *Better Teachers, Better Schools* (Washington: Thomas B. Fordham Foundation, 1999).

45. Lowell Milken, *Growth of the Teacher Advancement Program: Teaching as the Opportunity 2002* (Santa Monica, Calif.: Milken Family Foundation, 2002).

46. See Armor and others, *Analysis of the School Preferred Reading Program in Selected Los Angeles Minority Schools;* and Murnane, *Impact of School Resources on the Learning of Inner-City Children.* They identify total teacher effects as discussed above and relate them to principals' evaluations.

47. David K. Cohen and Richard J. Murnane, "Merit Pay and the Evaluation Problem: Understanding Why Most Merit Pay Plans Fail and a Few Survive," *Harvard Educational Review,* vol. 56, no. 1 (1986), pp. 1–17.

48. Eric A. Hanushek and others, *Making Schools Work: Improving Performance and Controlling Costs* (Brookings, 1994).

49. For consideration of the available evidence on teacher merit pay, see Elizabeth Lueder Karnes and Donald D. Black, *Teacher Evaluation and Merit Pay: An Annotated Bibliography* (New York: Greenwood Press, 1986); David K. Cohen and Richard J. Murnane, "The Merits of Merit Pay," *Public Interest,* vol. 80 (1985), pp. 3–30; Cohen and Murnane, "Merit Pay and the Evaluation Problem"; Dale Ballou and Michael Podgursky, "Teachers' Attitudes toward Merit Pay: Examining Conventional Wisdom," *Industrial and Labor Relations Review*, vol. 47, no. 1 (1993), pp. 50–61; Ballou and Podgursky, *Teacher Pay and Teacher Quality*; Elchanan Cohn, "Methods of Teacher Remuneration: Merit Pay and Career Ladders," in William E. Becker and William J. Baumol, eds., *Assessing Educational Practices: The Contribution of Economics* (MIT Press, 1996); and James A. Brickley and Jerold L. Zimmerman, "Changing Incentives in a Multitask Environment: Evidence from a Top-Tier Business School," *Journal of Corporate Finance,* vol. 7 (2001), pp. 367–96.

50. See Hanushek and others, *Making Schools Work.*

51. William L. Sanders and June C. Rivers, *Cumulative and Residual Effects of Teachers on Future Student Academic Achievement* (University of Tennessee, Value-Added Research and Assessment Center, November 1996).

52. Hanushek, "The Trade-off between Child Quantity and Quality," p. 106.

53. I am indebted to Haggai Kupermintz of the University of Colorado for sharing this observation.

54. Dale Ballou, "Sizing Up Test Scores," *Education Next* (Summer 2002), p. 12.

55. Education Commission of the States, "Spring Steering Committee Meeting: Linda Darling-Hammond–Chester Finn Jr. Quality Teaching Debate" (March 26, 2000) (www.ecs.org/ [October 21, 2003]).

56. Daniel Aaronson, Lisa Barrow, and William Sander, "Teachers and Student Achievement in Chicago Public Schools," mimeo (Federal Reserve Bank of Chicago, 2003).

57. Wayne and Youngs, "Teacher Characteristics and Student Achievement Gains."

Why Some Schools Have More Underqualified Teachers Than Others

RICHARD M. INGERSOLL

The failure to ensure that the nation's classrooms are all staffed with qualified schoolteachers is one of the most important problems in contemporary American education. Over the past two decades, dozens of reports and national commissions have focused attention on this problem, and, in turn, numerous reforms have been initiated to upgrade the quality and quantity of the teaching force.[1]

To address the quality issue, many states have pushed for more rigorous preservice and in-service teacher education, training, and certification standards. In response to the quantity issue, a host of initiatives and programs has been implemented that attempt to increase the supply of teachers by recruiting new candidates into teaching. A wide range of alternative licensing programs has been implemented to ease entry into teaching. Programs such as Troops-to-Teachers attempt to entice professionals into midcareer changes to teaching. Other programs, such as Teach for America, seek to lure the "best and brightest" into the occupation. Some school districts have resorted to recruiting teaching candidates from overseas. Finally, financial incentives such as signing bonuses, student loan forgiveness, housing assistance, and tuition reimbursement have been instituted to aid teacher recruitment.[2]

This chapter draws from research supported by grant R305T010592 from the U.S. Department of Education, Office of Educational Research and Improvement, National Institute on Educational Governance, Finance, Policymaking, and Management. Opinions reflect those of the author and do not necessarily reflect those of the granting agency. Thanks are due for helpful comments and feedback from Caroline Hoxby and Adam Scrupski and the many participants of the 2003 annual Brookings conference on education policy.

Concern with the quality and qualifications of teachers is neither unique nor surprising. Elementary and secondary schooling is mandatory in the United States, and the quality of teachers and teaching is undoubtedly one of the most important factors shaping the learning and growth of students. Moreover, the largest single component of the cost of education in any country is teacher compensation.

The responsibility for ensuring that the nation's classrooms are all staffed with qualified teachers is a perennially important issue in schools, but the thesis of this paper is that it is also among the least understood. Like many similarly worthwhile reforms, recent efforts alone will not solve the problems of underqualified teachers and poor-quality teaching in the United States because they do not address some of their key causes.

One of the least recognized of these causes is the phenomenon known as out-of-field teaching—teachers assigned to teach subjects for which they have little education or training. This is a crucial factor because highly qualified and well-trained teachers may become highly unqualified if, once on the job, they are assigned to teach subjects for which they have little background. Educators have long been aware of the existence of out-of-field teaching. James Conant, former president of Harvard University and father of the SAT, called attention to the widespread "misuse of teachers" through out-of-field assignments in his landmark 1963 study *The Education of American Teachers*. Albert Shanker, the late leader of the American Federation of Teachers, condemned out-of-field teaching as education's "dirty little secret" in a 1985 opinion piece in the *New York Times*. But this practice has been largely unknown to the public, policymakers, and many educational researchers. Until recently, almost no empirical research has been conducted with representative data on out-of-field teaching. Few writers on teacher quality or school organization even acknowledge the existence of this practice.[3] An absence of accurate data on out-of-field teaching contributed to this lack of recognition. This situation was remedied with the release, beginning in the early 1990s, of the Schools and Staffing Survey (SASS), a major new survey of the nation's elementary and secondary teachers conducted by the National Center for Education Statistics (NCES) of the U.S. Department of Education.

In previous research I have presented SASS data showing that out-of-field teaching is an ongoing and serious problem across the nation, especially in secondary schools.[4] These findings on out-of-field teaching have been replicated. Other researchers have calculated levels of out-of-field teaching using the same, or similar, data sources and, although different analysts have focused on a wide range of different measures of out-of-field teaching, all have reached the same conclusion—that there are high levels of out-of-field teaching in American schools.[5]

These findings have been featured in a number of major education reports and been widely reported in the national media.[6] As a result, the problem of out-of-field teaching has become a major concern in the realm of educational policy. The elimination of out-of-field teaching is, for example, an important objective of the No Child Left Behind Act. However, there has been little research on a key question: What are the reasons for the prevalence of out-of-field teaching in American schools? Empirically exploring this question is the objective of this analysis.

The Sources of Out-of-Field Teaching

Both education researchers and the education policy community generally believe that out-of-field teaching, like other types of underqualified teaching, is largely a result of either inadequate training on the part of teachers or shortages of qualified teachers.[7] From this viewpoint—hereafter referred to as the teacher deficit perspective—the source of the problem of out-of-field teaching primarily lies in deficits in either the quality or the quantity of teachers.

In the first case, out-of-field teaching is assumed to be a problem of poorly prepared teachers. In this view, the preparation of teachers in college or university training programs lacks adequate rigor, breadth, and depth, resulting in high levels of out-of-field teaching. Proponents of this view typically propose more rigorous teacher education, training, and certification as the remedy.[8] A common variant of this first view assumes that the problem is a lack of academic and substantive coursework, in particular, on the part of new teachers. Hence the remedy lies in requiring prospective teachers to complete a "real" undergraduate major in an academic discipline.[9]

In the second case, the problem of out-of-field teaching is assumed to be a result of teacher shortages. In this view, shortfalls in the number of available teachers, because of increasing student enrollments and a graying teaching work force, have forced many school systems to lower standards to fill teaching openings. Schools have resorted to hiring underqualified candidates or shifting existing staff trained in one field to teach in another,

Figure 1. Two Perspectives on the Causes and Consequences of Out-of-Field Teaching

Teacher deficit perspective
Inadequate teacher supply   →
Inadequate teacher training   →   Out-of-field teachers   →   Decreases in school performance

Organizational and occupational perspective
Administrative practices and
organizational characteristics   →   Out-of-field teachers   →   Decreases in school performance

causing out-of-field teaching. Proponents of this view typically propose enhanced teacher recruitment as a remedy.[10]

In contrast to the teacher deficit perspective, this study proposes an alternative perspective—one focused on the character of the organization of schools and occupation of teaching, to explain the sources of out-of-field teaching. My central hypothesis is that out-of-field teaching does not solely, or even primarily, stem from deficits in either the quality or the quantity of teachers. Instead, it is rooted in the manner in which schools are organized and in which teachers are employed and utilized. From this viewpoint, schools are not simply victims of low-quality teacher-training problems or of larger macro-demographic trends of supply and demand. To fully understand the problem of out-of-field teaching, the design and management of the organizations within which teachers work must be examined (see figure 1).

An Organizational and Occupational Perspective

Unlike those employed in the traditional professions, teachers have only limited authority over many key workplace decisions. National data have long documented, for example, that teachers have little influence or input into which courses they are assigned to teach. The data reveal that decisions concerning the selection and the allocation of teachers to course and program assignments are primarily the responsibility and prerogative of principals and other building-level school administrators.[11] These administrators are charged with the often-difficult task of providing a broad array of programs and courses with limited resources, limited time, a limited budget, and a limited teaching staff. Along with these limitations, building administrators' staffing decisions can be constrained by numerous factors, such as teachers union work rules, teacher seniority issues, school district regulations, class-size guidelines, and contractual obligations concerning the number and type of class assignments that can be allocated to teaching employees. For example, in a typical secondary school, teacher employment contracts stipulate that full-time teaching staff must be assigned to teach five classes in a normal seven class-period day. Maximizing the match between the content of teachers' assignments and the qualifications of the teachers themselves is only one of many demands and constraints administrators must weigh in the making of these decisions.

The resulting tension between multiple demands and limited resources is not new. Since the mid-twentieth century this appears to have increased as the expectations placed on schools by state and federal governments have steadily risen. Increasingly schools have been required to perform tasks once reserved for families, churches, and communities and to address both the academic learning and the social well-being of youngsters.[12] However, field research has shown that within these constraints school principals often have an unusual degree of discretion in staffing decisions.[13] Whereas pre-service teacher training is subject to an elaborate array of state licensing requirements, there is far less regulation of how teachers are utilized once on the job.[14] In this context, principals may find that assigning teachers to teach out of their fields is often not only legal, but also more efficient and less expensive than the alternatives. Simply put, out-of-field teaching is used by administrators because it is a cheap and convenient way of closing the gap between demands and resources; that is, of making ends meet.

For example, instead of trying to find and hire a new science teacher for a new state-mandated, but underfunded, science curriculum, a principal may find it more convenient to assign a couple of English and social studies teachers to cover a section or two in science. If a teacher suddenly leaves in the middle of a semester, a principal may opt to hire a readily available, but not fully qualified, substitute teacher instead of instigating a formal search for a new fully qualified teacher. When faced with the choice between hiring a fully qualified candidate to teach English and hiring a less-qualified candidate who is also willing to coach a major varsity sport, a principal may find it more expedient to do the latter. If a full-time music teacher is under contract, but student enrollment is sufficient to fill only three music classes, the principal may find it both necessary and cost-effective in a given semester to assign the music teacher to teach two classes in English, in addition to the three classes in music, to employ the teacher for a regular full-time complement of five classes per semester. If a school has three full-time social studies teachers but needs to offer seventeen social studies courses, or the equivalent of three and two-fifths full-time positions, and also has four full-time English teachers but needs to offer only eighteen English courses, or the equivalent of three and three-fifths full-time positions, one solution would be to assign one of the English teachers to teach three English courses and two social studies courses.

Faced with a myriad of such trade-offs and judgments, some degree of teacher misassignment by principals is probably unavoidable. However, while the SASS data have shown that out-of-field teaching is widespread, these data also show large school-to-school differences in this practice.[15] This raises an important question: What accounts for school differences in levels of out-of-field teaching?

Administrative Practices, Organizational Characteristics, and Out-of-Field Teaching

This analysis seeks to build on earlier work by empirically exploring the reasons that particular kinds of schools have more or less out-of-field teaching. It investigates the relationships between the degree of out-of-field teaching in schools and a number of possible factors suggested by the teacher deficit perspective, such as the extent to which schools experience difficulties in recruiting qualified teaching staff for their teaching job openings, and suggested by an organizational and occupational perspective, including a number of administrative practices and organizational characteristics.

Hiring Policies

While data from SASS show that school principals have a great deal of control over teacher hiring decisions, the data also show that the central administrations of public school districts often impose minimal standards on school-level decisions concerning new hires. For example, the data show that about two-thirds of all school districts formally require new teacher hires to hold a college major or minor in the main field to be taught. Such regulations would be expected to constrain the capacity of school principals to hire out-of-field candidates for openings.

The degree to which a school is faced with teacher recruitment and hiring difficulties and the kinds of regulations imposed by district-level administrators may shape a principal's hiring and staffing decisions. An organizational perspective, however, suggests an overlooked role exists for the leadership skills of principals in the employment, assignment, and utilization of teachers. This analysis will explore this factor by examining whether there is a positive association between the general leadership skill of principals and the degree of out-of-field teaching in schools.

Staffing Practices

Depending upon the constraints within which principals work, the degree of discretion allowed to them, and their leadership skills, numerous options and strategies could be available to principals in regard to teacher hiring and assignment. When faced with difficulty in finding qualified candidates to fill openings, school principals might opt to hire an available but underqualified teacher at the cost of a regular teacher salary, might choose to reassign an existing teacher to cover part or all of the hard-to-staff classes at no additional salary, or might decide to employ a long-term substitute teacher at a relatively low salary. Each of these choices would be expected to result in significantly more out-of-field teaching.

Alternatively, principals might opt to leave some hard-to-staff positions unfilled and shift student enrollment to existing classes. This would create larger classes, save salary costs, and, presumably, result in less out-of-field teaching. In other cases, administrators might have the budgetary resources and flexibility available to enhance recruitment efforts by providing better starting salaries or pay incentives.

Why are particular schools more likely to have out-of-field teachers? To address this question, this study compares and examines two explanations— the dominant teacher deficit perspective focuses on deficits in the quantity and quality of teacher supply and the organizational and occupational perspective focuses upon the manner in which schools are organized and teachers are employed and utilized. These perspectives are not necessarily mutually exclusive; both may help account for school variation in out-of-field teaching.

Data and Methods

The data for this study come from NCES' Schools and Staffing Survey. This is the largest and most comprehensive data set available on the staffing, occupational, and organizational characteristics of elementary and secondary schools. The survey was specifically designed to remedy the lack of nationally representative and comprehensive data on these issues.[16]

The U.S. Census Bureau collects the SASS data for NCES from random samples stratified by state, sector, and school level. To date, four independent cycles of SASS have been completed: 1987–88, 1990–91, 1993–94, and 1999–2000.[17] Each cycle of SASS includes several sets of separate, but linked, questionnaires for school administrators and for a random sample of teachers within each school. The response rate has been relatively high: 86 percent for teachers and 94 percent for administrators.

The data used in this study are primarily from the 1993–94 SASS. The sample contains about 46,700 teachers employed in about 9,000 public elementary, secondary, and combined (K–12) schools. Throughout, this analysis uses data weighted to compensate for the over- and undersampling of the complex stratified survey design. Each observation is weighted by the inverse of its probability of selection to obtain unbiased estimates of population parameters.

Representing a wide range of information on the characteristics of teachers, schools, and school districts across the country, SASS is particularly useful for addressing research questions on access to qualified teachers. Teachers reported their certification status and the major and minor fields of study for degrees earned at both the undergraduate and graduate levels. In addition, for each teacher sampled, data were collected on the subject taught, grade level, and number of students enrolled for each class period in the school day. From administrators, SASS obtained a wide range of information on school and district demographic characteristics, staffing procedures, teacher recruiting difficulties, administrative practices, and organizational characteristics.

There are two stages to my data analysis and data presentation. The first stage documents levels of teacher qualifications and out-of-field teaching across different types of schools. The second stage investigates the sources of school-to-school variations in out-of-field teaching.

I begin with a presentation of descriptive statistics on levels of teacher education and teacher certification, and the extent to which these levels vary across different types of schools. This stage of the analysis also presents data on levels and variations of out-of-field teaching. It focuses on establishing the role of out-of-field teaching as a major source of underqualified teachers.

One of the difficulties encountered in researching the problem of under-qualified and out-of-field teachers has been a lack of consensus on the best standard by which to define a qualified teacher. Few would argue that teachers need not be qualified. Moreover, teaching, unlike many other occupations, has an extensive body of empirical research documenting the proposition that the qualifications of teachers are tied to student outcomes.[18] But controversy has long swirled around how much education, what types of training, and which kinds of preparation teachers ought to have to be considered qualified in any given field.[19]

This study assumes that teachers, especially at the secondary level and in the core academic fields, to be considered adequately qualified, ought to have, as a minimal prerequisite, an undergraduate or graduate major or minor in the fields they are assigned to teach. Having a major or minor in a field does not guarantee one is a quality teacher, or even that one is a qualified teacher. I assume, however, that a major or minor is a necessary, if not sufficient, requirement of both.[20]

The first stage of the analysis focuses on the proportion of those teaching in five different fields without an undergraduate or graduate major or minor in that field. The five fields are general elementary education (at the elementary level) and mathematics, English, social studies, and science (at the secondary level). In this measure of out-of-field teaching I count both education and academic majors and minors as qualification to teach; for example, a major either in math or in math education counts as being qualified to teach math.

Some critics do not give equal status to education degrees, such as math education, science education, or social studies education as compared with degrees in math, science, or history. Such critics have argued that subject area education degrees have tended to be overloaded with required courses in pedagogy to the neglect of coursework in the subject itself. Over the past two decades, because of such problems, many states have upgraded teacher education by, among other things, requiring education majors to complete substantial coursework in an academic discipline. For instance, at many teacher-training institutions, a degree in math education currently requires as much coursework in the math department as does a degree in math itself. Hence there are good reasons to count both subject area and academic degrees. But, it is important to recognize that this particular measure, like most indicators of out-of-field teaching, captures a mix of both subject and pedagogical knowledge in its definition of an in-field teacher—something often missed by observers who often have wrongly assumed that measures of out-of-field teaching refer solely to a lack of subject knowledge in a field.[21]

Having documented cross-school levels of out-of-field teaching, the second stage of the analysis seeks to explain why particular schools are more or less likely to have different levels of out-of-field teaching. In particular, the analysis focuses on the link between the degree of out-of-field teaching in schools and factors representing both the teacher deficit perspective and the organizational and occupational perspective. This second stage begins with a summary of recent trends in overall levels of teacher supply, demand, and shortages; the numbers of schools that experience difficulty recruiting qualified faculty to fill their teaching openings; and the extent to which these difficulties affect levels of out-of-field teaching. The analysis then turns to a more advanced statistical analysis of the relative association of various factors with out-of-field teaching at the secondary level. The secondary subsample includes 23,867 public school teachers in grades seven through twelve. It includes all those teaching in any of eight fields, parallel to conventional departmental divisions at the secondary level: English, mathematics, social studies, science, art and music, physical education, foreign language, and vocational education. It excludes those employed in middle schools.

The dependent variable in this portion of the analysis is a second measure of out-of-field teaching—for each secondary-level teacher, the percentage of his or her daily classes in which he or she does not have an academic or education undergraduate or graduate major or minor in the field taught.[22] The purpose of this second portion of the analysis is to use multiple regression to examine whether this measure of out-of-field teaching is related to a number of aspects of school administration and organization characteristics, while controlling for two groups of independent variables: school contextual characteristics and school recruiting and hiring difficulties. Box 1 provides definitions, and table 1 provides mean teacher and school characteristics associated with the teachers in the sample.

For measures of school contextual characteristics, the analysis includes measures of school poverty enrollment, school urbanicity, both district size and school size, and whether there is a teachers union in the school district. These represent factors that are largely fixed and not amenable to the control of administrators, with the possible exception of school size. The latter has become a major policy issue and could be considered a manipulable aspect of the administration and organization of schools in my analysis.

Here I primarily treat size as an environmental and contextual variable but will also test its direct effects on out-of-field teaching in schools.

For school recruiting and hiring difficulties, the analysis includes a measure to control for whether schools had teaching job openings in the year of the survey and a measure to gauge the extent of difficulty these schools experienced with recruiting qualified faculty to fill their openings for thirteen teaching fields. Finally, after controlling for the teacher and school factors, the analysis includes a number of factors reflecting administrative practices and organizational characteristics. These latter measures include a variable assessing whether the school district has informal or formal rules stipulating that new teacher hires have a major or minor in the main field to be taught; a measure representing the mean school ratings by all of the teachers sampled in each school of the leadership skills of their principals; a measure of the extent to which a school covers hard-to-fill teaching openings by hiring underqualified teachers, reassigning teachers of another subject or grade level, or using short-term or long-term substitutes; a measure of the school's average class size; a measure of whether the school district provides pay incentives for teachers to enhance their education or training through in-service or college coursework; and the normal yearly starting salary provided by the district for new, inexperienced teachers.

The data in the analysis are couched at two levels—teacher level and school level. Hence this analysis uses a regression program, SAS' PROC MIXED (SAS here stands for Statistical Analysis System), that adjusts for the clustering of teachers within schools resulting from the complex, multilevel design of the SASS sample. PROC MIXED has the additional advantage of allowing for the inclusion of the survey's design weights.

SASS is a cross-sectional database. Each cycle represents new and independent teacher and school samples. However, some schools do appear in more than one of the four cycles of SASS and some of the questionnaire items used in this analysis also appear in more than one cycle. Ostensibly, these school characteristics could be traced over time and then examined to determine whether they predict changes in the dependent variable over time. This kind of analysis could be used to speak to the issue of causality and is worth exploring, but I will not attempt to do so here. The repeated schools are not a true panel, are not representative, and do not support inferences of the larger population. Moreover, the teacher sample has little overlap between cycles. The results of the multivariate findings in this chapter represent associations between particular teacher and school measures and the

Box 1. Definitions of Measures Used in the Multiple Regression Analysis of Out-of-Field Teaching at the Secondary Level

Out-of-field teaching

> **Percent secondary classes out of field**—for each seventh- through twelfth-grade teacher, percentage of classes in which teacher does not have an undergraduate or graduate major or minor in field taught. Both academic and education majors or minors are counted (for example, math and math education). Measure includes all those teaching in any of eight fields, parallel to conventional departmental divisions at the secondary level—English, mathematics, social studies, science, art or music, physical education, foreign language, and vocational education. It excludes those employed in middle schools. For more detail on this measure, see R. Ingersoll, *Teacher Supply, Teacher Qualifications, and Teacher Turnover* (Washington: National Center for Education Statistics, 1995).

School contextual characteristics

> **Poverty enrollment**—percentage of students receiving the federal free or reduced-price lunch program for students from families below poverty level.
>
> **Rural**—a dichotomous variable where 0 = central city or urban fringe/large town and 1 = rural/small town.
>
> **Suburban**—a dichotomous variable where 0 = rural/small town or central city and 1 = urban fringe/large town.
>
> **District size**—student enrollment of district. Divided by 1,000, to make units refer to increments of 1,000 students.
>
> **School size**—student enrollment of school. Divided by 100, to make units refer to increments of 100 students.
>
> **Presence of teacher union**—a dichotomous variable where 0 = school district has no teacher union and 1 = school district does have one.

School recruiting and hiring difficulties

> **Teaching job openings**—a dichotomous variable where 0 = school had no teaching job opening(s) that year and 1 = school had teaching job opening(s) that year.
>
> **Hiring difficulties**—on a scale of 0 to 13, sum of 13 teaching fields for which school administrator reported "somewhat difficult," "very difficult," or "could not fill" in response to item that asked, "How difficult or easy was it to fill the vacancies for this school year in each of the following fields?" The latter include special education; English

as a Second Language; English for speakers of other languages; bilingual education; English; mathematics; social studies; physical science; life science; music; foreign languages; business or marketing; industrial arts; home economics; trade and industry; and agriculture.

Administrative practices and organizational characteristics

Major/minor required of hires—on a scale of 1 = not used, 2 = used, 3 = required, school district requirement for new hires having college major or minor in field to be taught, as reported by school administrators.

Principal leadership—on a scale of 1 = strongly disagree to 4 = strongly agree the school mean of six items asked of all teachers about whether their principal recognizes staff members for good work; knows what kind of school he or she wants; communicates his or her expectations; is supportive and encouraging; backs up teachers; and communicates with teachers about instructional practices. This measure is based on the school mean of the reports of all teachers sampled in each school, not only those misassigned. Factor analysis (with varimax rotation method) was used to develop this measure. Item loadings of 0.4 were considered necessary for inclusion. Items in the factor had high internal consistency (a > 0.7).

Hiring or assigning underqualified—on a scale of 0 to 4, sum used of four possible methods to cover vacancies, as reported by school administrators—hire a less than fully qualified teacher; assign teacher of another subject or grade level to teach the class; assign administrator or counselor to teach the class; use short-term or long-term substitutes. To avoid missing observations, this variable is calculated for all schools, even those without vacancies or without hiring difficulties that, by definition, would not have indicated use of these strategies.

Average class size—school's mean student enrollment per classroom.

Pay incentives—district use of pay incentives for teachers' completion of in-service training or college credits.

Starting teacher salary—normal yearly base salary for teacher with a bachelor's degree and no experience, as reported by school administrators. Divided by 1,000, to make units refer to increments of $1,000.

Table 1. Means and Standard Deviations for Variables Used in Multiple Regression Analysis of Out-of-Field Teaching at the Secondary Level, 1993–94

Variable	Mean	Standard deviation
Percent secondary classes out of field	16	35
School contextual characteristics		
Poverty enrollment (percent)	23	22.8
Rural (percent)	43	...
Suburban (percent)	32	.
District size	45,745	105,597
School size	1084	640
With teachers union (percent)	73	...
School recruiting and hiring difficulties		
Schools with teaching job openings (percent)	87	...
Hiring difficulties (scale of 0–13)	1.5	1.9
Administrative practices and organizational characteristics		
Major or minor required of hires (scale of 1–3)	2.6	0.60
Principal leadership (scale of 1–4)	2.1	0.68
Hiring or assigning underqualified (scale of 0–4)	0.31	0.61
Average class size	23	8
With pay incentives (percent)	17	...
Starting teacher salary (dollars)	23,177	3,358

degree to which individual teachers are given out-of-field assignments in schools.

Levels of Teacher Qualifications and Out-of-Field Teaching

The data show that most public elementary and secondary teachers have basic education and training (see table 2). Almost all public school teachers have completed a four-year college education. Ninety-nine percent of public school teachers hold at least a bachelor's degree, and almost half have obtained graduate degrees. Moreover, 94 percent of public school teachers have regular or full state-approved teaching certificates.

The data also reveal some distinct cross-school differences in the qualifications of teachers. Schools with high poverty enrollments and those in urban areas sometimes have less access to qualified teachers. For example, teachers in high-poverty schools are less likely to have graduate degrees than teachers in low-poverty schools. However, little difference is evident

Table 2. Percentage of Elementary and Secondary Public School Teachers, by Highest Degree Earned and by Highest Type of Certification, by Type of School, 1993–94

	Less than bachelor's degree	Bachelor's degree	Master's degree or more	No certification	Less-than-regular certification	Regular certification
Total	0.7	52	47	2	4	94
Poverty enrollment						
Low	0.9	45	54	1.5	3	96
High	0.6	56	43	4	6	90
School size						
Small	0.9	61	38	1.7	3	95
Large	0.9	49	50	2	4	94
Community						
Rural	0.8	58	41	2	3	95
Suburban	0.7	46	53	2	3	96
Urban	0.7	49	50	3	5	92

Note: Less-than-regular certification includes all those with emergency, temporary, alternative, or provisional certification. Regular certification includes all those with probationary, regular, standard, full, or advanced certification. (Probationary refers to initial license issued after satisfying all requirements except completion of probationary period.) Low poverty refers to schools where 15 percent or less of the students receive publicly funded free or reduced-price lunches. High poverty refers to schools where over 80 percent do so. Small schools are those with fewer than three hundred students. Large schools are those with six hundred or more students. Middle categories of size and poverty enrollment are not shown.

between suburban and urban schools in the percentage of teachers with graduate degrees. But, it is also important to recognize that these data disclose little of the quality of these qualifications; there may be differences in teacher qualifications not revealed here.

The most glaring and prominent source of inadequate access to qualified teachers is not a lack of basic education or training of teachers, but a lack of fit between teachers' preparation and teachers' class assignments: the phenomenon of out-of-field teaching. Whereas most teachers have a bachelor's degree and a regular teaching certificate, many teachers at both the elementary and the secondary levels are assigned to teach classes in fields that do not match their educational background.

At the elementary school level, the data show that 12 percent of those who teach regular pre-elementary or general elementary classes do not have an undergraduate or graduate major or minor in the fields of pre-elementary education, early childhood education, or elementary education (see column 1 of table 3).[23] There are also cross-school disparities: Elementary teachers in poor schools are less likely to have a major or minor in the field.

However, the standard by which one defines a qualified elementary teacher impacts the amount of out-of-field teaching found in elementary schools. Out-of-field levels drop significantly when looking at those without teaching certificates, in contrast to those without majors or minors. In background analyses (not shown here), I have found that only 5 percent of regular elementary teachers did not have regular certificates in the fields of pre-elementary education or elementary education.

The data also show that levels of out-of-field teaching are higher at the secondary level than at the elementary level.[24] For example, about a third of all public secondary school math teachers have neither a major nor a minor in math, math education, or related disciplines, such as engineering or physics. About one quarter of all secondary school English teachers have neither a major nor a minor in English or related subjects, such as literature, communications, speech, journalism, English education, or reading education. In science, slightly lower levels—about one-fifth of all public secondary school teachers—do not have at least a minor in one of the sciences or in science education. Finally, about a fifth of social studies teachers are without at least a minor in any of the social sciences, in public affairs, in social studies education, or in history (see columns 2–8 of table 3).[25]

As is true in elementary schools, large cross-school differences are found in out-of-field teaching in secondary schools. In most fields, teachers in high-poverty schools are more likely to be out of field than are teachers in more affluent schools, although more affluent schools are not free of out-of-field teaching. For example, almost a third of social studies teachers in high-poverty schools, as opposed to 16 percent in low-poverty schools, do not have at least a minor in social studies or a related discipline. Moreover, small schools (less than three hundred students) have more out-of-field teaching than do large schools (six hundred or more students). These cross-school findings are consistent across all four cycles of SASS and with analyses that use other measures of out-of-field teaching, such as the percentage of classes or the percentage of students taught by out-of-field teachers.[26]

At the secondary level, out-of-field teaching levels are similar for teachers whether one is looking at those without a major or minor, or looking at teachers without certification, in their assigned fields. For example, I have found in other analyses that about a third of public secondary math teachers do not have teaching certificates in math, a figure similar to those lacking a major or minor in math.[27] But focusing on those without certificates can lead one to underestimate the amount of underqualified teaching within

Table 3. Percentage of Public School Teachers in Each Field without a Major or a Minor in That Field, by School Type, 1993–94

				Secondary				
	Elementary (1)	English (2)	Math (3)	All sciences (4)	Life science (5)	Physical science (6)	All social sciences (7)	History (8)
Total	12.2	24.1	31.4	19.9	32.9	56.9	19.3	53.1
Poverty enrollment								
Low	11.6	21.8	27.5	17.2	28.9	50.6	16.2	47.1
High	20.8	20.1	37.6	28.0	39.4	68.4	29.6	36.6
School size								
Small	6.6	30.4	41.2	25.5	38.1	64.5	25.5	62.8
Large	15.1	22.4	27.5	17.6	30.1	53.7	17.2	48.1
Community								
Rural	8.3	23.1	30.2	19.5	34.1	60.2	19.5	56.8
Suburban	14.5	21.8	29.6	21.5	32.1	55.1	16.9	50.6
Urban	14.7	25.3	33.1	16.7	31.8	50.5	21.1	48.0

Note: Elementary includes all those teaching in the fields of pre-kindergarten, kindergarten, or general elementary in grades K–8. It includes those teaching in self-contained classes, where the teacher teaches multiple subjects to the same class of students all or most of the day. It includes K–8 teachers employed in middle schools. It excludes departmentalized teachers who teach subject matter courses to several classes of different students all or most of the day. Elementary teachers with a major or minor in the fields of pre-elementary, early childhood, or elementary education are defined as in-field.

The teaching fields of English, math, science, and social studies include only departmentalized teachers in grades seven through twelve. It excludes those employed in middle schools. For details on definitions of these assignment fields and the major and minors defined as in-field in each, see R. Ingersoll, "The Problem of Underqualified Teachers in American Secondary Schools," *Educational Researcher*, vol. 28, no. 2 (1999), pp. 26–37.

The estimates for life science, physical science, and history represent the percentage of teachers without at least a minor in those particular subfields. For example, in science, teachers who hold a minor in any one of the sciences are defined as in-field. In physical science—which includes physics, chemistry, space science, and geology—teachers must hold a minor in one of those physical sciences to be defined as in-field, not simply a minor in any science.

Low poverty refers to schools where 15 percent or less of the students receive publicly funded free or reduced-price lunches. High poverty refers to schools where over 80 percent do so. Small schools are those with fewer than three hundred students. Large schools are those with six hundred or more students. Middle categories of poverty and size are not shown.

broad fields, such as science and social studies, that have many disciplines. Teachers in these fields are routinely required to teach any of a wide array of disciplines and subfields within the department. However, simply having a certificate in the larger field may not mean that teachers are qualified to teach all of the subjects within the field. For example, a teacher with a degree in biology and a certificate in science may not be qualified to teach physics. In science and in social studies, as shown in columns 5, 6, and 8 in table 3, there are high levels of within-department, but out-of-subfield, teaching. Over half of those teaching physical science classes (chemistry, physics, earth, or space science) are without a major or minor in any of the physical sciences. Given that most social studies teachers are expected to teach history in middle school and high school, it is worth noting that more than half of all those teaching history are without either a major or a minor in history.

Several points must be stressed concerning the validity of these data on out-of-field teaching. On the one hand, some of these out-of-field teachers undoubtedly may be qualified even though they do not have a minor or major in the field. Some may be qualified by virtue of knowledge gained through previous jobs, through life experiences, or through informal training. Others may have completed substantial college coursework in a field and have a teaching certificate but lack a major or minor in that field.

On the other hand, these measures represent a relatively low standard by which to define a qualified teacher. To many observers, even a moderate number of teachers lacking the minimal prerequisite of a college minor signals the existence of serious problems in schools. When I upgrade the definition of a qualified teacher to include only those who hold both a college major and a teaching certificate in the field, the amount of out-of-field teaching substantially increases.[28] Moreover, the numbers of students affected are not trivial: Every year in each of the fields of English, math, and history well over four million secondary-level students are taught by teachers with neither a major nor a minor in the field.

It is also important to recognize the implications of these data for explaining the sources of out-of-field teaching. One variant of the teacher deficit perspective assumes that out-of-field teaching is largely a problem of poorly prepared teachers. In this view, a lack of adequate rigor, breadth, and depth, especially in academic and substantive coursework, in college or university teacher-training programs results in more out-of-field teaching. The data show, however, that most teachers have at least a bachelor's degree and a full teaching certificate. To be sure, many of these teachers have education, not academic, degrees. But having an education degree does not mean a teacher lacks content training in a particular subject or specialty. SASS data show that few teachers have only a generic major or minor in education, such as in secondary education or curriculum. Most have subject area education majors or minors, such as in math education or English education.[29] And the latter increasingly requires substantial academic subject coursework.[30]

My point is not to dismiss the importance of teacher preparation reforms. There is no doubt the teaching force has and can continue to benefit from more rigorous higher education and training standards. My point is that this view of out-of-field teaching misses the distinction between teachers' training and teachers' assignments and confounds two different types or sources

Figure 2. Percentage of Public Secondary School Teachers (Grades Seven through Twelve) in Each Field without a Major or Minor in That Field, 1993–94 and 1999–2000

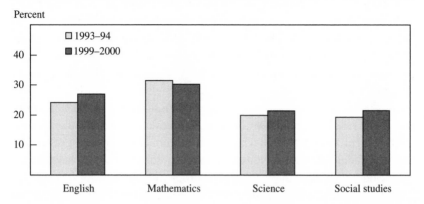

of underqualified teaching. The data show that those teaching out of field at either the elementary or secondary level are typically veterans with an average of fourteen years of teaching experience. Furthermore, about 45 percent of out-of-field teachers hold graduate degrees in disciplines other than the subjects in which they have been assigned to teach. Hence out-of-field teachers are typically experienced and qualified individuals who have been assigned to teach in fields that do not match their training or education. This is a widespread and chronic practice and has shown little change in levels over the past decade (see figure 2). The data show that each year some out-of-field teaching takes place in well over half of all U.S. secondary schools and each year over one-fifth of the public secondary teaching force does some out-of-field teaching. At the secondary level, these misassignments typically involve one or two classes out of a normal daily schedule of five classes.

The Sources of Out-of-Field Teaching

These data raise questions. If not because of inadequacies in the training of teachers, what is the reason for out-of-field teaching? What accounts for the degree to which school administrators misassign teachers?

Teacher Shortages

Do teacher shortages account for out-of-field teaching? Data from SASS and other NCES data sources show that, consistent with the shortage predictions, demand for teachers has increased since the mid-1980s.[31] Since 1984, student enrollments have increased, most schools have had job openings for teachers, and the size of the teacher work force (K–12) has increased, although the rate of these increases began to decline slightly in the late 1990s.[32] Most important, substantial numbers of schools with teaching openings have experienced difficulties with recruitment. For example, in both 1990–91 and 1993–94 about 47 percent of schools with openings reported some degree of difficulty finding qualified candidates in one or more fields.

The data also show there are several problems with teacher shortages as an explanation for out-of-field teaching. First, shortages cannot explain the high levels of out-of-field teaching that exist in English and social studies, fields that have long been known to have teacher surpluses. Second, even when the rates of student enrollment increases were at their peak in the mid-1990s, only a minority of the total population of schools experienced recruitment problems in any given field. As expected, the data also indicate that levels of out-of-field teaching were higher in schools reporting more difficulties in finding qualified candidates for their job openings. But about half of all misassigned teachers in any given year were employed in schools that reported no difficulties whatsoever finding qualified candidates for their job openings that year. Moreover, in any given year a great deal of out-of-field teaching takes place in schools that did not have vacancies or openings for teachers in that year. In sum, the data show that some schools face difficulties finding qualified teachers to fill positions, and this problem leads to out-of-field teaching assignments. But the data suggest that shortages and their attendant hiring difficulties are not the sole, or even primary, factor behind out-of-field teaching. Instead of simply focusing on macrodemographic sources of this problem, this analysis hypothesizes that out-of-field teaching is also rooted in the manner in which schools are organized and administered.

Predictors of Out-of-Field Teaching

This section presents the results of multiple regression analyses estimating the relative association between the dependent variable—each teacher's

Table 4. Multiple Regression Analysis of Percent Secondary-Level Classes Out of Field

Variable	Model 1 (b)	Model 1 (se)	Model 2 (b)	Model 2 (se)	Model 3 (b)	Model 3 (se)
Intercept	18.3*	1.36	19.4*	1.58	36.6*	3.28
School contextual characteristics						
Poverty enrollment	0.09*	0.016	0.09*	0.016	0.09*	0.016
Rural	–3.2*	0.93	–3.2*	0.93	–3.0*	0.932
Suburban	–0.6	0.95	–0.62	0.95	–0.55	0.95
District size (by 1,000)	0.01*	0.003	0.011*	0.003	0.01*	0.003
School size (by 100)	–0.30*	0.06	–0.30*	0.06	–0.09	0.06
Presence of teachers union	–0.09	0.899	–0.10	0.747	0.53	0.797
School recruiting and hiring difficulties						
Teaching job openings			–1.4	1.01	–1.4	1.01
Hiring difficulties			0.13	0.182	0.06	0.183
Administrative practices and organizational characteristics						
Major or minor required of hires					–1.5*	0.561
Principal leadership					–1.6*	0.377
Hiring or assigning underqualified					1.1*	0.533
Average class size					–0.67*	0.033
Pay incentives					–0.41	0.672
Starting teacher salary (by 1,000)					0.11	0.108
Proportion of school-level variance explained (Rsq)	0.16		0.16		0.16	
Sample size (*N*)	18,770		18,770		18,770	

Note: Unstandardized coefficients displayed.
* $p < 0.05$

percentage of out-of-field classes—and three groups of independent variables: school contextual characteristics, school recruiting and hiring difficulties, and school administrative practices and organizational characteristics. These three groups of predictors are introduced progressively in three models in table 4. This part of the analysis focuses solely on the secondary level: grades seven through twelve. The data in the previous stage of the analysis (table 3) indicated that levels of out-of-field teaching are more pronounced in secondary schools than in elementary schools. Moreover, to many observers, the problem in secondary schools is a more compelling case because classes at the secondary level usually require a greater level of subject matter mastery and training on the part of teachers than do those at the elementary school level, and, hence, being taught by an out-of-field teacher could be more consequential for students at that level.

Model 1 focuses on the school background variables. It shows that teachers in high-poverty schools are more often out of field, after controlling for other factors. While teachers in urban schools are more often out of field than teachers in rural schools, the difference between out-of-field teaching in urban and suburban schools is not statistically significant (at a 95 percent level of confidence). Both district size and school size are related to out-of-field teaching, but in opposite directions. Larger districts have more out-of-field teaching, while larger schools have less. Small schools, by definition, usually have fewer overall resources, including teaching staff, than do larger schools.[33] That smaller schools have more out-of-field teaching than do larger schools could be because the former find it more difficult to allow staff specialization, and, hence, teachers in these schools are more often required to be generalists.

The presence of a teachers union is associated with less out-of-field teaching, but the coefficient is not statistically significant. This undermines the claims of some opponents of teachers unions who have directly blamed such organizations for the prevalence of out-of-field teaching. In this view, self-serving work rules promulgated by teachers unions, especially seniority rules, are the main reason that classrooms are staffed with underqualified teachers. The use and abuse of such rules are especially prevalent, this argument holds, in times of teacher oversupply, when school officials face the need to cut or shift staff because of fiscal cutbacks or declining enrollments. In such situations, "last-hired, first-fired" union seniority rules require that more experienced teachers be given priority, regardless of competence. As a result, veteran teachers are often given out-of-field assignments, in-field junior staff are transferred or laid off, and students suffer accordingly.[34] The data do not support this viewpoint.

As shown in model 2, surprisingly, school hiring and hiring difficulties themselves do not appear to be the major underlying factors related to the amount of out-of-field teaching in schools, as held by the teacher deficit perspective. A significant bivariate positive correlation exists between the degree to which a school has difficulty finding qualified candidates to fill its openings and the degree of out-of-field teaching in the school. But after controlling for other factors, this relationship becomes weak and statistically insignificant, as shown in table 4.

The question of particular interest here is: After controlling for these characteristics of schools, what administrative practices and organizational characteristics of schools have an independent association with the average amount of out-of-field teaching in schools? The analysis in model 3 shows that several aspects of schools are related to misassignment. It also shows that the addition of this third group of variables brought little change in the coefficients of the earlier groups of predictors in models 1 and 2. One notable exception is the decrease in the school-size effect, suggesting that these aspects of school administration account for the lower amount of out-of-field teaching that large schools have.

School districts vary in the extent to which they impose standards on the teacher hiring process, and these hiring regulations are related to the average degree of out-of-field teaching in schools. The SASS data show that about two-thirds of school districts require that new teacher hires hold a college major or minor in the field to be taught, and, as shown in table 4, teachers in schools governed by these district-level policies do less out-of-field teaching.

The data also show that an additional factor associated with the degree of out of-field teaching in a school is the perceived leadership effectiveness of the principal. Schools vary in how well their faculty as a whole rate the performance of their principals on attributes of good leadership (for example, principals who recognize good teaching, communicate well, are supportive, and back up teachers). The data in table 4 show significantly less out-of-field teaching occurring in schools in which all of the teachers (regardless of whether they are misassigned or not) highly rate the leadership performance of their principals. It is unclear from this finding which aspects of principals' behavior may be related to their staffing assignment practices and whether the attitudes of teachers toward principals are a cause or effect of such practices. That is, principals who rarely misassign teachers may be appreciated for this and thus earn high ratings from the faculty as a whole, or highly rated principals may be more effective at avoiding misassigning their teachers.

While difficulty in filling teaching vacancies does not have an independent effect on the degree of out-of-field teaching, how school administrators choose to cope with their hiring difficulties does. Of those schools with teaching openings, about one-third reported the use of one or more of the following strategies to cover their vacancies: hiring less than fully qualified teachers, reassigning teachers trained in another field to teach the unstaffed classes, or using substitute teachers. Almost by definition these strategies result in out-of-field teaching, and, as expected, the analysis shows more out-of-field teaching in schools that employed more of these methods to fill their vacancies. This may seem a redundant finding, but it is necessary to control for this factor because the data indicate that misassignment takes place in schools without hiring difficulties and even without vacancies. Moreover, it is also necessary to include this factor because it is not the only strategy administrators might use in the face of difficulties.

In contrast, other school administrators might opt to expand class sizes or cancel classes instead of using misassignment to cope with staffing difficulties. The analysis shows that average class sizes are strongly related to the degree of out-of-field teaching in schools. Schools with larger classes tend to have less out-of-field teaching, after controlling for other factors. A negative association exists between whether districts provide pay incentives to teachers for training and the amount of out-of-field teaching— incentives are associated with less out-of-field teaching—but it is not of statistical significance. Finally, higher starting teacher salaries are also not significantly related to levels of out-of-field teaching.

Several cautions and limitations need to be stressed. This is an exploratory analysis and the regression models account for only a portion of school-to-school differences in out-of-field teaching. Further research is needed to refine and verify these exploratory findings. If borne out by further analysis, these findings do, however, suggest important implications for both theory and policy concerning the problem of out-of-field teachers.

Implications

This study tests the extent to which the problem of out-of-field teaching has to do with the manner in which schools are organized and teachers are employed and utilized once on the job. The analysis shows that out-of-field teaching is a common administrative practice whereby otherwise qualified teachers are assigned by school principals to teach classes in subjects that do not match their fields of training. This practice takes place as often as not in schools that do not suffer from teacher recruitment problems. Hence this analysis suggests that reform strategies that solely focus on teacher preparation or supply, while perhaps highly worthwhile, will not eliminate the problem of underqualified teaching unless they also address the problem of misassignment. In short, recruiting large numbers of new candidates into teaching and mandating more rigorous training requirements for them will not solve the problem of underqualified teaching if large numbers of teachers continue to be assigned to teach subjects other than those for which they were trained.

Focusing blame on teachers, on teacher-training institutions, or on inexorable, macro-demographic trends suggests that schools are simply victims and diverts attention from an important root of the problem—the way schools are organized and teachers are managed. A central objective of this analysis is to explore which aspects of the organization and administration of schools factor into the degree of misassignment in schools. My results suggest that the way school administrators, especially school principals, respond to and cope with staffing decisions and challenges affects the levels of out-of-field teaching more than does the extent to which schools face teacher shortages and attendant hiring difficulties. When facing difficulty finding qualified candidates to fill teaching job openings, some school principals resort to hiring less than fully qualified teachers, assigning teachers of one subject or grade level to teach classes in others, or employing substitute teachers to cover hard-to-staff classes. These decisions result in more out-of-field teaching. Sometimes these choices are unavoidable, and some out-of-field teaching must be expected. But the results also show that school principals vary in their staffing strategies. Sometimes, top-down district regulations shape the choices available. For example, school districts that have formal regulations concerning minimal training requirements for new hires have less out-of-field teaching. One of the stronger predictors of the amount of out-of-field teaching in schools is the leadership performance of principals. The measure used for the latter was a composite indicator based on evaluations by teachers and, hence, could be highly subjective. Like the other factors, however, it is also highly suggestive.

What all of these findings collectively suggest is a role for managerial choice, agency, and responsibility—elements often overlooked in the educational literature on the sources of underqualified teachers. One strategy for raising teaching quality in schools would be to improve the assignment of teachers already employed in schools. This would be a low-cost alternative or complement to strategies aiming to modify the quality or quantity of teacher-training graduates. It would also be an intervention that could be undertaken immediately, as opposed to the lag time it takes for modifications in the output of teacher-training institutions to bring about changes in classroom practice in schools.

While this analysis suggests some alternative staffing strategies for school leaders, it does not suggest any of these options will be easy or cost-free.

Staffing decisions involve some difficult trade-offs and tough choices for school administrators. For example, lowering class sizes, currently a popular reform idea, appears to come at the expense of increasing out-of-field teaching.[35] Likewise, the data suggest that reducing the size of schools, another currently popular reform idea, may also result in more out-of-field teaching. The results also contradict the view that teachers unions are a major source of out-of-field teaching. Schools with unions do not have more out-of-field teaching. Union work rules certainly have an impact on the management and administration of schools, but eliminating teachers unions will not eliminate out-of-field teaching.

Future Research Possibilities

The large-scale survey data analyzed here provide an overall portrait of the levels and sources of out-of-field teaching and can suggest which factors are associated with out-of-field teaching. But they have obvious limits for understanding the processes behind school staffing. Follow-up field investigations are needed to illuminate the decisionmaking processes surrounding the hiring, assignment, and utilization of teachers in particular kinds of schools. What are the hidden incentive systems within which administrators make staffing decisions? How do particular teachers come to be teaching particular classes? What are the reasons behind the misassignment of teachers?

Although this analysis has begun to explore the factors related to school-to-school differences in out-of-field teaching, it does not address adequately a larger question: Why is out-of-field teaching prevalent across the American K–12 education system as a whole? In addition to close-up, micro-level field studies, a second avenue for further research is macro-level, historical, and comparative investigation of the roots of this mode of organizing the work of teachers. One hypothesis is that the prevalence of out-of-field teaching is rooted in the semiprofessional status of teaching—a predominantly female occupation.

Unlike Canada and many European and Asian nations, the U.S. elementary and secondary school teaching force is largely treated as lower-status, semiskilled workers, especially those working in disadvantaged schools. Since the end of the nineteenth century American educators have promoted the view that teaching, like the traditional male-dominated professions, is highly complex work requiring specialized knowledge and skill and, like these professions, deserves commensurate prestige, authority, and compensation. These efforts have, however, met with only limited success.[36] The comparison with traditional professions is stark. Few would require cardiologists to deliver babies, real estate lawyers to defend criminal cases, chemical engineers to design bridges, or sociology professors to teach English. This also applies to the high-skill blue-collar occupations. Few, for example, would ask an electrician to solve a plumbing problem. The commonly held assumption is that such traditional male-dominated occupations and professions require a great deal of expertise and, hence, specialization is necessary. In contrast, underlying out-of-field teaching, I hypothesize, is the assumption that female-dominated, precollegiate school teaching requires far less skill, training, and expertise than these traditional professions, and, hence, specialization is less necessary. The continuing status of teaching as a semiprofession has resulted in what the data reveal: Out-of-field teaching is not simply an emergency condition, but a common and accepted administrative practice in many schools in the United States. From this perspective, the long-term solution to upgrading the quality of teaching is to upgrade the quality of the teaching occupation. A well-paid, well-respected profession would be less likely to lower standards as a coping mechanism.

Comment by Caroline M. Hoxby

In the United States, serious concern has arisen about out-of-field teaching among elementary and, especially, secondary teachers. While long-standing, it has been on the short list of key education issues since the publication of *A Nation at Risk*, twenty years ago.[37] Concern about out-of-field teaching is currently so great that the No Child Left Behind legislation promulgated in 2002 contains strong incentives for schools to eliminate it. (These incentives fall under the "Highly Qualified Teachers" section of Title I.)

Richard M. Ingersoll does not address the question of whether out-of-field teaching has a negative effect on student achievement. Answering this question convincingly is extremely difficult because schools are not randomly assigned to have out-of-field teachers. It is easy to think that one is looking at the effects of out-of-field teaching when one is merely looking at the effects of the correlates of out-of-field teaching. Thus far, no credible evidence has been published about the causal effects of out-of-field teaching, and this is problematic. Education researchers must rely on their common sense, which suggests that teachers are unlikely to be effective if they have little or no formal education in the subject they teach. Nevertheless, in reading Ingersoll's paper, one must keep in mind that the effect of out-of-field teaching remains unknown. The supposition that it is negative is based on introspection and correlational data that do not reveal causal effects. Because school administrators should logically react to the effects, not the negative appearance, of out-of-fielding, one should always be mindful that no understanding has been reached about those effects when evaluating administrators' management of their teacher work force.

The Deficit Hypothesis and the Organizational Hypothesis

All this is by way of introduction to Ingersoll's paper, written by a leading scholar who accounts for much of the existing knowledge about the prevalence of out-of-field teaching. Ingersoll attempts to explain why out-of-field teaching takes place by examining the circumstances of schools that do and do not practice it. He describes two hypotheses about why out-of-field teaching occurs: the deficit hypothesis and the organizational hypothesis. He shows that no obvious evidence exists to support the deficit hypothesis. This is a very important finding because the deficit hypothesis is thought to be so obviously correct that it does not need to be debated. The deficit hypothesis dominates education schools and policy circles. By showing that it is probably not correct, Ingersoll opens the door for the organizational hypothesis. He also offers some direct evidence that the organizational hypothesis is correct, but the latter evidence must be described as suggestive instead of causal.

Essentially, supporters of the deficit hypothesis argue that out-of-field teaching is the result of too few prospective teachers being trained in a subject area. Also, they argue, teacher pay is too low generally, and this leads to teacher shortages. The consequence of the shortages is that schools fill vacancies with underqualified teachers—specifically, teachers who may be certified or prepared in an area but who are not certified or prepared in the field to which they are assigned.

In contrast, supporters of the organizational hypothesis argue that plenty of prospective teachers are certified in subject areas, but school districts mismanage their resources so that they end up assigning teachers to classes in which their subject area knowledge is slight. Such mismanagement may occur because administrators have weak incentives to manage their teaching staffs well or because districts may face high costs (in particular, costs associated with labor unrest) of changing rigid work rules or salary contracts to attract qualified teachers. Consider a district that attempts to rewrite its teachers' contract so that teachers who have math or science skills get paid a substantial premium for filling math and science assignments in secondary schools. (Math and science skills are noteworthy because they earn significant rewards in the private sector.) In a state with laws that are highly supportive of unions (mandatory bargaining, union shops, dues checkoff, and so on), a district that tries to rewrite its contract in this way is likely to face great union resistance and perhaps labor strife. No major U.S. teachers union supports pay premia for teachers with math and science skills. As a consequence, an administrator may decide that dealing with the consequences of out-of-field teaching is less troublesome than facing the consequences of labor unrest. The administrator may therefore assign teachers to subjects in which their preparation is slim, but he or she does so knowingly.

Two Other Theories on Why Out-of-Field Teaching Occurs

At least two other possible hypotheses can be cited for why out-of-field teaching occurs. First, it may be that teachers' subject area skills are mismeasured and that most teachers who appear to be teaching without subject area knowledge do, in fact, have subject area knowledge. Such mismeasurement is most likely to occur with teachers in grades seven through nine, where one could plausibly have ample subject area knowledge without having either minored or majored in the subject in college. For instance, any graduate of a selective liberal arts college should have math and language arts knowledge that is sufficient to teach a typical seventh-grade mathematics or English class. Moving from grade seven to grades ten through twelve, it is less plausible that a person without substantial college-level coursework in a subject could have learned enough about that subject to be an effective teacher of that subject. Similarly, moving from teachers who attended very selective colleges to teachers who attended nonselective colleges, it is less plausible that a person without a major or minor in a subject could know the subject well enough to teach it.

The potential mismeasurement problem does affect Ingersoll's evidence. He measures out-of-field teaching in secondary school by grouping grades seven through twelve together. It would be helpful to have separate statistics by grade. Much of the out-of-field teaching that he identifies likely is middle school teaching. Also, it would be helpful to have some information on whether out-of-field teachers are usually from more selective colleges or less selective colleges.

Second, out-of-field teaching may not be harmful. After all, the evidence on the effects of out-of-field teaching does not come from carefully evaluated policy experiments. Instead, the evidence comes from the normal variation among schools in their use of out-of-fielding, and the schools that use it are not selected randomly. Out-of-field teaching could be correlated with lower student achievement without causing lower student achievement. For instance, out-of-field teaching might appear to lower achievement because it is correlated with parents' dedication to education in the school. Parents' dedication is not observed, however, so education researchers might attribute its effect to out-of-field teaching, in the absence of a true policy experiment. In any case, if the out-of-field teaching that occurs is not harmful, then administrators may be using it wisely to flexibly manage their staff.

Descriptive Evidence and Causal Evidence

One of the persistent difficulties for education researchers is that they rarely get to evaluate true experiments or even the partial experiments that some policy changes provide. That is, they rarely work with clean variation in the policy that interests them—in this case, out-of-field teaching. Instead, they work with variation that is tainted by or can be confounded with other factors, such as the environment in which a school operates. For instance, determining how unions affect out-of-field teaching is difficult, because unions tend to arise in districts that are disproportionately large and urban. But the factors that cause unions to arise may also have independent effects on whether out-of-field teaching occurs. A large school, for example, is unlikely to find itself with the enrollment or staffing fluctuations that produce an environment ripe for out-of-field teaching.

Ingersoll routinely runs into the problem of correlation versus causation. Put another way, the paper is at its best at providing descriptive evidence or evidence of correlations. It is not at its best when attempting to give such descriptive evidence a causal interpretation. Sometimes descriptive evidence is helpful, such as when Ingersoll is trying to determine whether much support exists for the deficit hypotheses. If the supposition is that the overwhelming reason for out-of-field teaching is a deficit of suitable candidates, then there ought to be fairly obvious evidence of a correlation between out-of-field teaching and measures of teaching deficits. If such a correlation were apparent, it would not be proof that the deficits caused out-of-field teaching, but it would be consistent with the deficit hypothesis. If there were not much of a correlation between out-of-field teaching and indicators of teaching deficits, then deficits would unlikely be the major cause of the phenomenon. For Ingersoll, correlational evidence is more useful for disproving a hypothesis than it is at proving one.

Ingersoll is interested in showing not only that the deficit hypothesis is wrong, but also that the organizational hypothesis is right. Here, the descriptive evidence is more problematic.

EVIDENCE AGAINST THE DEFICIT HYPOTHESIS. Suppose the deficit hypothesis were correct. A school that could not find a qualified candidate for a subject area teaching job could do one of two things. First, it could leave the vacancy open and either not cover the classes or cover the classes in a catch-as-catch-can way. That is, out-of-field teaching may or may not be seen in schools that report vacancies. Second, the school could close the vacancy and fill the job with an out-of-field teacher. In this case, schools without vacancies would have more out-of-field teaching. Thus one cannot build a convincing test of the deficit hypotheses by looking at the correlation between vacancies and out-of-field teaching. In short, the statistically insignificant coefficients on the "teaching job openings" variable in Ingersoll's table 4 do not convince me that the deficit hypothesis is wrong.

In contrast, one can build a convincing test by looking at the correlation between a school reporting hiring trouble and out-of-field teaching. Regardless of whether a school fills or leaves open vacancies, a school that has out-of-field teaching because of a deficit should report that it has trouble hiring. Thus the single most important result Ingersoll finds is the statistically insignificant coefficient on "hiring difficulties" in model 2 of table 4. A positive, statistically significant correlation between reported hiring difficulties and out-of-field teaching is the minimum required evidence for the deficit hypothesis. Seeing that lack of correlation, I find it very hard to believe that difficulty in hiring qualified teachers is the primary reason that schools have out-of-field teaching.

EVIDENCE FOR THE ORGANIZATIONAL VIEW. The first variables in the multiple regression analysis presented in table 4 are the school contextual characteristics. Some of these variables—such as poverty, ruralness, and district size—are clearly outside a school's control and are therefore properly viewed as exogenous forces on whether out-of-field teaching occurs. However, even the coefficients on these variables are difficult to interpret as causal relationships. For instance, does a school's being rural really make it substantially less likely to have out-of-field teaching? This seems unlikely because a school in a sparsely populated area would presumably find it structurally hardest to hire a teacher for every subject class. Also, large districts have more out-of-field teaching. This is peculiar because, structurally, a large district should be most able to reallocate teachers to meet subject area demands. In addition, large districts experience less unpredictable variation in their enrollment (simply because of the law of large numbers). This should enable them to plan better for future staffing needs.

In short, one suspects that the reason that the coefficients are as they are is that big, urban districts are the ones with substantial out-of-field teaching. They do not have out-of-field teaching for structural reasons (because these go against them), but for reasons of governance perhaps. It now becomes difficult to interpret the coefficient on the presence of a teachers union (which is insignificant) as evidence that unions have no effect on out-of-field teaching. Teachers unions arise disproportionately and are disproportionately strong in big, urban districts. So, perhaps teachers unions have no effect or perhaps the coefficients on district size and urbanness are picking up their true effect (because they are certainly not picking up the causal effects of size and population sparsity).

In short, I am not persuaded that I have learned much about the causal effects of schools' contextual characteristics from table 4. This is an example of how hard it is to interpret correlations as evidence of causation.

The variables in table 4 that I have not yet discussed are the administrative practice and organizational variables. These include whether a college major or minor is required of subject area teachers, a subjective rating of the principal's leadership, whether the school hires or assigns underqualified teachers, average class size, whether incentive pay exists, and the starting teacher salary. Of these variables, only one—the starting teacher salary—is arguably exogenous to a school. That is, a district with limited funds may have no choice but to pay lower starting salaries than it would like.

The remaining variables are determined simultaneously with whether to allow out-of-field teaching. For instance, schools that require a college major or minor from subject area hires, not surprisingly, have less out-of-field teaching. After all, the two variables have an almost mechanical relationship: If a school does not hire teachers except when they have subject area degrees, something would have to go terribly wrong with staff management before much out-of-field teaching occurred. But, the fact that a school hires only those with subject area degrees and consequently has little out-of-field teaching is likely caused by a third factor that is not understood.

Similar difficulties arise with "hiring or assigned underqualified teachers." A school that engages in this practice almost mechanically has out-of-field teaching. Indeed, one might have thought the variable was a measure of out-of-field teaching. Principals' ratings are also difficult to interpret causally. A good principal may figure out how to avoid out-of-field teaching, or a poorly circumstanced school forced to have out-of-field teaching may end up with disgruntled teachers who give their principal a low rating, even though he or she is not responsible for the overall level of resources.

In summary, on the one hand, the correlations in table 4 do not suggest that the organizational hypothesis is wrong. On the other hand, they do not constitute much evidence that it is right.

Where to Go from Here

To establish whether the organizational hypothesis is correct, an empirical strategy that focuses on policy changes would probably be useful. For instance, Ingersoll might, in the future, use multiple waves of the Schools and Staffing Surveys to form panel data. He might then investigate whether out-of-field teaching changes when a school gets unionized, takes on a new principal, or changes its hiring policies. He might use statewide class-size reduction policies to determine whether class-size reduction causally raises out-of-field teaching. He might examine changes in states' minimum pay scales to see whether out-of-field teaching among new teachers drops significantly in the year after a state pay scale rises substantially.

The most important policy changes, for determining both the effects and causes of out-of-field teaching, are those occurring because of the No Child Left Behind Act. Given that their previous research stimulated the "Highly Qualified Teachers" clauses, Ingersoll and other scholars should evaluate the consequences of the legislation. Evaluating new strictures on out-of-field teaching will undoubtedly be the best way to learn about the consequences of such strictures.

Finally, consider the larger implications of the fact that the deficit hypothesis appears to be wrong. If schools that do not have trouble hiring nevertheless practice out-of-field teaching, undue rigidities must exist in the way that teachers are allocated to classes. One suspects that these rigidities may be built into teachers' contracts. Out-of-field teaching makes it easier for a union to protect its members with long tenure, at the expense of less senior teachers with subject area knowledge.

Comment by Adam F. Scrupski

Richard M. Ingersoll maintains that out-of-field teaching assignments are not the consequence of an insufficiency of certified teachers or inadequate teacher education. Instead, he says they are the consequence of school organizational factors leading to dysfunctional administrative adaptation to particular personnel problems (the employment of teachers uneducated or uncertified for the positions to which they are assigned). But before granting him the core of his thesis, the problems and issues that the thesis reveals should be examined in some detail.

Ingersoll's enumeration of expedient ways of assigning teachers to vacancies includes the distribution of increments of student clientele among other sections of the same course. This practice has the unfortunate consequence of increasing class size and diminishing morale among the teachers who get the extra students (flouting the teacher group's demand for equal treatment). A second option involves covering classes of additional students through hiring what Ingersoll calls "long-term substitutes." However, the latter seems hardly to be an acceptable option. No pools of such substitutes exist, and hiring a long-term substitute means hiring someone per diem for a long, perhaps a semester-long, term. In New Jersey, regulations forbid the hiring of noncontractual substitutes for long-term service (no substitute teacher in New Jersey may teach for more than twenty consecutive school days). While the former alternative seems not to be seriously considered by Ingersoll, he seems to believe that the latter is a real danger and an often-chosen alternative for expediency-minded school administrators.

In his examination of the parameters of out-of-field teaching, Ingersoll attends first to a definition of out-of-field teaching based on a teacher's major. He begins with elementary school teaching and notes that 12 percent of those who teach pre-elementary or general elementary classes do not have any kind of education major and are therefore out-of-field placements.

But the phenomenon of education major seems to be a disappearing academic identity. At Rutgers, the State University of New Jersey, where I professed for thirty-three years, there has not been an education major since the 1940s. Only students with majors in the arts and sciences may apply to the Rutgers teacher preparation programs. Since 1986, New Jersey's state regulations for teacher certification also require an arts and sciences major. At about the same time, the Holmes Group, an elite collection of professional education units at research universities, called for the abolition of the education major. A steady erosion of the education major has been seen since then. The American Association of Colleges for Teacher Education estimates that thirty-eight states now insist on a major drawn from arts and sciences for teacher certification program enrollees. The appropiate identity, in this case, is not the major but the certification status, as Ingersoll himself notes: "Out-of-field placements drop significantly when looking at those without teaching certificates, in contrast to those without majors or minors." What is the big deal? one might ask. Ed major or teacher certification program? Each signifies a number of courses in pedagogy, curriculum, and foundations of education. The answer is that the inaccuracy identifies cases of out-of-field placement among elementary teachers where they do not exist, in cases in which teachers major in arts and sciences and still enroll in teacher certification programs.

Also, the practice can mask a problem that should be uncovered. For example, at Rutgers two-thirds of elementary certification program enrollees, complying with the requirement for a major drawn from the arts and sciences, major in psychology. (I have been told that is the case at other institutions as well.) And psychology is a thirty-six-credit major. How much psychology does one need to teach school? Surely the two required courses in educational psychology and developmental psychology are sufficient for the general elementary teacher. The remaining psychology credits are taking curricular room that might be occupied by studies in history, literature, music, math, biology, and other content-related areas.

To continue this digression a little further, the solution to the problem of the appropriate major for the elementary teaching aspirant may lie in some form of general liberal arts major composed of six to nine or so credits each in history, literature, math, science, and music (perhaps including piano, to counter the noisy, joyless hooks of the electric guitar). Some of my colleagues and I at Rutgers tried to subvert the psychology major by including in a revised elementary certification program a requirement for fifteen credits of a subject that is taught in the elementary school, such as those subjects noted above. However, when the new certification program was implemented, the requirement, which had been approved unanimously by the school's faculty, was not included. (I had left the program's directorship by that time, but when I asked why the fifteen-credit item was omitted, I was told that it seemed to be one new requirement too many.) The point here is that the problem of inadequate teacher capability in this case seems not to lie in day-to-day administrative expedience but in the very domain that Ingersoll abjures, teacher education and certification.

To illustrate further the complexity of organizational adaptations as they relate to the supply of teachers, consider Ingersoll's treatment of secondary out-of-field placements in the area of history, a phenomenon recently addressed by Diane Ravitch.[38] Again, terminological phenomena seem to control. It is surely lamentable, as Ingersoll notes, that over half of those reported to be exclusively teaching history are without a major or minor in the subject. However, before attributing complete chicanery, insanity, or plain sloth to those administrators responsible for such a sin of teacher assignment, note that existing social studies certification regulations in most states permit history to be taught by majors in one of the social sciences (or even a kind of interdisciplinary major called social studies) and permit history to be taught through eighth grade in a self-contained fashion by certified elementary teachers or in specialized way, usually at seventh- and eighth-grade levels, by elementary certificants as well.

What Ingersoll has revealed is an apparent weakness in the knowledge of history per se on the part of those assigned to teach the subject as specialists, a weakness whose correction lies not in the hands of day-to-day school administrators, but with state boards and teacher educators. In many cases the problem is being solved at the college certification program level. In New Jersey, despite the state-level regulations that permit any social science major to be certified to teach social studies (which includes history), Rutgers social studies teaching aspirants major in history as a consequence of advisement, and at the College of New Jersey such students are required to major in history.

But Ingersoll has performed a significant service in pointing out that a teacher's nominal identity as even a history major does not necessarily imply a subject matter background fitting him to teach any high school course in the field of history. It appears that the appropriate adaptation to such a situation lies in the hands of local school administrators who must balance the intracurricular strengths of their nominally qualified certificants.

Ingersoll's most puzzling findings are the high levels of out-of-field teaching found in secondary (grades seven through twelve) English and social studies, fields that, as he notes, have long been known to exhibit surpluses of certified teachers. Ingersoll reports that a quarter of secondary-level English teachers have neither a major nor a minor in English or related subjects and "a fifth of social studies teachers are without at least a minor in any of the social sciences, in public affairs, in social studies education, or in history." Most would perceive such findings as indicative of a travesty on secondary education. Are educational decisionmakers in the area of personnel assignment really so delinquent?

The inclusion of grades seven and eight in the category of secondary level, an organizationally related designation traceable to the long-ago days of the grades seven to nine junior high school, could provide an alternative explanation to one that implies serious culpability on the part of expediency-minded school administrators. In most states, elementary certification extends through grade eight. A teacher so certified can legitimately teach all subjects at any grade level through eighth grade. Such a teacher also is certified to teach any single subject, say social studies or English, in a specialized way, but not beyond the eighth-grade level.

Many school administrators and many teachers seem to find that experienced K–8 certified elementary teachers, such as those "veterans with an average of fourteen years of teaching experience" whom Ingersoll found commonly teaching out of field, are better teachers of English or social studies at seventh- or eighth-grade levels than relatively inexperienced certified secondary English or social studies teachers. Because those veteran elementary K–8 teachers are certified to teach English and social studies to seventh or eighth graders, the principal assigns them so to teach. (Schools and Staffing Survey data for 1999–2000 show very high percentages of middle school students learning English and social studies from teachers without a major or credential in the respective subjects, the consequence of elementary teachers assigned to teach the two subjects in either a self-contained or specialized fashion.)

Why might experienced certified elementary teachers be better adapted to teach special subjects, particularly English and social studies, to seventh and eighth graders than specialist-trained high school teachers? Prospective answers to such a question are related to the organizational features of the school as a singular institution, those that Ingersoll said he would rely on to explain out-of-field teaching. Students of the school as an organization and even experienced school personnel can offer at least three reasons.

1. Many educators believe that at seventh- and eighth-grade levels, transitional stages between elementary and high school, students should have teachers who commonly relate to students in more personally diffuse and particularistic ways, as elementary teachers have learned to do, than the more subject-oriented high school teachers are used to doing. It is also believed that experienced elementary school teachers take a greater range of responsibility for student behavior and achievement than do high school teachers, whose reference group instructionally speaking is more likely to be the higher education professoriate, who tend to take a more limited responsibility for student performance.

2. Some secondary administrators like to place seventh and eighth graders in core curriculum arrangements in which a single person teaches both humanities-related subjects, English and history (called social studies). One central New Jersey district (whose high school seniors have on occasion had the highest SAT scores in the state and which has an extremely demanding parent clientele) so organizes seventh and eighth grades, asking that its English-teaching certified specialists gain elementary certification so that they can teach history, too, and that its social studies specialists gain elementary certification so they can also teach English, even though each would be considered out of field in teaching one of the subjects.

3. Classroom discipline problems are considered to be greatest in seventh and eighth grade (before disaffected students reach school-leaving age and can be persuaded, perhaps by a retention or two, to drop out). Also, social studies and English are largely talk courses with a good deal of classroom discussion that places a strain on pupil attention and teacher control. Elementary teachers are believed to be better disciplinarians, more likely to monitor their own behavior for disorder-stimulating propensities and generally taking a greater range of responsibility for classroom happenings. They are more likely to call for parent conferences to alert parents to their children's weaknesses and to enlist parents in dealing with them. They also are less apt to readily refer out-of-order pupils to a principal, a course of

action that Willard Waller called "system building" and which tends to weaken the authority of both teacher and principal.[39] If the purviews and objectives of the middle school curricular and pedagogical adaptations are valid, as they seem to be, the solution is hardly a requirement for dual specialized subject certification supported by a major in both subjects. But it may suggest a preservice preparatory academic program of a humanities-oriented nature, including substantial components of curricular-related work in history and literature, again a case of teacher education, not everyday administrative action.

One implication of the preceding observations is that the Schools and Staffing Survey indicants of teacher qualification in a given subject may be too general, too merely nominal, to be of value in identifying weaknesses in a teacher's preservice instructional program and, therefore, in relating the resultant credential to measures of pupil performance—the last a demonstration that Ingersoll gives short shrift to in his paper. While he asserts in his paper that "teaching . . . has an extensive body of empirical research documenting the proposition that the qualifications of teachers are tied to student outcomes," the three studies cited lend only limited support to the proposition. The most recent comprehensive study on the effect of teacher certification on students' achievement found a relationship only in the area of mathematics. Results for both history and English were indeterminate.[40]

I might offer one suggestion drawn from my years as a middle school principal during a period of genuine teacher shortage (early 1960s). Completion of a certification program may imply more than effective training in pedagogy. Much evidence suggests that teachers are not so instrumentally affected by that pedagogical training. Comparing certification program completers with provisionally certified teachers, many with strong subject matter backgrounds, I found the former considerably more serious about and more committed to teaching. Perhaps their certificates and the academic and clinical experiences they signified were a kind of occupational ante, ensuring embracement of teaching roles. Or perhaps the certification program courses were a testing ground for diligence, independent action, assumption of serious responsibility, attention to detail, and self-monitoring, all necessary for the systematic planning, confident classroom management, and continual assessment of pupil performance that effective public school teaching entails. I found that the provisional-type teachers, for whom the selection of teaching as an occupation (a career change for some) was more a matter of immediacy—not the culmination of long-term aspirations and programmatic preparation, but a kind of occupational trying on of the teacher persona (or their conception of the teacher persona) to see if it fit the personality—were less likely to embrace the rigors, the hard demands, of the teacher role, however temporarily enacted.

To the extent that school administrators, in making assignments of teachers, are mobilizing functional teacher propensities (say, general intelligence, alertness to what might be considered the gestalt of the classroom as an instructional arena, sensitivity, verbal capability) that are independent of teachers' major or credentialed status, they will contribute to its lack of relationship to student performance.

Ingersoll, after making his case for organizational sources of out-of-field placements, suggests that schools simply need to improve the assignment of teachers already employed. In a presumptive reference to Dan Lortie's insightful study of autonomy and control in elementary school teaching, Ingersoll seems to rely on the title of the book (*The Semi-Professions and Their Organization*) containing Lortie's essay to suggest that the upward mobility of the teaching occupation itself, not an ameliorative upgrading of its laggard incumbents, is required for raising the standards of professional service and ultimately obviating out-of-field teaching. Ingersoll would have been better advised to cite Lortie's genuinely organizationally related observations concerning the strength of the teacher informal group, whose intrinsic reward structure and professional egalitarianism allow it to wield sanctions vis-à-vis the principal that enforce teacher demands for such measures as conformity with official (state-level) regulations that affect teachers' classroom performance. In an incisive application of social exchange theory, Lortie says the teacher group gives the principal the school if the principal gives the teachers the classroom, where teachers' intrinsic rewards are situated. The principal's reciprocal gift giving includes the teachers' specific classroom teaching assignments. Thus an organizationally related explanation of administrative maintenance, not subversion, of certification regulations is found.

Hanging together for Ingersoll as potential explainers of out-of-field placements that vary by school are poverty level: the less the poverty, the fewer the out-of-field placements; presence of hiring standards (essentially an indicant of superordinate administrative base-touching): the more explicit the standards, the fewer the out-of-field placements; and leadership effectiveness of the principal: the greater the teachers' satisfaction with principal performance, the fewer the out-of-field assignments. All of these factors suggest a school or district of greater administrative accountability (explicit standards), higher teacher morale and work satisfaction (greater satisfaction with principal behavior), and more scrutinizing (higher-income) parents; in short, a better integrated social system, in Parsonian terms.

What do these characteristics imply? I suggest that they imply a discerning, demanding parental clientele—a clientele with a removable stake in the school's success, not easily cowed by the school bureaucracy—and that the parental demand is the essential factor in the appropriate placement of teachers. As one long-experienced middle school teacher once told her principal, "Our supervisors are the demanding parents in this district; if we satisfy them, we don't have to worry about you." Such parents will not tolerate expedient out-of-field teacher placements. Nor should any parents.

How can a school's parents be empowered? How can parents as individuals and as a collectivity be made into effective mediators vis-à-vis the school? Only a greater stake in the effectiveness of the school, it seems, can make a difference. What seems in order is some alteration in institutional structure that transforms the identity of the desirable parent from that of a homework supervisor and Parent-Teacher Association member to that of an everyday social capitalizer, empowered client of the school, and integral member of the school's client community. This is an age of private, independent action on the part of parents as stewards of their children's education, and it is that private option that needs to be supported in all the dimensions it requires.

Notes

1. For example, National Commission on Excellence in Education, *A Nation at Risk: The Imperative for Educational Reform* (Washington: Government Printing Office, 1983); National Academy of Sciences, *Toward Understanding Teacher Supply and Demand* (Washington: National Academy Press, 1987); National Commission on Teaching and America's Future, *What Matters Most: Teaching for America's Future* (New York: 1996); and National Commission on Teaching and America's Future, *Doing What Matters Most: Investing in Quality Teaching* (New York: 1997).

2. See E. Hirsch, J. Koppich, and M. Knapp, *Revisiting What States Are Doing to Improve the Quality of Teaching: An Update on Patterns and Trends* (University of Washington, Center for the Study of Teaching and Policy, 2001); E. Feistritzer, *Alternative Teacher Certification: A State-by-State Analysis 1997* (Washington: National Center for Education Information, 1997); and W. Kopp, "Reforming Schools of Education Will Not Be Enough," *Yale Law and Policy Review,* vol. 10 (1992), pp. 58–68.

3. Notable exceptions to this include G. W. Haggstrom, L. Darling-Hammond, and D. Grissmer, *Assessing Teacher Supply and Demand* (Santa Monica, Calif.: RAND Corporation,

1988); and T. Sizer, *Horace's Compromise: The Dilemma of the American High School* (Boston: Houghton Mifflin, 1992).

4. See R. Ingersoll, *Teacher Supply, Teacher Qualifications, and Teacher Turnover* (Washington: National Center for Education Statistics, 1995); R. Ingersoll, *Out-of-Field Teaching and Educational Equality* (Washington: National Center for Education Statistics, 1996); R. Ingersoll, "The Problem of Underqualified Teachers in American Secondary Schools," *Educational Researcher,* vol. 28, no. 2 (1999), pp. 26–37; and R. Ingersoll, *Out-of-Field Teaching, Educational Inequality, and the Organization of Schools: An Exploratory Analysis* (University of Washington, Center for the Study of Teaching and Policy, 2002).

5. See, for example, S. Bobbitt and M. McMillen, *Qualifications of the Public School Teacher Workforce* (Washington: National Center for Education Statistics, 1995); L. Lewis and others, *Teacher Quality: A Report on the Preparation and Qualifications of Public School Teachers* (Washington: National Center for Education Statistics, 1999); and M. McMillen and others, *Qualifications of the Public School Teacher Workforce: 1987–88 to 1999–2000* (Washington: National Center for Education Statistics, 2002).

6. See, for example, Education Trust, *Education Watch* (Washington: American Association for Higher Education, 1996); Education Trust, *Education Watch* (Washington: American Association for Higher Education, 1998); National Commission on Teaching and America's Future, *What Matters Most*; National Commission on Teaching and America's Future, *Doing What Matters Most*; Education Week, *Quality Counts: A Report on Education in the Fifty States*, 1997, 1998, 2000, and 2003.

7. For a review, see Ingersoll, "The Problem of Underqualified Teachers in American Secondary Schools."

8. See, for example, L. Darling-Hammond, *Teacher Quality and Student Achievement: A Review of State Policy Evidence* (University of Washington, Center for the Study of Teaching and Policy, 1999); American Council on Education, *To Touch the Future: Transforming the Way Teachers Are Taught* (Washington: 1999); S. Soler, *Teacher Quality Is Job One: Why States Need to Revamp Teacher Certification* (Washington: Progressive Policy Institute, 1999); T. Toch, "Why Teachers Don't Teach: How Teacher Unions Are Wrecking Our Schools," *U.S. News and World Report,* February 26, 1996, pp. 62–71; Bill Clinton, *State of the Union Address* (Washington: Government Printing Office, 1999); and Committee for Economic Development, *American Workers and Economic Change* (New York: 1996).

9. This viewpoint is especially common among news columnists. See, for example, the syndicated columns of David Broder, Thomas Sowell, and Maggie Gallagher the week of September 14–20, 1996.

10. See, for example, National Commission on Teaching and America's Future, *What Matters Most*; and National Commission on Teaching and America's Future, *Doing What Matters Most*.

11. R. Ingersoll, *Who Controls Teachers' Work? Power and Accountability in America's Schools* (Harvard University Press, 2003).

12. M. Kirst, *Who Controls Our Schools? American Values in Conflict* (New York: W. H. Freeman Co., 1984); and J. Coleman and T. Hoffer, *Public and Private Schools: The Impact of Communities* (Basic, 1987).

13. B. Delany, "Allocation, Choice, and Stratification within High Schools: How the Sorting Machine Copes," *American Journal of Education,* vol. 99, no. 2 (1991), pp. 181–207; and Allen Ruby, "An Implementable Curriculum Approach in Improving Science Instruction in Urban Schools," paper presented at the annual meeting of the American Educational Research Association, Montreal, Canada, 1999.

14. Education Week, *Quality Counts,* 2000; and V. Robinson, *Making Do in the Classroom: A Report on the Misassignment of Teachers* (Washington: Council for Basic Education and American Federation of Teachers, 1985).

15. Ingersoll, "The Problem of Underqualified Teachers in American Secondary Schools."

16. Haggstrom, Darling-Hammond, and Grissmer, *Assessing Teacher Supply and Demand.*

17. For information on the Schools and Staffing Survey, see S. Choy and others, *Schools and Staffing in the U.S.: A Statistical Profile, 1990–91* (Washington: National Center for Education Statistics, 1993); or R. Henke and others, *America's Teachers: Profile of a Profession, 1993–94* (Washington: National Center for Education Statistics, 1997).

18. See, for example, R. Ferguson, "Paying for Public Education: New Evidence on How and Why Money Matters," *Harvard Journal on Legislation,* vol. 28 (1991), pp. 465–98; R. Greenwald, L. Hedges, and R. Laine, "The Effect of School Resources on Student Achievement," *Review of Educational Research,* vol. 66 (1996), pp. 361–96; and S. Raudenbush, R. Fotiu, and Y. Cheong, "Synthesizing Results from the Trial State Assessment," *Journal of Educational and Behavioral Statistics,* vol. 24, no. 4 (1999), pp. 413–38.

19. See, for example, E. Haertel, "New Forms of Teacher Assessment," in G. Granted, ed., *Review of Research in Education,* vol. 17 (Washington: American Educational Research Association, 1991), pp. 3–29; W. Haney, G. Madus, and A. Kreitzer, "Charms Talismanic: Testing Teachers for the Improvement of American Education," in Ernst Z. Rothkopf, ed., *Review of Research in Education,* vol. 13 (Washington: American Educational Research Association, 1987), pp. 169–238; and M. Kennedy, "The Problem of Improving Teacher Quality While Balancing Supply and Demand," in E. Boe and D. Gilford, eds., *Teacher Supply, Demand, and Quality* (Washington: National Academy Press, 1992), pp. 63–126.

20. For further discussion of the debate over the necessity of teacher qualifications, see R. Ingersoll, "Misunderstanding the Problem of Out-of-Field Teaching," *Educational Researcher,* vol. 30, no. 1 (2001), pp. 21–22.

21. Previous studies have used a number of different measures of out-of-field teaching, representing a range of standards. Some measures focus on whether teachers have a teaching certificate in the fields they teach, others focus on whether teachers have an undergraduate or graduate degree, and still others focus on whether teachers have both a certificate and a degree in the fields they are assigned to teach. Measures of out-of-field teaching also vary according to whether they focus on the numbers of teachers doing it or the numbers of students exposed to it and according to which fields and subjects are examined and which grade levels are investigated. This study uses several different measures of out-of-field teaching, drawn from this previous work. For a detailed review and evaluation of a variety of different measures of out-of-field teaching, see R. Ingersoll, "Measuring Out-of-Field Teaching," 2002, available from the author.

22. For more detail on this second type of out-of-field teaching measure, see Ingersoll, *Teacher Supply, Teacher Qualifications, and Teacher Turnover.*

23. The data in column 1 of table 3 refer to public elementary and middle school (kindergarten through grade eight) teachers whose assignment is pre-elementary or general elementary and who teach in self-contained classes. The latter refers to those who teach multiple subjects to the same students for all or most of the day. This excludes departmentalized elementary teachers and specialists such as those who teach art, music, physical education, math, or special education to different students throughout the day.

24. The data in columns 2–8 of table 3 refer to public secondary school (grades seven through twelve) teachers who are departmentalized. The latter refers to those who teach subject matter classes to different classes of students for all or most of the day. It excludes departmentalized teachers employed in middle schools.

25. For details on these particular measures, see Ingersoll, "The Problem of Underqualified Teachers in American Secondary Schools"; and Ingersoll, "Measuring Out-of-Field Teaching."

26. See, for example, K. Haycock, "Good Teaching Matters . . . A Lot," *Thinking K–16: A Publication of the Education Trust,* vol. 3, no. 2 (1998), pp. 3–14; K. Haycock, "No More Settling for Less," *Thinking K–16: A Publication of the Education Trust,* vol. 4, no. 1 (2000), pp. 3–12; Ingersoll, *Out-of-Field Teaching and Educational Equality*; C. Jerald and R. Ingersoll, *All Talk, No Action: Putting an End to Out-of-Field Teaching* (Washington: Education Trust, 2002); and R. Ingersoll, *Out-of-Field Teaching and the Limits of Teacher Policy* (University of Washington, Center for the Study of Teaching and Policy, 2003).

27. Ingersoll, "The Problem of Underqualified Teachers in American Secondary Schools"; and R. Ingersoll, *Can the No Child Left Behind Act Solve the Teacher Quality Problem?* (Washington: National Governors' Association, 2003).

28. Ingersoll, "Measuring Out-of-Field Teaching."

29. Ingersoll, "The Problem of Underqualified Teachers in American Secondary Schools."

30. National Association of State Directors of Teacher Education and Certification, *Manual on Certification and Preparation of Educational Personnel in the United States and Canada* (Sacramento, Calif.: 1997).

31. See, for example, Ingersoll, "The Problem of Underqualified Teachers in American Secondary Schools"; and R. Ingersoll, "Teacher Turnover and Teacher Shortages: An Organizational Analysis," *American Educational Research Journal,* vol. 38, no. 3 (2001), pp. 499–534.

32. D. Gerald and W. Hussar, *Projections of Education Statistics to 2008* (Washington: National Center for Education Statistics, 1998); and T. Snyder, C. Hoffman, and C. Geddes, *The Digest of Education* (Washington: National Center for Education Statistics, 1997), pp. 12–13.

33. D. Monk, "Secondary School Size and Curriculum Comprehensiveness," *Economics of Education Review,* vol. 6, no. 2 (1987), pp. 137–50.

34. For example, Toch, "Why Teachers Don't Teach."

35. For insightful discussion of the unanticipated outcomes of elementary school class-size reduction reforms in California, see Haycock, "Good Teaching Matters . . . A Lot"; B. Stecher and others, "Class-Size Reduction in California: A Story of Hope, Promise, and Unintended Consequences," *Phi Delta Kappan,* vol. 82, no. 9 (2001), pp. 670–74; and G. Bohrnstedt, B. Stecher, and E. Wiley, "The California Class-Size Reduction Evaluation: Lessons Learned," in M. C. Wang and J. D. Finn, eds., *How Small Classes Help Teachers Do Their Best* (Temple University, Center for Research in Human Development and Education, 2000), pp. 201–26.

36. D. Lortie, "The Balance of Control and Autonomy in Elementary School Teaching," in A. Etzioni, ed., *The Semiprofessions and Their Organizations: Teachers, Nurses, and Social Workers* (Free Press, 1969), pp. 1–53; Burton Clark, "The High School and the University: What Went Wrong in America, Parts 1 and 2," *Phi Delta Kappan,* vol. 66 (1985), pp. 392–97, 472–75; and R. Ingersoll, "The Status of Teaching as a Profession," in Jeanne Ballantine and Joan Spade, eds., *Schools in Society: A Sociological Approach to Education* (Belmont, Calif.: Wadsworth Press, 2000), pp. 115–29.

37. National Commission on Excellence in Education. *A Nation at Risk.*

38. Diane Ravitch, "The Educational Backgrounds of History Teachers," in P. N. Stearns, P. Seixas, and S. Wineburg, eds., *Knowing, Teaching, and Learning History* (New York University Press, 2000), pp. 143–55.

39. Willard Waller, *The Sociology of Teaching* (John Wiley, 1957).

40. Andrew Wayne and Peter Young, "Teacher Characteristics and Student Achievement Gains: A Review," *Review of Educational Research,* vol. 73, no. 1 (Spring 2003), pp. 89–122.

The Ed School's Romance with Progressivism

DAVID F. LABAREE

Progressivism became the natural ideology of education professors in the twentieth century—shaping their language and the language of American education, even though it had little impact on the practice of teacher educators and researchers or on the practice of teachers in schools. And although this ideology represents an approach to issues of teaching and learning in the public schools that is well suited to the needs of education professors, it is antithetical to the aims of the current standards-based reform movement.

The struggle for control of American education in the early twentieth century was between two factions of the movement for progressive education. The administrative progressives won, and they reconstructed the organization and curriculum of American schools in a form that has lasted to the present day. Meanwhile, the pedagogical progressives failed miserably in shaping what is done in schools, but they succeeded in shaping how to talk about schools. Professors in schools of education were caught in the middle of this dispute, and they ended up in an awkwardly compromised position. Their hands were busy, preparing teachers to work within the confines of the educational system established by the administrative progressives and carrying out research to make this system work more effi-

This paper is drawn from the final two chapters of my book *The Trouble with Ed Schools*, which is scheduled for publication by Yale University Press in 2004. I am deeply grateful to the following colleagues for the insightful critical readings they gave of earlier versions of these chapters: Tom Bird, Jeffrey Mirel, Lynn Fendler, and Barbara Beatty. In addition, I want to thank E. D. Hirsch Jr., Barbara Beatty, and Diane Ravitch for their insightful comments on the earlier draft of this paper, which I presented at the Brookings conference on education policy, held in May 2003. I also benefited from the comments of a number of other participants at that conference.

ciently. But their hearts were with the pedagogues. So they became the high priests of pedagogical progressivism, keeping this faith alive within the halls of the education school and teaching the words of its credo to generations of new educators.

In the lingo of American education today, progressivism means pedagogical progressivism. It means basing instruction on the needs, interests, and developmental stages of the child; teaching students the skills they need to learn any subject, instead of focusing on transmitting a particular subject; promoting discovery and self-directed learning by the student through active engagement; having students work on projects that express student purposes and that integrate the disciplines around socially relevant themes; and promoting values of community, cooperation, tolerance, justice, and democratic equality. In the shorthand of educational jargon, these traits are capsulized in phrases such as "child-centered instruction," "discovery learning," and "learning how to learn." And in the current language of American education schools, a single label captures this entire approach to education: constructivism.

As Lawrence A. Cremin has pointed out, by the 1950s this progressive approach to education had become the dominant language of American education.[1] Within the community of professional educators—that is, classroom teachers and the education professors who train them—progressivism provides the words used to talk about teaching and learning in schools. And within education schools, progressivism is the ruling ideology. It is hard to find anyone in an American education school who does not talk the talk and espouse the principles of the progressive creed.

This situation worries some educational reformers. Progressivism runs directly counter to the main thrust of educational reform efforts in the United States in the early twenty-first century. Reform is moving toward establishing rigorous academic frameworks for the school curriculum, setting performance standards for students, and using high-stakes testing to motivate students to learn the curriculum and teachers to teach it. Education schools and their progressive ideals stand in strong opposition to all of these reform efforts. In addition, reformers are seeking to reduce government regulation of access to teaching, by supporting alternative modes of teacher preparation, while ed schools strongly defend their role as the gatekeepers to the profession. To today's reformers, therefore, with their strong orientation toward standards and deregulation, ed schools look less like the solution than the problem.

But these reformers should not be so worried—for two reasons. First, this form of progressivism has had an enormous impact on educational rhetoric but very little impact on educational practice. This conclusion was reached by historians of pedagogy, such as Larry Cuban and Arthur Zilversmit, and by contemporary scholars of teaching practice, such as John I. Goodlad and David K. Cohen.[2] Instruction in American schools is overwhelmingly teacher-centered; classroom management is the teacher's top priority; traditional school subjects dominate the curriculum; textbooks and teacher talk are the primary means of delivering this curriculum; learning consists of recalling what texts and teachers say; and standardized tests measure how much of this students have learned. What signs exist of student-centered instruction and discovery learning tend to be superficial or short-lived. Educators talk progressive, but they do not teach that way. In short, traditional methods of teaching and learning are in control of American education. The pedagogical progressives lost.

Second, reformers should not worry about contemporary progressivism because its primary advocates are lodged in education schools, and nobody takes these institutions seriously. Those teaching in the university think of those in ed schools as being academically weak and narrowly vocational. They see ed school teachers not as peers in the world of higher education but as an embarrassment, who should not be part of a university at all. To them the ed school looks less like a school of medicine than a school of cosmetology. The most prestigious universities often try to limit the ability of the education school to grant degrees or even eliminate the school altogether. I do not have space to explain the historical roots of the education school's lowly status in the United States. But take my word for it: Education schools rank at the very bottom.[3] As a result of this, ed school educators have no credibility in making pronouncements about education. They are solidly in the progressive camp ideologically, but they have no ability to promote progressive practices in the schools. In fact, they do not even practice progressivism in their own work, as seen in the way they carry out research and the way they train teachers.

I will not propose ways to resolve the standoff between ed schools and the reform movement. Ed schools are unlikely to convert to the standards ideology and the reform movement is unlikely to convert to ed school progressivism. Each is more apt to seek to make the other irrelevant, as each attempts to bypass instead of transform the other. And in such a contest, ed schools will continue to lose, as they have always done, because the only part of education they dominate is the rhetoric, whereas the reformers are aiming to control the core elements of curriculum, testing, and governance. I will explore the nature of the ed school's rhetorical commitment to progressivism and its roots in the history of this beleaguered institution. My hope is that this analysis will be helpful to participants on both sides of the policy divide.

The Roots of the Ed School's Ties with Progressivism

Why do American education professors have such a long-standing and widely shared commitment to the progressive vision? The answer can be found in the convergence between the history of the education school and the history of the child-centered strand of progressivism during the early twentieth century. Historical circumstances drew them together so strongly that they became inseparable. As a result, progressivism became the ideology of the education professor.

Education schools have their own legend about how this happened, which is a stirring tale about a marriage made in heaven, between an ideal that would save education and a stalwart champion that would fight the forces of traditionalism to make this ideal a reality. As is the case with most legends, there is some truth in this account.

But here I want to tell a different story. In this story, the union between pedagogical progressivism and the education school is not the result of mutual attraction but of something more enduring: mutual need. It was not a marriage of the strong but a wedding of the weak. Both were losers in their respective arenas. Child-centered progressivism lost out in the struggle for control of American schools, and the education schools lost out in the struggle for respect in American higher education. They needed each other, with one looking for a safe haven and the other looking for a righteous mission. As a result, education schools came to have a commitment to progressivism that is so deeply rooted that, within these institutions, it is largely beyond challenge. At the same time, however, this progressive vision never came to dominate the practice of teaching and learning in schools—or even to penetrate the practice of teacher educators and researchers within education schools themselves.

How Dewey Lost: A Short History of Progressive Education

To examine the roots of the education school's commitment to a particular form of progressivism, the history of the progressive education movement in the United States in the first half of the twentieth century must be explored. Only then can an understanding be reached about the way that the institution and the ideology fell into each other's arms.

The progressive education movement in the United States was not a single entity but a cluster of overlapping and competing tendencies. All of the historians of this movement agree on this point, although they use different nomenclature. David Tyack talks about administrative and pedagogical progressives; Robert L. Church and Michael W. Sedlak use the terms *conservative progressives* and *liberal progressives*; Herbert Kliebard defines three groupings, which he calls social efficiency, child development, and social reconstruction.[4] I will use the administrative and pedagogical labels, which seem to have the most currency, with the understanding that the conservative and social efficiency groups fit more or less within the administrative category and the liberal and social reconstructionist groups fit roughly within the pedagogical, with child development straddling the two.[5]

Over time, the administrative progressives trounced their pedagogical counterparts. Ellen Condliffe Lagemann explains this with admirable precision:

> I have often argued to students, only in part to be perverse, that one cannot understand the history of education in the United States during the twentieth century unless one realizes that Edward L. Thorndike won and John Dewey lost. The statement is too simple, of course, but nevertheless more true than untrue and useful for several reasons. First, it suggests that, even if Thorndike and Dewey both spoke and wrote in the "progressive" idiom, the differences of view that separated them were large and significant. Beyond that, it calls attention to differences in the way each man's ideas were received. If Dewey has been revered among some educators and his thought has had influence across a greater range of scholarly domains—philosophy, sociology, politics, and social psychology, among them— Thorndike's thought has been more influential within education. It helped to shape public school practice as well as scholarship about education.[6]

What this means for my purposes here is that the pedagogical progressives had the most impact on educational rhetoric, whereas the administrative progressives had the most impact on the structure and practice of education in schools. A sign of the intellectual influence exerted by the pedagogical group is that its language has come to define what is now called progressivism. And this language has become the orthodox way for teachers and teacher educators to talk about classroom instruction. At the same time, however, the administrative progressives were most effective in putting their reforms to work in the daily life of schools.

THE TWO FORMS OF PROGRESSIVISM IN THE EARLY TWENTIETH CENTURY. A number of prominent leaders are counted among the pedagogical progressives, including Francis W. Parker, G. Stanley Hall, William H. Kilpatrick, George S. Counts, Harold O. Rugg, and Boyd H. Bode. However, John Dewey was the godfather of this movement. He was not particularly happy to be in this position. During his lifetime, he frequently complained about the misuse of his ideas by many of the pedagogical progressives, and he would not be pleased about many of the things that contemporary education professors espouse in his name. But, for better or for worse, most of the central ideas of the current progressive creed can be traced to his writings.

Perhaps the best way to characterize the central thrust of the pedagogical progressive view of education is to follow the lead of E. D. Hirsch Jr. and point to its essential romanticism. Hirsch sees two romantic beliefs in particular lying at the heart of educational progressivism.

> First, Romanticism believed that human nature is innately good, and should therefore be encouraged to take its natural course, unspoiled by the artificial impositions of social prejudice and convention. Second, Romanticism concluded that the child is neither a scaled-down, ignorant version of the adult nor a formless piece of clay in need of molding, rather, the child is a special being in its own right with unique, trustworthy—indeed holy—impulses that should be allowed to develop and run their course.[7]

Closely linked to these beliefs is "the idea that civilization has a corrupting rather than a benign, uplifting, virtue-enhancing effect on the young child."[8] From this perspective, traditional education is not just an ineffective method of instruction but one that is misdirected and damaging, by seeking to impose a fixed body of knowledge on the child at the will of the teacher. The romantic alternative is a naturalistic pedagogy (which arises from the needs, interests, and capacities of the child and responds to the will of the child) and a skill-based curriculum (which focuses on providing the child with the learning skills that can be used to acquire whatever knowledge he or she desires).

Two important components of the naturalism inherent in progressive pedagogy, according to Hirsch, are developmentalism and holistic learning. If learning is natural, then teaching needs to adapt itself to the natural developmental capacities of the learner, which requires a careful effort to provide particular subject matters and skills only when they are appropriate for the student's stage of development. Developmentally appropriate practices and curricula are central to the progressive vision. The second key extension of the naturalistic approach to teaching is the idea that learning is most natural when it takes place in holistic form, where multiple domains of skill and knowledge are integrated into thematic units and projects instead of being taught as separate subjects. This thus results in the progressive passion for interdisciplinary studies, thematic units, and the project method.

What held the pedagogical progressives together was a common romantic vision, but the vision that held the administrative progressives together was strictly utilitarian. And whereas the former focused on teaching and learning in the classroom, the latter focused on governance and on the structure and purpose of the curriculum. In addition to Thorndike, highly visible members of this group in the first half of the twentieth century included David Snedden, Ross L. Finney, Edward A. Ross, Leonard Ayres, Charles Ellwood, Charles H. Judd, Ellwood P. Cubberly, Charles C. Peters, W. W. Charters, John F. Bobbitt, Charles Prosser, and, in conjunction with the pedagogical progressives, G. Stanley Hall.

The organizing principle of the diverse reform efforts that arose from the administrative progressives was social efficiency. In one sense, this meant restructuring the governance and organization of schooling to make it run more efficiently, in line with business management practices. In another sense, social efficiency meant reorganizing education to make it more efficient in meeting the needs of economy and society, by preparing students to play effective adult roles in work, family, and community. This utilitarian vision was strikingly different from the romantic perspective of the pedagogical progressives, who wanted school to focus on the learning needs and experiences of students, in the present instead of the future, as children instead of as apprentice adults. It led to the administrative progressives' most distinctive contribution to American education: scientific curriculum making. This notion of curriculum was grounded in differentiation. It started with the developmental differences in students at different points in their social and intellectual growth, as spelled out in the work of psychologists such as Hall, and with the differences in intellectual ability of students at the same age, as measured by the apparently objective methods of the new intelligence quotient (IQ) testing movement. The idea then was to match these differences in the abilities of individual students with the different mental requirements of the vast array of occupational roles required by a complex industrial society. And the curriculum approach that linked these two came from the enormously influential learning theory of the psychologist Edward L. Thorndike.

According to Thorndike, skills learned in one kind of learning task did not carry over well to other kinds of tasks. This was in direct opposition to nineteenth-century faculty psychology. It also contradicted the psychological theory of the pedagogical progressives, who put primary emphasis on students' learning to learn and saw subject matter as a secondary concern, valuable mostly as a medium for skill acquisition rather than as the substantive focus of learning.[9] Thorndike's view had enormous consequences for the curriculum. It meant that a core curriculum, concentrated in a few academic disciplines, made no sense for schools, especially at the secondary level where students were getting closer to their adult roles. Instead, a vastly expanded array of curriculum options was needed, differentiated both by student abilities and by projected future occupation and focused on the specific knowledge and skills that the student can handle and that the job requires. From this perspective, then, all education was vocational.

The administrative progressives were enormously successful in putting through their agenda in two areas in particular—governance and curriculum. In governance, they succeeded in consolidating small school districts into larger units, centralizing control of schools in the district in the hands of a small elite school board that was buffered from politics, and in lodging daily management of the schools in a bureaucracy staffed with professional administrators.

They assembled their ideas on curriculum in a highly influential report published in 1918—*The Cardinal Principles of Secondary Education*—and they managed to put most of them into practice in the schools.[10] One measure of this was their success in transforming traditional disciplinary subjects (such as math, science, history, and English) into a form that was less narrowly academic and more broadly aligned with the diffuse social efficiency aims of *Cardinal Principles*. The most successful change along these lines was the reconstruction of history as social studies, but other successes included the invention and dissemination of general math and general science. Other signs of the impact of the social efficiency agenda were the sharp decline in classical languages and the more moderate but still significant drop in modern language enrollments.[11]

But the biggest impact was in the shift toward a curriculum that was vocational in purpose and differentiated in structure. As David L. Angus and Jeffrey E. Mirel show in their study of high school course enrollments in the twentieth century, most courses that students were taking in the 1930s were still nominally in traditional academic subjects, not in the new vocational, health, and home economics courses.[12] But these academic courses themselves had already undergone transformation into a social efficiency form, such as social studies and general science, and the purpose of the whole curriculum was now increasingly recast as an effort to prepare students for their vocational roles as workers and homemakers, whatever the particular course title. Most important, Angus and Mirel found that the curriculum was increasingly expanded to provide a wide array of academic and nonacademic courses at multiple ability levels, which were intended to meet the needs of students with widely differing occupational trajectories and academic skills. This differentiation of the curriculum, with accompanying segregation of studies by gender and social class, was the most striking and enduring of the consequences of the social efficiency agenda for schools.

The pedagogical progressives did not see all of this as bad news. The two forms of progressivism, for all their differences, had several key elements in common that allowed them to join forces on occasion or at least tolerate each other. One was a shared belief in developmentalism, which led them to call for education that was adapted to the capacities of students at particular stages of intellectual and social growth, although they took off from this basic position in different directions. The administrative progressives combined developmental differences with same-age differences in ability to provide the rationale for a radically differentiated curriculum, whereas the pedagogical progressives used developmentalism as a basis for opposing a standardized curriculum and supporting a learning process shaped by individual student interest and initiative. The strongest bond between the two strands of progressivism, however, was their common dissatisfaction with, and often active hostility toward, the traditional academic curriculum. In their opposition to discipline-based school subjects, the two stood together, although the grounds for their attacks were different. Administrative progressives saw academic subjects as an impediment to the acquisition of the useful knowledge needed to play adult social and economic roles. The pedagogical progressives saw these subjects as an imposition of adult structures of knowledge that would impede student interest and deter self-directed learning.

However, the main thrust of the social efficiency curriculum, with its emphasis on vocational training and differentiated outcomes, was diametrically opposite to the core principles of the pedagogical progressives. It mandated the kind of top-down curriculum that the latter abhorred, imposed on students to serve society's need for particular skills and knowledge, and forcing them to spend their time in schools being socialized for the adult social roles they would later play. This puts priority on learning particular subject matter instead of learning to learn; it elevates the interests of society and of school administrators over the interests of students; it makes the classroom a preparation for adulthood instead of an exploration of childhood; and, in the name of these social benefits, it risks extinguishing the child's engagement in learning and curiosity about the world. It was, in short, the kind of curriculum that Dewey deplored—"externally presented material, conceived and generated in standpoints and attitudes remote from the child, and developed in motives alien to him."[13]

Not only did the social efficiency curriculum threaten the kind of natural learning process treasured by the pedagogical progressives, but it also threatened the values of social justice and egalitarian community that were central to their beliefs. While this curriculum was radical in its challenge to traditional notions of academic education, it was profoundly conservative in its embrace of the existing social order and in its eagerness to prepare students for predetermined positions within that order.[14] It introduced tracking and ability grouping into American schools; it introduced ability testing and guidance as ways of sorting students into the appropriate classes; and it institutionalized the educational reproduction of social inequality by creating a system in which educational differences followed from and in turn reinforced differences in class, gender, and race.

While the administrative progressives enjoyed considerable and enduring success in implementing their program, pedagogical progressives did not. In general, the inroads they made on practice were small and fleeting. Zilversmit summarized his study of school districts in the Chicago area in a way that paralleled the view expressed by Dewey himself looking back on the progressive movement from the perspective of the early 1950s.[15] Zilversmit put it this way: "The ultimate failure was that so much of progressivism's apparent success was rhetorical. While some schools and individual teachers had heeded Dewey's call for a more child-centered school, most had given only lip service to these ideas while continuing older practices."[16] Schools that adopted progressive teaching with any depth and seriousness were few, and these efforts usually did not last. Private progressive schools popped up, flourished for a while, and then typically reverted to type when the founder died or moved on. Public school systems that took the plunge likewise slipped back to a more traditional academic curriculum over time.

WHY THORNDIKE WON. First, the administrative progressives' reform message appealed to people in power. Business and political leaders were attracted to a mode of educational reform that promised to eliminate waste, to organize and manage schools more efficiently, to tailor instruction to the needs of employers, to Americanize the children of immigrants, and to provide students with the skills and attitudes they would need to perform and to accept their future roles in society. For people who could make these reforms happen, this was the right message at the right time.

Second, the utilitarian quality of the administrative progressive agenda was easier to sell than the romantic vision of the pedagogical counterparts. Administrative progressives were offering a way to make schools work better in serving society's needs, whereas the pedagogical progressives were offering a way to make learning more natural, more intrinsically engaging, more authentic. In a contest between utility and romance, utility is usually going to win. It promises to give people something they need, not merely something they might like.

Third, the administrative progressives argued that their agenda stood on the authority of science. The pedagogical progressives also drew on science in making their claims (for example, Dewey published a book in 1929 called *The Sources of a Science of Education*), but they had a harder time demonstrating the empirical effectiveness of such diffuse notions as child-centered instruction and the project method. Meanwhile the social efficiency leaders adeptly deployed data from a flood of tests and statistics and school surveys to prove the value of their reforms.

Fourth, as Lagemann points out, Dewey lost the battle for the schools in part because he retired early from the field.[17] His direct involvement in schools lasted only eight years, from the founding of the Laboratory School in 1896 until the time he left Chicago and entered the philosophy department at Columbia University in 1904. After that, his work on education was spun out of memory and woven into theory, giving it an abstract and academic air, and these qualities became an enduring legacy for the pedagogical progressives. In contrast, the administrative progressives were deeply involved in the schools as administrators, policymakers, curriculum developers, and educational researchers. Empirically grounded, personally engaged, and resolutely practical, they enjoyed enormous credibility in promoting their reform agenda. Under these circumstances, it should be no surprise that Dewey's main effect was on educational rhetoric while Thorndike's main effect was on educational practice.

Finally, the administrative progressives' focus on the management of schools and the structure of the curriculum gave them an important power advantage over the pedagogical progressives, who focused on teachers and their practice in the classroom. Teachers were in a weak position to effect change in the face of opponents who were school administrators and educational policymakers. This was especially true when the latter had managed to define the administrative and curriculum structures within which teachers had to function. Even teachers who wanted to carry out child-centered instruction in their classrooms found themselves confined within a bureaucratic school system that mandated a differentiated and vocationally oriented curriculum nonconducive to this kind of teaching. Under these circumstances, it is no surprise that teachers were more likely to adopt some rhetoric from pedagogical progressivism and to inject some token activity and movement into their classrooms than they were to implement the full Deweyan agenda.

How the Rhetoric of Pedagogical Progressivism Came to Rest at the Ed School

So how did the triumph of the administrative progressives affect education schools? As Michael B. Katz has argued, academic units focused on education started out with a critical stance toward their subject, but by the 1930s they had evolved into a strictly functional role supporting the existing system of schooling.[18] By this time, schools were organized according to the principles of administrative progressivism. They were professionally managed organizations devoted to the production of socially efficient educational outcomes. They sorted students by academic ability and future job prospects and then provided a stratified curriculum designed to meet these highly divergent needs. The job of education schools was to prepare teachers and administrators who could operate efficiently within this model of schooling and to carry out research that would make the system run more smoothly.

It was a job, to be sure, but it was not much of a mission. Ed schools presented the education professor as a functionary, a cog in the new social efficiency education machine, but this left the professor with nothing to profess. Administrative progressivism promised a cold and scientific kind of educational efficiency. This was cause enough for some professors. Many of the administrative progressives were themselves education professors, particularly those in programs such as administration, educational psychology, and testing. Yet for most of the faculty, especially those involved in curriculum and instruction and teacher education, this was not the kind of cause that made them want to jump out of bed in the morning and race into work.

With their roles thus downscaled and de-skilled, it is easy to understand why the success of administrative progressivism reinforced the education faculty's attraction to pedagogical progressivism. The latter was a vision of education that could get an education professor's blood pumping. Pedagogical progressivism proposed to do much more than just make schools efficient. It called for turning education upside down, by having the purposes and interests of the student drive the curriculum instead of forcing the curriculum onto the student. It offered a way to free schools from artificial constraints and rigid disciplines and unleash the student's natural impulse to learn. It proposed to re-create the classroom as a model democratic community of learners, which could become a way to reduce injustice and enhance democratic equality in the larger society.

Pedagogical progressivism, therefore, may have lost the fight to shape practice in schools and even in education schools. But the vision was still alive, and in the education school it found an ideological safe haven. It offered most education professors the mission they needed to infuse meaning into their newly redefined work as teacher educators and functionaries in the educational machine. They did their teaching and research within the structure defined by Thorndike, but their hearts and minds belonged to Dewey. Not for nothing has Dewey's picture been found on the wall in so many education school offices for so many years.

This rhetorical entrenchment of pedagogical progressivism within the education school posed no serious threat to the accomplishments of the administrative progressives. Early on, the two groups in the progressive movement had in effect divided the territory between themselves, with one taking the ground and the other taking the air: The administrative progressives focused on organization and the pedagogues on rhetoric. As Lagemann suggests, it probably all started when Dewey left the lab school for the philosophy department. The control of the administrative progressives over organization, curriculum, and practice in schools was so secure that they could afford to have faculty members in education schools spouting the creed of child-centered instruction. The professors could teach the language of Dewey to teacher candidates, employ it in decorating their scholarship, and talk it up in their workshops in schools. Teachers, too, could come to talk the talk of pedagogical progressivism, but, like the professors, they also had to work within the differentiated and vocationally oriented structure of schooling created by the administrative progressives, so the consequences for this structure were minimal.

The persistence of a harmlessly rhetorical form of pedagogical progressivism within the education school also proved useful to the newly established administrative progressive order in schools by providing it with much-needed ideological cover. Social efficiency education, when examined closely from the perspective of American traditions of democratic equality and individual opportunity, was not an attractive sight. As a social process, it sorted students into ability groups based in part on social origins, provided them with access only to the knowledge deemed within their ability, and then sent them off to particular positions in the pyramid of jobs based on their academic attainments. As an educational process, it was mechanistic, alienating, and dull, with a dumbed-down curriculum and a disengaging pedagogy. This was a coldly utilitarian and socially reproductive vision of schooling, and the offer it made to students—learn a skill and take your place in the work force—was hard to get excited about and easy to refuse. Into this efficient and heartless environment, the romantic educational vision of the pedagogical progressives introduced welcome elements, such as natural learning, student-centered teaching, interest-based curriculum, and possibilities for personal fulfillment and social improvement. Therefore having education schools imbue student teachers with a commitment to this kind of engaging and optimistic form of teaching and learning helped make the whole prospect of social efficiency education seem a little more palatable.

The Consequences of Ed School Culture: Little Harm, Little Help

In light of the ed school's many failings, critics not surprisingly often identify it as a prime source of the problems with American schools. But I have some good news to report: The ed school is simply too weak to perpetrate such a crime. Institutionally it is clearly implicated in the work of schools, and rhetorically it provides support for some of the problems in schools, so it cannot claim to be innocent of their failings. But if a fair-minded jury examined the evidence for the charge that the ed school has ruined public education, it would find enough room for doubt to render a verdict of not guilty.

For many critics this charge rests on the ed school's deep attachment to progressive ideas. These ideas are dangerously wrong, they say, and the ed school has done its damage to the schools by forcing these ideas into the classroom through the media of teacher education and educational research. They see this impact occurring in two main areas. Ed school progressivism, they argue, has directly undermined the content of the curriculum in schools, promoting activity and skill training over the acquisition of substantive knowledge; and it has undermined the commonality of the curriculum, promoting differentiated access to knowledge and thus sharply increased social inequality. In exploring this indictment of the ed school, I draw on two prominent books that make this case with vigor, *The Schools We Need and Why We Don't Have Them*, by E. D. Hirsch Jr., and *Left Back: A Century of Failed School Reforms*, by Diane Ravitch.[19]

Undermining Academic Content

On the issue of identifying the ed school's role in undermining content, no one has been more effective than Hirsch, who sees the root of the problem in what he calls the formalism and naturalism of the progressive approach to education. His reaction to the progressives' formalism—their love affair with the learning process—is to assert that learning has to be about something, namely, the subject matter in the school curriculum.

> It is a fallacy, then, to claim that the schools should or could teach all-purpose reading, thinking, and learning skills. But paradoxically, adequate attention to the transmission of broad general knowledge actually does lead to general intellectual skills. The paradox is quite stunning. Our emphasis on formal skills has resulted in students who are deficient in formal skills, whereas an appropriate emphasis on transmitting knowledge results in students who actually possess the skills that are sought by American educators—skills such as critical thinking and learning to learn.[20]

In response to the progressive vision of a naturalistic pedagogy, Hirsch argues that nothing necessarily natural exists about the kind of learning children are expected to do in school. Children learn spoken language on their own through informal interaction with family and friends, he acknowledges, but learning to read is something different, because it requires systematic instruction to accomplish it effectively and efficiently. He argues that learning is too important to be left to the discretion of minors, that developmentalism leads to delaying and differentiating students' access to knowledge, and that holistic, project-based instruction fails to establish a solid basis for learning in the individual disciplines.

This critique makes considerable sense to me. Something is dangerous about the way pedagogical progressives emphasize process over content, treating curriculum as an open category to be filled by whatever substantive knowledge is convenient in hopes of teaching students to learn on their own. Hirsch, however, is more effective in explaining the potential damage that progressive ideas might have on the content of the curriculum than in demonstrating that they have had this effect. The problem is in trying to show that the ed school—the sad sack of American higher education—has had the muscle to inflict so much damage. Hirsch acknowledges the weakness of ed schools; in fact, he emphasizes this issue. But he tries to spin the weakness of ed schools into a form of strength. After detailing how education professors are held in low esteem by their colleagues at the university, he argues, "The plight of education schools in the universities is counterbalanced by their enormous importance in the sphere of teacher certification and their huge ideological influence in the nation's schools."[21]

He suggests two factors that give ed schools the leverage to suppress academic learning in American classrooms: their structural role in certifying teachers and their ideological dominance in the education community.

THE ED SCHOOL'S CONTROL OF TEACHER CERTIFICATION. Ed schools do occupy the central position in the structure for certifying teachers, which potentially gives them considerable power, and they use this position to try to convert their student teachers to the progressive view of teaching—as an inquiry-based, child-centered, and activity-oriented practice aimed at promoting learning skills rather than at transmitting an academic curriculum. However, several factors severely undercut that power. For one thing, prospective teachers can get into the classroom in several ways without first passing through an ed school teacher education program, which include pursuing one of several different alternative certification programs and getting hired with little or no formal training by means of a temporary, provisional, or emergency license.[22]

But the most important factor that belies the ed school's "enormous importance in the sphere of teacher education" is the consistent finding in the research on teacher education that these programs exert remarkably little impact on the way their graduates teach. In a review of the literature on teacher change, Virginia Richardson and Peggy Placier report that teacher education programs are more effective at moving "students to the point of indicating on a short-answer or multiple-choice test that they have acquired academic knowledge about teaching and learning" than at changing their fundamental views about teaching.

> What we see expressed in these current studies of teacher education is the difficulty in changing the type of tacit beliefs and understandings that lie buried in a person's being. These cognitions and beliefs drive everyday classroom practice within local contexts.[23]

One study after another reported "that students did not change their beliefs and assumptions about good teaching during the course of their teacher education programs." Instead, studies found "that the novices' perspectives tended to solidify rather than change over the course of the student teaching experiences."[24] (I explain some of the reasons for this elsewhere.)[25]

Prospective teachers learn about teaching from a sixteen- or seventeen-year apprenticeship of observation as students, which provides them with a powerful attachment to an image of teaching that several years in a teacher preparation program can do little to change.[26] Compounding this resistance to the teacher ed message is the strong belief among prospective teachers and the public at large that teaching is natural and easy and therefore does not require extensive professional training. Finally, student and novice teachers are quickly drawn into the culture of practice in the schools, which to them represents the compelling practical story about teaching in contrast with the less useful theoretical version they get in the ed school.

So, contrary to Hirsch's claim, the ed school's structural position as the conduit for teacher preparation and certification has not given it the kind of power that would be required to divert schools from academic learning to the progressive focus on learning to learn. But what about its ideological position as the mother church of the progressive creed?

THE ED SCHOOL'S CONTROL OF EDUCATIONAL RHETORIC. Here Hirsch is on stronger ground. The primary accomplishment of the ed school's pedagogical progressives in the first half of the twentieth century was to gain hegemony over educational discourse in the United States. About this point there does not seem to be much disagreement.

Looking closely at most of the claims people make about the dominance of ed school progressivism over American education, the strongest evidence is found in rhetoric instead of practice. For example, Jeanne S. Chall, in *The Academic Achievement Challenge*, mounts a book-length attack on progressivism for undermining academic achievement in schools. This book provides a useful analysis of the central differences between progressive and traditional ideas about pedagogy and curriculum, but it never demonstrates that the former established itself in school practice at the expense of the latter. In chapter 7, "Student-Centered Education: From Theory to Practice," Chall seeks to address this issue directly. She begins by noting that "some researchers have found that progressive education was not as widely implemented in practice as was thought earlier," citing in particular the work of John I. Goodlad and Larry Cuban.[27] She then goes on to say, "And yet, it would seem that most schools were influenced in some ways by progressive education. This influence was reflected by their accepting certain concepts and beliefs from progressive education without necessarily implementing the broader program."[28]

This is hardly a strong claim about the impact of progressivism on practice, is it? She talks about how "it would seem" progressivism had an impact "in some ways," especially given that the impact was primarily on "accepting certain concepts and beliefs" rather than "implementing the broader program." In the rest of the chapter she does little to show the effect of theory on practice, presenting instead a series of examples that for the most part demonstrate the way educators talk about schooling, using progressive ideas such as "readiness," "naturalness," and "the whole child."

Consider other examples. From within the ed school community, John Goodlad's 1983 study of more than one thousand classrooms in thirty-eight elementary and secondary schools in all regions of the United States presents a detailed portrait of teaching that fits the traditional model much better than the progressive model.[29] Or a recent study by the Manhattan Institute purports to show the impact of progressive ideas on teacher's practice (the title is *What Do Teachers Teach?*), but it is based on a survey of teacher beliefs about teaching, not their practices, and thus it confirms only the familiar point that teachers talk about what they do in the language of progressivism.[30]

Differentiating Access to Knowledge

In *Left Back*, historian Diane Ravitch argues, parallel to Hirsch, that, over the course of the twentieth century, ed school progressivism undermined the academic content of the curriculum in American schools. But she emphasizes another related aspect of its negative impact on learning—the way progressivism produced a differentiated access to knowledge and thereby destroyed the democratic promise inherent in public education.

> As enrollments in school increased in the early twentieth century, there was a decided split between those who believed that a liberal education (that is, an academic curriculum) should be given to all students and those who wanted such studies taught only to the college-bound elite. The latter group, based primarily in the schools of education, identified itself with the new progressive education movement and dominated the education profession in its formative years.[31]

Curriculum in American schools is differentiated, especially at the secondary level; on that point there is wide agreement. Students are exposed to different kinds of knowledge, and this differentiation takes three forms: tracking within schools, ability grouping within classrooms, and tracking between schools. Ravitch's concern about this differentiated curriculum, similar to the concern expressed by Hirsch in the bestseller *Cultural Literacy*, is that it prevents students from acquiring the common body of knowledge that they need to function effectively as citizens in a democracy.[32] The problem with ed school progressivism, she argues, is not only that it undercuts the academic curriculum in general in favor of vocational and student-initiated studies, but also that it limits access to this rich resource to only a few of the most privileged students in the top tracks and at the best schools. For the less privileged students, the curriculum becomes diffused, dumbed down, vocationalized, and socially limiting.

This is a familiar argument in the research literature in education, but it has usually come from the political left. An entire body of work known as social reproduction theory emerged in the 1960s, which argued that schooling serves to reproduce social inequality by sorting students according to their social origins, tracking them into stratified classes that gave them access to different levels of knowledge, and then channeling them into jobs at different levels in the stratified occupational structure, with the result that students from the various social classes and ethnic groups end up in positions similar to the ones occupied by their parents.[33]

The difference in *Left Back* is that Ravitch does not present the pattern of stratified learning and stratified social outcomes as the result of the basic inequality in the structure of American society, but instead as the result of misguided curriculum ideas promulgated by ed school progressives. On this point we disagree. She portrays the whole progressive movement as the cause of the problem, whereas I lay the blame primarily on the administrative progressives. In the struggle for the control of the progressive movement, the administrative progressives succeeded in exerting the greatest impact on practice, while the pedagogical progressives had the greatest impact on rhetoric.

Administrative Progressives Did It

Curriculum differentiation arises from two central principles of the administrative progressives—developmentalism and social efficiency. According to the developmental approach, education can be effective only if it is tailored to the developmental needs of the individual student. From this perspective, a common academic curriculum is counterproductive, because it fails to take into account what kind of learning students will be able to accomplish in light of their cognitive capabilities at a given point. Pitching the curriculum too fast or too slow, too high or too low for a particular student will produce frustration and failure instead of learning. Therefore, a student's level of learning must be assessed through systematic testing and then that student should be assigned to the appropriate curriculum. And as a practical matter, given that individualized instruction is unrealistic in a classroom of twenty-five or thirty students, this means assigning each student to an appropriate ability group or tracked class along with other students who are at approximately the same developmental level.

The principle of social efficiency operates at two levels in the administrative progressive approach to curriculum. At the societal level, social efficiency means that schools need to produce graduates who are capable of filling the full array of occupational positions in a complex social structure if the society is going to function efficiently. Because different jobs require substantially different kinds of knowledge and skill, schools need to differentiate the curriculum in a way that approximately matches the differential knowledge requirements of these jobs. Under these circumstances a common academic curriculum is dysfunctional, both because the commonality of learning fails to meet the needs of a differentiated society and because the academic nature of learning fails to prepare students for the practical demands of work. At the school level, social efficiency means that schools need to organize themselves in a manner that allows them to manage this complex instructional task efficiently. A heterogeneous collection of students needs to be assigned into grades by age and then assigned into ability groups and tracks by development level. To do this, a system of testing and a stratified array of course options, whose number and distribution are a function of the capabilities of the students and the capacities of the staff, are required. Because this system embeds ability in track level more than grade level, and because students tend to stay in the same track during their school careers, social promotion must be instituted to keep students moving through the grades and out the door.

The administrative progressives' devotion to developmentalism and social efficiency led not only to a curriculum that was differentiated but also to one whose academic content was substantially lower than before. If school subjects have to be adjusted to the capacities of students and to the requirements of the job market, and if most students have modest capacities and most jobs have modest skill requirements, then only a few classes need provide a rigorous academic content for the college-bound elite, while most students need classes that are less academic, less demanding, and better suited to their modest future roles in society. This is a straightforward prescription for diluting academic content. As a result, the administrative progressives were responsible for turning the meat of academic subjects into meatloaf, with such inventions as social studies, general science, and home economics. The recommendations of the *Cardinal Principles* report, the canonical statement of the administrative progressive view of the curriculum, defined the seven goals of education as almost everything but academic learning—"health," "command of fundamental processes," "worthy home membership," "vocation," "citizenship," "worthy use of leisure," and "ethical character."[34] The report was explicit on the centrality of vocational studies and the marginality of the academic.

> The range of such curriculums should be as wide as the school can offer effectively. The basis of differentiation should be, in the broad sense of the term, vocational, thus justifying the names commonly given, such as agricultural, business, clerical, industrial, fine-arts, and household-arts curriculums. Provision should be made also for those having distinctively academic interests and needs.[35]

Therefore, on the charge that ed school progressives ruined schools by eradicating academic content, I say they tried but failed. On the charge that they ruined schools by differentiating the curriculum, I say, flat out, they did not do it. In fact, they were philosophically opposed to this effort. The real culprits in both cases were the administrative progressives, who had motive and opportunity, and whose guilt is well supported by the evidence.

Ed Schools Did Not Even Do It to Themselves

Although the rhetoric of ed schools is unrelentingly progressive, their practice is not. At these institutions both the production of research and the preparation of teachers take place under a veneer of pedagogical progressivism, but in each case the internal machinery supports the operation of the social efficiency structure of schooling, with one supplying its technology and the other its technicians.

First, consider the practice of research. At the end of her authoritative history of American educational research, Ellen Condliffe Lagemann concludes that this research took an early direction whose legacy for education is "deeply troubling."

> To look at the history of education research is to discover a field that was really quite shapeless circa 1890 and quite well shaped by roughly 1920. By that date, research in education had become more technical than liberal. It was more narrowly instrumental than genuinely investigatory in an open-ended, playful way.[36]

What emerged from this foundation was the tradition of research on teacher effectiveness that became the dominant form of educational research in the twentieth century, as Alan R. Tom and Lee S. Shulman show in their respective surveys of the subject.[37]

By the end of the century, this type of work was under fire from other researchers, who advanced alternative forms of research that were less prescriptive and more interpretive and that fostered a pedagogy that was more progressive.[38] But a good case can be made that the instrumental approach is still alive and well and continues to occupy a strong position in the field. In his review of the research literature, Robert E. Floden finds considerable "evidence that research on teaching effects is vital and highly regarded."[39] A key reason for that is that many policymakers and funding agencies are now asking researchers for more evidence regarding effects on student learning.[40] The No Child Left Behind Act (P.L. 107-110), signed into federal law in 2002, included language mandating scientifically based research to support programs with proven effectiveness, which led to the establishment of guidelines for authoritative research about effective methods in the Education Department's What Works Clearinghouse and which also quickly prompted the education research community to come up with its own defense in *Scientific Research in Education*.[41]

This is a good case of how structural imperatives trump rhetorical commitments for educational researchers. Ed professors may prefer the progressive approach to teaching and learning, but all of the mandates and incentives from policymakers, school administrators, and funding agencies line up behind a demand for research that shows "what works"—in particular what techniques and curricula demonstrably raise the scores of students in tests of academic achievement.[42] Throughout the twentieth century, progressive-minded researchers have dutifully lined up to play a supporting role in this effort.

A similar pattern is evident in the practice of teacher preparation. The university education school, in its formative phase in the early twentieth century, adapted itself organizationally to the emerging structure of professional roles in the school systems created by the administrative progressives. In so doing, it traded critical distance for lasting functionality. As Michael Katz suggested, education professors could have treated their field as a discipline, establishing for themselves a role in generating innovative ideas about education and in providing independent criticism of the way things are done in schools.[43] But this would have meant ceding the main work of preparing educational practitioners to the teachers colleges, thus permanently confining university ed schools to the margins of the burgeoning educational enterprise. So, instead, the education faculty adopted the model of the professional school, organized around the production of practitioners for the socially efficient school system, a strategy that opened up large and lasting opportunities for creating faculty positions and attracting research dollars. This gave ed schools a sizable, visible, and enduring role in the vast arena of public education, but it locked them firmly in place within the existing educational structure. Their critical stance toward education was reduced to a pedagogical progressivism that necessarily remained primarily rhetorical, while they focused their instructional efforts on preparing students to work in the real world of schools.

Thus in the preparation of teachers as well in the production of research, structural realities triumphed over rhetorical ideals for the American ed school. Education professors may prefer to produce teachers who will carry out the progressive ideal of student-centered, integrated, and inquiry-based learning, but they have accommodated themselves, however reluctantly, to the role pushed on them, which is to prepare teachers who will fit into the existing pattern of teacher-centered, differentiated, and curriculum-driven instruction in schools.

Ed Schools Are Easy to Blame but the Fault Lies Elsewhere

Ed schools are an obvious and easy target for anyone who wants to place blame for problems with American education. They are obvious because they are so clearly in the middle of things, preparing teachers and producing research, purveying the talk that educators talk. They are easy because their social standing is so low, because their progressive rhetoric is so close to self-parody, and because their weakness leaves them in no position to fight back effectively.

The problem with this situation is that blaming ed schools for these problems is simply wrong. Education professors love to talk like John Dewey, but, like everyone else in education, they walk in the path of Edward Thorndike. If their progressive rhetoric were faithfully put into practice in American classrooms, the impact on teaching and learning might be negative in significant ways. I agree with critics that the progressive emphasis on classroom process over curriculum content and on discovery by students over instruction by teachers could be harmful to teaching and learning. But these critics can relax. The impact has been minimal. The mistake that critics have made is in taking education professors at their word instead of watching them in action, in listening to teachers talk about their practice instead of observing what they do in the classroom.

Comment by E. D. Hirsch Jr.

David F. Labaree's historical analysis of progressivism belongs in the tradition of Larry Cuban, Arthur Zilversmit, and, most recently, Ellen Condliffe Lagemann. That tradition readily concedes that romantic progressivism has permeated education schools to the point of intellectual monopoly, but, according to these historians of education, romantic progressivism has never taken over the public schools as a method of teaching. As proof of this they show that a considerable amount of whole class instruction is still going on, that students' seats are still arranged in rows, and that students are still asked to complete exercises in workbooks. I am inclined to concede this point, as I think all education historians probably should, given the believable observational reports, most recently from Jay Matthews. I have always assumed that this claim of progressive apologetics was probably right in a narrow sense.

At the same time, I have long thought that this narrow point is almost completely irrelevant to the most important historical influence of progressivism, which is less its influence on pedagogy than its influence in diluting and fragmenting the elementary curriculum to a truly harmful and indefensible degree.

One of the troublesome features of the discipline of history is that, although it may carry the trappings of punctilious scholarship, its interpretation of the potentially infinite data is not something that can be given by the data themselves. The data supporting one historical interpretation are never the same as the data supporting another. Thus, without declining into facile postmodernism, one can accept the disconcerting, long-conceded point recently made once again by Arthur Schlesinger Jr. when reviewing a new biography of Andrew Jackson: History is an unending conflict of conversations. Regarding the conversation about the influence of progressivism, this history clearly is very different when looked at through one filter than it is when looked at through another.

Cuban's book, which founded the tradition in which Labaree now writes, is entitled *How Teachers Taught*. Cuban's point, like Labaree's, was that teachers are on the whole still teaching the same way they did in 1890. Hence progressivism, despite all the complaints leveled at it, has had negligible real effects in the schools.

But turn a different filter on the data, and consider a somewhat different topic about the history of American elementary schools, namely, what teachers taught. This is a curiously understudied historical topic. Some data on the topic in the form of preserved tests from earlier days, and earlier textbooks, suggest that elementary students in the public schools received a demanding and coherent set of learnings. But this is, as I say, a neglected topic, and I believe it is hugely significant that Cuban, and Labaree, and the dominant tradition of ed school–generated history have disregarded the subject of what teachers taught.

The resulting focus on pedagogy and the resulting neglect of content in historical studies themselves may be owing to the progressivist sympathies of the historians, who seem to assume, in concord with the ideas of progressivism, that the specific content of the elementary curriculum is not of central historical or educational importance.

But I believe most people would think that the subject has high historical significance. Granted that a golden age of American education has never existed, was there nonetheless a time during the pre-progressive era when a typical public school determined specifically what content children should learn in first grade, second grade, third grade, and so on, so that the content of one grade could build on the previous one in a cumulative, nonrepetitive way? To those outside of the progressive dispensation, this would seem to be a significant historical question. And I believe and predict that when historians get around to studying this question in depth the answer will prove to be, "Yes, there was a time when the elementary school curriculum was specific, cumulative, and nonrepetitive."

By contrast, this has certainly not been the case in recent decades, under the dominant progressive dispensation. I know that at first hand, because for the past decade I have been visiting schools that wish to adopt the Core Knowledge curriculum, and until the recent advent of the state standards movement, those schools have had no difficulty adopting it while still following their vague district guidelines. This strange fact first caused the Core Knowledge movement to come to national notice. A reporter from the *Wall Street Journal* had heard about a public school in Florida that had decided to adopt the Core Knowledge curriculum. On the scene, the reporter asked the principal what curriculum the Core Knowledge curriculum had replaced. When the principal said that it had not replaced anything, that the school was still following the local guidelines and teaching Core Knowledge at the same time, the reporter, a hard-headed investigative type, pressed further. "Look, it had to replace something," he repeatedly said. "No," persisted the principal, "we're still following the district guidelines, we're just putting in some definite content."

What the principal said was true, and under the progressive dispensation it has been true until recently in nearly every district in the nation. There has been essentially no elementary curriculum in the ordinary meaning of the term. The district guidelines typically said: "The student will learn about distant lands and customs." "The student will practice critical thinking." Into such rubrics almost any content could be fit, with the result that the actual curriculum received by students has often consisted of numbing repetitions of lessons about the rain forest and *Charlotte's Web* and glaring gaps where there should have been instruction about photosynthesis and the American Revolution.

Labaree and Lageman want to blame all this on the so-called administrative progressives fathered by Edward L. Thorndike instead of the romantic progressives fathered by John Dewey. But, in a telling passage in Labaree's paper, he discusses the implications of Thorndike's ideas. Thorndike had exploded the notion that studying hard subjects such as Latin disciplined the mind, enabling it to tackle other, unfamiliar hard subjects. No, according to Thorndike, transfer of skill from one subject matter or discipline to another is not evident, and this finding is still strongly supported today. And what are the curricular implications of Thorndike's argument? Many cognitive psychologists would say that his finding supports the idea of a broad general early education in the humanities, arts, and sciences, precisely because skills are not transferred, and nobody can predict what specific line of endeavor a student will later pursue. But, as Labaree points out, this inference was not drawn by either the administrative or the romantic progressives. The administrative types thought that what children should study would be determined by their intelligence quotients (IQs) or their parents' station in life. The romantic types thought that what children should study would be determined by their individual temperaments and stages of development. Both left content up for grabs. Labaree makes an important admission: This general tendency against defining any curriculum was agreeable to both parties—both the administrators whom he blames and the romantics whom he exculpates by suggesting they had no influence. But this is a crucial concession regarding the influence of both kinds of progressivism, because the abandonment of a common democratic elementary curriculum whether in the name of social pseudoscience or in the name of romantic individualism was the most crucial change that the movement wrought.

But that point about content aside, I think it is wrong to suggest that progressivism had no significant effect upon pedagogy. Three familiar examples from recent decades prove this point. First, the whole language method of teaching reading was disastrous. Reading pedagogy belongs to the sphere of pedagogical method. The whole language method, the grandchild of the whole word method sponsored by William H. Kilpatrick and other progressives in the 1920s, is an idea that must be laid at the feet of the ed schools. Ed schools indoctrinated teachers in the virtues of this method of teaching reading. Not only that, ed schools, with their characteristic intolerance of dissent, directed heavy scorn against those who, like my former ed school colleague Connie Juel, dared to suggest that the scholarship went the other way. A gentle person, she was upset constantly to be called derisively a "phonicator." The whole language movement was a child of the ed schools, hatched and nurtured there, successfully pressed upon future teachers, and still, miraculously, widely advocated there.

Second, teaching critical thinking skills was advocated at the expense of definite content. This pedagogical idea has been adopted by both administrative and romantic progressives. That such abstract methods should be attributed to the tradition of Thorndike is paradoxical, because the idea of transferable critical thinking skills contradicts his central and most important finding, namely, that there are few abstract, transferable thinking skills. Modern psychology has upheld his finding, but that has done little to dampen the persistent and influential promulgation of this idea to fledgling teachers in ed schools.

Other examples would include the anti-procedural pedagogy for teaching mathematics and the anti-grammar pedagogy for teaching writing. These pedagogies have been born and bred in ed schools. They were not the independent inventions of teachers.

Finally, the most important pedagogical influence of all is the derogation of mere fact and the consequent failure to insist upon subject matter knowledge by teachers. This is an ed school sin of omission, not commission, and therefore could easily be overlooked by apologetic historians. But the ill-education of teachers, their lack of general knowledge, must be the gravest influence that the ed schools have exercised on the schools. Among the few reliable findings in educational research is the correlation of student gains in achievement and skill with the subject matter knowledge of their teachers. The influence of progressivism in perpetuating teacher ignorance should not be omitted from the historical account, nor should it be forgiven.

While conceding some of the shortcomings of romantic progressivism, Labaree seems content to say that ed schools have, after all, been fairly harmless. He seems willing to leave the matter there. He agrees that conformist pressure exists in ed schools for all faculty to adhere to the dominant progressivist ideology, yet he does not call for a new, more vigorous culture of debate and dissent or of self-criticism.

His most astonishing concession is that ed schools make essentially no difference. He says that teachers teach the same way whether they go to ed school or not. Why, then, send teachers to ed school, when they might be learning history or math—to the future benefit of their students? So the defense of ed schools has come to this. Do not pick on them. They are harmless. They do not do much good, but neither do they do much harm. I wonder if this may be the last gasp of public self-defense of ed schools. It conflicts with the standard defense that ed schools ensure teacher quality. Accepting Labaree's arguments would mean throwing that dubious defense away. If they are as impotent and ineffectual as he insists, why, then, have ed schools at all and why should states require future teachers to gain degrees from them?

But, in fact, ideas are not so harmless as Labaree avers. The ideas with which teachers are forced to be indoctrinated to teach are a mixture of false-hoods and half-truths that have had the historical effect of depressing student achievement and widening the gap between advantaged and disadvantaged children. John Maynard Keynes was right when he said that "soon or late, it is ideas, not vested interests, which are dangerous for good or evil."

Comment by Barbara Beatty

David F. Labaree is brave to be so critical of education schools. He comes from the ed school world, and while he tries to get ed schools off the hook for some of the many things for which they have been blamed, he admits that ed schools have little to show for themselves. The best he can say is that they have done little harm, faint praise indeed. This will win him no friends among his colleagues, and his exoneration of the ed school on grounds of incompetence will not endear him to its critics, as E. D. Hirsch Jr.'s remarks suggest.

I teach in an education department in a liberal arts college, so this is my world, too. But it does not feel quite the same, which is one of my main cri-tiques of Labaree's provocative piece. Teacher education programs are not all alike, whether they are located in an ed school or a department of edu-cation, and this variation matters.

I am grateful for the comments of Linda Eisenmann, Ken Hawes, Patricia Graham, and Geoff Tegnell and other members of the Boston-area history of education study group and of David F. Labaree and other participants at the Brookings conference on education policy, held in May 2003.

Nor did the rhetoric of pedagogical progressivism win out in ed schools as decisively as Labaree argues. Many contenders have appeared for the hearts and minds of teacher educators, many from outside of ed schools. And ed schools may, and might, have had more impact on teachers than Labaree argues, in both helpful and harmful ways. So, depending on one's view of what is educationally desirable, critics such as Hirsch and Diane Ravitch and others who say that ed schools have impeded the movement toward higher standards and achievement may be partly right.[44] But ed schools also deserve some credit for moving the standards movement along and for some other things as well.

Labaree's basic argument is that ed schools should not be blamed for dumbing down the academic curriculum, because pedagogical progressives who espoused child-centered education were too weak to have had much impact on schools. Instead, a second group of bad administrative progressives did the damage. This assumes that all ed schools were the same, that the ideas of ed school progressives fit neatly into these two types, that pedagogical progressives dominated ed school rhetoric, and that these were the only main actors in teacher education. I think the story is more complex.

First, following the Carnegie classification of institutions of higher education, big differences exist among ed schools and departments in first-, second-, and third-tier public and private colleges and universities. These institutions attract different calibers of students and faculty, have more or less students majoring in education, and are more or less dependent on the tuition of teacher education enrollments, which affects the status of teacher education programs within the institution. Urban, suburban, and rural location, religious affiliation, and the race, gender, and social class background of the student body can matter significantly, too, and many other variables give institutions distinct character, as I know Labaree knows. To discuss ed schools as a uniform archetype ignores this variation and its historical origins.[45]

Progressivism also comes in many varieties, as Labaree knows. I am not sure that the typologies that historians use when discussing progressive education generally fit as well for teacher education, because it was so influenced by psychology, which has a different history. When psychology evolved at the end of the nineteenth century, it rapidly "colonized" teacher education.[46] This happened because teachers turned to psychologists for help, because many believed that a science of education could be created, because education had a weak knowledge base and low status, as Labaree correctly emphasizes, and because psychologists needed jobs. In 1898 Harvard University psychology professor Hugo Münsterberg wrote to Columbia University Psychology Department chair James McKeen Cattell, "My elementary psychology course has … 360 students—what will this country do with all these psychologists?"[47] The answer was that many of them would work in teacher education programs. Almost three quarters of the recipients of doctorates in psychology from Clark University in the 1890s, where G. Stanley Hall was president, found work in teachers colleges, training schools, or child study departments.[48] Hall, John Dewey, Edward L. Thorndike, and many if not most of the prominent progressives involved in education were psychologists by training, as were so many other theorists whose ideas have influenced teacher education.

It seems unfair to make ed schools bear full responsibility for the effects of ideas that came from psychology, though educators adapted and used these theories selectively. Nor should ed schools be blamed for the consequences of depending on psychology, when psychology is written into most teacher certification regulations. The Massachusetts Regulations for Teacher Licensure, for instance, require "knowledge of human development to identify learning activities appropriate to the specific discipline, age, and range of materials being taught."[49] Federal education policy relies more heavily than ever on appeals to scientifically based, psychologically derived knowledge about education. But this knowledge is difficult to leverage, because psychology has its own research agendas and is often taught to teachers by psychologists who come from psychology departments, not ed schools.

Another important effect of this colonization is that, because psychology was pluralistic from its inception, many different, often conflicting types of psychology competed for teacher educators' and teachers' attention. Sociology, anthropology, and other fields also invaded ed schools. The result has been a lack of consensus, what former Harvard Graduate School of Education dean Patrica Albjerg Graham has called a "cacophony" of constantly changing views.[50]

These "plural worlds of educational research," to borrow Ellen Condliffe Lagemann's phrase, overlapped within ed schools, such as Teachers College, where student teachers might be reading Dewey while also taking courses with Thorndike.[51] Diverse strains of psychology replicated and recombined through hiring patterns in ed schools and departments throughout the country. Influenced by the senior psychologists under whom they trained, successive generations brought their varying allegiances with them to the ed schools and departments where they worked.[52] The rhetoric of teacher education programs and theories that teachers were taught about teaching and learning could differ considerably depending on the varieties of psychology represented on the faculty.[53]

As these strains of psychology evolved and spawned hybrids and as new psychologies emerged, they became encrusted in teacher education. Because this was a cumulative, not an empirical, process, theories piled up, creating a wildly eclectic mixture from which teacher educators and teachers could pick and choose. Over the course of the thirty years that I have been involved in teacher education, I have taught student teachers about Ivan Pavlov's schedules of reinforcement, Sigmund Freud's mechanisms of defense, B. F. Skinner's behavior modification, Jean Piaget's stages of development, and more. Most educational psychology texts contain remnants of these different views, along with newer ideas from cognitive psychology. As these psychologies have accreted, they have taken up more space in the teacher education curriculum, space that arguably might be used for other, more productive purposes.

I am not lumping these theories together intellectually, but given that all of these psychologies ended up in ed schools, why should ed schools as institutions be blamed for some of the ideas they harbored and not others? Deweyan pedagogical progressivism was undoubtedly preached in many ed schools and became much more pervasive after it coalesced with Piagetian developmentalism and other views in the 1980s to form constructivism. But Thorndike's rhetoric was also very influential in ed schools and in the grade schools and high schools themselves.

I disagree with Hirsch, however, who says that Thorndike, like the pedagogical progressives, was lax about defining curricula. In fact, Thorndike developed a carefully sequenced arithmetic series, *The Thorndike Arithmetics*, which became standard texts in many American elementary schools, and similar curricula were developed in reading and other subjects.[54] The kind of coherent, common content, the loss of which Hirsch bemoans, was created by some progressives.

But it was not taught democratically. Labaree, Hirsch, and Ravitch are right that Thorndike and the administrative progressives advocated a social efficiency curriculum, which tracked all but a few elite students into low-level vocational courses. "It is wasteful," Thorndike wrote in 1903, "to attempt to create and folly to pretend to create capacities and interests which are assumed or denied to an individual before he is born."[55] This comes from his text *Educational Psychology,* which was used in many teacher education programs. Here the long arm of the psychological debate about the heritability of intelligence reached deeply into ed schools and grade schools and high schools.

Thorndike was also the father of subject-specific, standardized achievement tests, which are one of the main levers for raising academic achievement in American schools today. Lagemann and Labaree are right that Thorndike was responsible for much of why American education is the way it is, increasingly standardized and test-driven.[56] So, depending on one's views, ed schools deserve credit for advancing this mechanism of education reform. Thorndike's ideas have had great impact, and it may not have been all bad. But standardized testing is a double-edged sword, which highlights individual differences in ability, some of which may be difficult to diminish and provides a rationale for curriculum differentiation and tracking, at the same time that it provides a yardstick and prod for academic progress.

I will not belabor the point about the lack of child-centered, progressive pedagogy in schools, which Hirsch concedes. But as to derogating facts, Thorndike was all about facts. As he wrote at the end of his last book, "facts no matter how uninspiring" were more useful for improving society than anything else.[57]

I agree with Labaree that this reliance on standardized curriculum, testing, and potentially boring facts was also responsible for some dumbing down. As David Tyack documents, the "one best system" of standardization, at least at the school and district levels, was in place in most urban school systems for years, and Thorndike's rhetoric, curricula, and methods certainly had plenty of time to take effect.[58] Suffice it to say that the legacy of the progressives was complicated, contradictory, and mixed and will continue to be the source of historical debate.

And I differ with Hirsch that ed schools should bear the full burden for teachers' lack of general knowledge. Along with psychologists, a broader group of academic actors are implicated in the outcomes of teacher education. If teachers do not know enough subject matter to teach academically challenging content, ed schools should not solely take the blame. Ed schools can and should be criticized for not requiring the equivalent of at least a double major in education and an academic subject, or a minor in education and a major in arts and sciences. But ed school professors do not teach these content courses. Arts and sciences professors do, and they have been notoriously difficult to engage in the work of teacher preparation. Many of the elite liberal arts colleges and universities from which alternative teacher certification programs hope to draw candidates do not have distribution requirements, and they do not require students who may become teachers to take a mathematics course, for instance. The kind of survey courses that give prospective teachers a broad sweep of the content they need to cover state curriculum requirements has also gone out of style, especially at elite institutions.

As Sandra Stotsky argues in her paper, state certification requirements can stipulate that student teachers acquire this general knowledge, as Massachusetts's new regulations do. But it is neither realistically possible nor necessarily desirable to get control over the specific content of courses in the arts and sciences, especially at elite institutions. As Stotsky notes, some professors will argue that this violates their academic freedom. A large part of the attraction of being a college professor is the opportunity to teach content in which one is intellectually interested. This autonomy is a main reason that smart, highly educated people will work for relatively low pay. Having the freedom to choose courses based on intrinsic interest is also a large part of the attraction and promise of a liberal arts education for students. As with psychology, getting more leverage on the content of courses in the arts and sciences is going to be difficult.

I want to end with the example of the education of a teacher. Geoff Tegnell, who teaches eighth-grade social studies and English in Brookline, Massachusetts, received a bachelor's degree and a master's degree in European history from Wesleyan College. He then obtained a master of arts in teaching from Suffolk University in Boston, where he was certified, and a doctorate in the history of education from the Harvard Graduate School of Education. Unlike some teachers, Tegnell has very strong subject matter preparation in his field and high verbal ability, another characteristic that most researchers agree is correlated with teacher quality.[59] In some ways this background makes Tegnell's perspective more useful, as it is harder to dismiss. When I asked him if his teacher preparation at Suffolk, which is not elite like the other institutions he attended, had been helpful, he said yes, and more than twenty years later he was able to recall what he had been taught in remarkable detail.[60]

Like for most teachers, Tegnell's teacher education consisted of a mixture of courses. He studied educational and developmental psychology; the teaching of reading; classroom methods, including assessment and classroom management; and subject-specific methods in social studies. He also student taught. When he mentioned theorists, they were mostly what Labaree might call modern pedagogical progressives, such as Carl Rogers, Piaget, and Lawrence Kohlberg. But Tegnell also mentioned learning Benjamin Bloom's famous taxonomy of educational objectives and studying standardized tests and measurement. These are all psychologists, from psychology's many strains.

When I asked Tegnell how his teacher training had affected his teaching, he described numerous ways. The student teachers I have worked with say this, too, though such evidence is anecdotal. Education researchers are having difficulty finding evidence of lasting effects, which supports Labaree.[61] Tegnell said that the skills he had learned, along with the support of a good principal and some good in-service programs, "quite literally saved my teaching career!" He added that he thought that teachers without sufficient pedagogical preparation were more likely to quit during their first few years, something that data on graduates of some alternative certification programs support.[62]

The multiple messages of Tegnell's training were apparent when he talked about his teaching. Like other teachers, Tegnell uses many vocabularies. Drawing upon his subject matter knowledge, he employs disciplinary language from history and English to talk about curriculum content. He uses terminology from his education methods courses, which tends to be progressive and student-centered, to talk about his pedagogy, though he says he does plenty of lecturing. He uses technical terms from educational psychology when he talks about his students' test scores, which he says all teachers know in their heads. He sounds like a sociologist or an anthropologist when he describes the cultural and socioeconomic backgrounds of the students he teaches at Brookline's most diverse school, which has a substantial population of racial and linguistic minorities and students from low-income families. And when a student does not progress as much as Tegnell hopes, he sometimes uses language from developmental psychology, saying that the student was not "developmentally ready" to reason analytically at that level. Tegnell is also aware that some of his students do not work hard enough, and he lets them and their parents know this.

A potential downside to these different idioms is that they may cancel each other out. Pedagogy can obscure content, low test scores and socioeconomic data can limit expectations, and lack of developmental readiness and appropriateness can serve as excuses for not finding out why students are having difficulty, for not holding them to higher standards, and for not challenging them with more sophisticated subject matter.

So what are some of the policy implications of this complexity? Labaree's cautionary tale explains much about the current standoff between the child-centered constructivism of many teacher education programs today and the high-stakes testing advocated by many in the standards movement, which is now mandated by much state and federal education policy. Historians should be cautious about drawing direct connections between history and policy.[63] With this caveat, I think that the eclecticism of psychological influences and lack of consensus within and among ed schools can be healthy, as long as student teachers are introduced to a full range of methods. Teachers need to be able to pull ideas from many sources, and principals should be able to hire teachers with different views, to complement the mix in a school. The current convergence around constructivism may be problematic, however, as Hirsch argues, if student teachers are not also taught how to teach phonics and encouraged to try direct teaching methods in mathematics and other subjects. Teacher educators and policymakers need to move beyond these teaching wars and make sure that all student teachers are exposed to the breadth of pedagogical research and practice a wide range of teaching methods.

As to policies to promote stronger subject matter knowledge, here college and university presidents need to become more involved. Until top administrators at the top institutions that enroll the top students communicate the crisis in subject matter preparation to deans and department chairs, arts and science faculty are not likely to do much about it. As Labaree argues, ed schools and departments do not have enough status to press the issue. And teacher educators are busy working with schools, where even more should be done. Reinstituting some distribution requirements and survey courses would help. Getting more arts and science faculty engaged in teacher education, as advisers, as co-teachers of courses about how to teach disciplinary content, and as co-supervisors of student teachers would help. Giving them outside and institutional support for clinical fellowships to do pedagogical research and spend time in schools would help. Subsidizing scholarships and forgivable loans and fifth-year programs to encourage more highly qualified students to go into teaching and for graduates to return for coursework toward certification would help. Staffing ed schools and departments so that student teachers can learn in smallish groups would help, too, although it would be expensive, and probably resisted, as ed school tuitions often subsidize other more costly, prestigious departments.

I do not think that doing away with ed schools, turning teacher education over to the disciplines, and making elementary education some kind of second-class field, as Stotsky suggests, is the answer, although it may work in a few institutions. Most arts and science faculty do not have the time or know-how to make connections with schools, though some senior faculty well past tenure may want to take on more of this responsibility and should be encouraged to do so, by deans and by education faculty. Most clinical adjunct faculty have low status and thus little ability to bridge the chasm between the world of academia and the school. Tegnell was adamant that doing away with ed schools was a bad idea, and his response relates to the many vocabularies teachers use. "Abolish ed school, and we will erode the common culture on which collaboration among guidance, instructional, specialist, and administration collaboration is founded."[64]

But Tegnell agreed with me that the most difficult problem is teachers' lack of access to subject matter knowledge. He described a large new federal grant that he had helped get from Teaching American History, through which sixty teachers from different towns in Massachusetts will meet over the course of three summers with senior historians to read primary sources and design new lessons. More in-depth collaboration such as this around subject matter needs to happen at the undergraduate and graduate levels and after, in colleges, universities, and schools. Student teachers, teachers, teacher educators, psychologists, and other arts and science faculty need to work together on such projects. Distributing responsibility for teacher education more widely and getting the many actors involved to focus on specific academic content, along with strategies for teaching that content, would be a step toward helping attract more of "the teachers we need."

Notes

1. Lawrence A. Cremin, *The Transformation of the School: Progressivism in American Education, 1876–1957* (Vintage, 1961), p. 328.

2. Larry Cuban, *How Teachers Taught: Constancy and Change in American Classrooms, 1890–1980,* 2d ed. (New York: Teachers College Press, 1993); David K. Cohen, "A Revolution in One Classroom: The Case of Mrs. Oublier," *Educational Evaluation and Policy Analysis,* vol. 12 (1990), pp. 311–29; John I. Goodlad, *A Place Called School* (McGraw-Hill, 1983); and

Arthur Zilversmit, *Changing Schools: Progressive Education Theory and Practice, 1930–1960* (University of Chicago Press, 1993).

3. David F. Labaree, "The Trouble with Ed Schools," *Educational Foundations*, vol. 14 (1996), pp. 1–19; and David F. Labaree, *The Trouble with Ed Schools* (Yale University Press, forthcoming 2004).

4. David Tyack, *The One Best System* (Harvard University Press, 1974); Robert L. Church and Michael W. Sedlak, *Education in the United States* (New York: Free Press, 1976); and Herbert Kliebard, *The Struggle for the American Curriculum, 1893–1958* (New York: Routledge, 1986).

5. See, for example, John L. Rury, *Education and Social Change: Themes in the History of American Education* (Mahwah, N.J.: Lawrence Erlbaum, 2002).

6. Ellen Condliffe Lagemann, "The Plural Worlds of Educational Research," *History of Education Quarterly,* vol. 29, no. 2 (1989), pp. 185–214.

7. E. D. Hirsch Jr., *The Schools We Need and Why We Don't Have Them* (Doubleday, 1996), p. 74.

8. Hirsch, *The Schools We Need and Why We Don't Have Them*, p. 75.

9. Striking similarities exist between the faculty psychology that supported learning of traditional academic subjects and the skill-oriented learning theory of the pedagogical progressives, which is ironic because faculty psychology was the grounding for the classical curriculum that the pedagogical and administrative progressives so strongly opposed.

10. Commission on Reorganization of Secondary Education, *Cardinal Principles of Secondary Education,* Bulletin 35 (Department of Interior, Bureau of Education, 1918).

11. Edward A. Krug, *The American High School, 1880–1920* (University of Wisconsin Press, 1964); and Edward A. Krug, *The American High School, 1920–1941* (University of Wisconsin Press, 1972).

12. David L. Angus and Jeffrey E. Mirel, *The Failed Promise of the American High School, 1890–1995* (New York: Teachers College Press, 1999).

13. John Dewey, "The Child and the Curriculum," in Philip W. Jackson, ed., *The School and Society and the Child and the Curriculum* (University of Chicago Press, 1902/1990), p. 205.

14. Cremin, *The Transformation of the School;* Church and Sedlak, *Education in the United States;* Diane Ravitch, *Left Back: A Century of Failed School Reforms* (Simon and Schuster, 2000); and Rury, *Education and Social Change.*

15. John Dewey, "Introduction," in Elsie Ripley Clapp, ed., *The Uses of Resources in Education* (New York: Harper and Brothers, 1952), pp. vii–xi.

16. Zilversmit, *Changing Schools*, p. 168.

17. Lagemann, "The Plural Worlds of Educational Research."

18. Michael B. Katz, "From Theory to Survey in Graduate Schools of Education," *Journal of Higher Education,* vol. 36 (1966), pp. 325–34.

19. Hirsch, *The Schools We Need and Why We Don't Have Them*; and Ravitch, *Left Back.*

20. Hirsch, *The Schools We Need and Why We Don't Have Them*, p. 219.

21. Hirsch, *The Schools We Need and Why We Don't Have Them*, pp. 115–16.

22. According to one report, more than one quarter of teachers are not fully licensed. See National Commission on Teaching and America's Future, *What Matters Most: Teaching for America's Future* (New York: 1996), p. 15.

23. Virginia Richardson and Peggy Placier, "Teacher Change," in Virginia Richardson, ed., *Handbook of Research on Teaching,* 4th ed. (Washington: American Educational Research Association, 2002), pp. 905–47, especially p. 915.

24. Richardson and Placier, "Teacher Change," p. 915.

25. Labaree, *The Trouble with Ed Schools*, chap. 3; and David F. Labaree, "On the Nature of Teaching and Teacher Education: Difficult Practices That Look Easy," *Journal of Teacher Education,* vol. 51 (2000), pp. 228–33.

26. Dan C. Lortie, *Schoolteacher: A Sociological Study* (University of Chicago Press, 1975).

27. John I. Goodlad, *A Place Called School* (McGraw-Hill, 1983); and Cuban, *How Teachers Taught.*

28. Jeanne S. Chall, *The Academic Achievement Challenge: What Really Works in the Classroom?* (New York: Guilford, 2000), p. 114.

29. Goodlad, *A Place Called School*, pp. 123–24.

30. Christopher Barnes, *What Do Teachers Teach? A Survey of America's Fourth and Eighth Grade Teachers* (Manhattan Institute, 2002).

31. Ravitch, *Left Back*, pp. 14–15.

32. E. D. Hirsch Jr., *Cultural Literacy: What Every American Needs to Know* (Vintage, 1988).

33. Samuel Bowles and Herbert Gintis, *Schooling in Capitalist America* (Basic Books, 1976); Jeannie Oakes, *Keeping Track: How Schools Structure Inequality* (Yale University Press, 1985); and Jean Anyon, "Social Class and School Knowledge," *Curriculum Inquiry,* vol. 11 (1981), pp. 3–42.

34. Commission on Reorganization of Secondary Education, *Cardinal Principles of Secondary Education*, pp. 10–16.

35. Commission on Reorganization of Secondary Education, *Cardinal Principles of Secondary Education*, p. 22.

36. Ellen Condliffe Lagemann, *An Elusive Science: The Troubling History of Educational Research* (University of Chicago Press, 2000), p. 236.

37. Alan R. Tom, *Teaching as a Moral Craft* (New York: Longman, 1984); and Lee S. Shulman, "Paradigms and Research Programs in the Study of Teaching: A Contemporary Perspective," in Merlin C. Wittrock, ed., *Handbook of Research on Teaching*, 3d ed. (Macmillan, 1986), pp. 3–36.

38. David Hamilton and Erica McWilliam, "Ex-centric Voices That Frame Research on Teaching," in Virginia Richardson, ed., *Handbook of Research on Teaching,* 4th ed. (Washington: American Educational Research Association, 2001), pp. 17–43.

39. Robert E. Floden, "Research on Effects of Teaching: A Continuing Model for Research on Teaching," in Virginia Richardson, ed., *Handbook of Research on Teaching,* 4th ed. (Washington: American Educational Research Association, 2001), p. 13.

40. Floden, "Research on Effects of Teaching," pp. 13–14.

41. Department of Education, What Works Clearinghouse [w-w-c.org [May 2003]); and National Research Council, *Scientific Research in Education*, ed. Richard J. Shavelson and Lisa Towne, Committee on Scientific Principles for Education Research (Washington: National Academy Press, 2002).

42. *What Works* is the title of a booklet summarizing research about teaching and learning that was widely distributed by the Department of Education in 1986. See Department of Education, *What Works: Research about Teaching and Learning* (Government Printing Office, 1986). A website, the What Works Clearinghouse (w-w-c.org), was established by the department in 2002 for the purpose of promoting science-based standards for evaluation of educational research.

43. Katz, "From Theory to Survey in Graduate Schools of Education."

44. See Hirsch, *The Schools We Need and Why We Don't Have Them;* and Ravitch, *Left Back.*

45. David F. Labaree uses the term *archetype* in the book manuscript from which his paper is drawn, *The Trouble with Ed Schools*. For an overview of some of these differences, see John I. Goodlad, Roger Soder, and Kenneth A. Sirotnik, eds., *Places Where Teachers Are Taught* (San Francisco, Calif.: Jossey-Bass, 1990).

46. The concept of colonization came from a personal conversation with Sheldon H. White. My understanding of the history of psychology and its influence on education is greatly influenced by White's work. See, for instance, Sheldon H. White, "Developmental Psychology in a World of Designed Institutions," in Willem Koops and Michael Zuckerman, eds., *Beyond the Century of the Child: Cultural History and Developmental Psychology* (University of Pennsylvania Press, 2003), pp. 204–25.

47. Hugo Münsterberg to James McKeen Cattell, February 25, 1898, Hugo Münsterberg Papers, Boston Public Library, in Jo Anne Brown, *The Definition of a Profession: The Authority of Metaphor in the History of Intelligence Testing, 1890–1930* (Princeton University Press, 1992), p. 65.

48. John M. O'Donnell, *The Origins of Behaviorism: American Psychology, 1879–1920* (New York University Press, 1985), p. 154.

49. Commonwealth of Massachusetts Department of Education, "603 CMR 7.00 Regulations for Educator Licensure and Preparation Program Approval, Draft Regulations with Changes Incorporated, October 28, 2002," p. 39.

50. Patricia Albjerg Graham, "Schools: Cacophony about Practice, Silence about Purpose," *Daedalus,* vol. 113, no. 4 (1984), pp. 29–57. Many others have described the stew of ideas that have been imported into education. See, especially, Cremin, *The Transformation of the School*; and Kliebard, *The Struggle for the American Curriculum.* On the pluralism of psychology, see Sheldon H. White, "Three Visions of a Psychology of Education," in L. T. Landesman, ed., *Culture, Schooling, and Psychological Development* (Norwood, N.J.: Ablex), pp. 1–38. Lagemann uses the term *cacophony* as well in *An Elusive Science,* p. 99.

51. Ellen Condliffe Lagemann, "The Plural Worlds of Education Research," *History of Education Quarterly,* vol. 29, no. 2 (1989), pp. 185–214.

52. On the history of these psychological allegiances, see, among others, Edward G. Boring, *A History of Experimental Psychology,* 2d ed. (Englewood Cliffs, N.J.: Prentice-Hall, 1950); Brown, *The Definition of a Profession*; Kurt Danziger, *Constructing the Subject: The Historical Origins of Psychological Research* (New York: Cambridge University Press, 1990); and O'Donnell, *Origins of Behaviorism.*

53. Barbara Beatty, "Rethinking the Role of Psychology," in David Olson and Nancy Torrance, eds., *The Handbook of Education and Human Development* (Oxford, England: Blackwell, 1996), pp. 100–16.

54. Edward L. Thorndike, *The Thorndike Arithmetics, Books 1–3* (Chicago: Rand-McNally, 1917).

55. Edward L.Thorndike, *Educational Psychology* (New York: Lemcke and Buechner, 1903), p. 44. See also Barbara Beatty, "From Laws of Learning to a Science of Values: Efficiency and Morality in Thorndike's Educational Psychology," *American Psychologist,* vol. 53, no. 10 (October 1998), pp. 1145–52.

56. Lagemann, "The Plural Worlds of Educational Research," p. 185.

57. Edward L. Thorndike, *Human Nature and the Social Order* (Macmillan, 1940), p. 963. On the continuity of teacher-centered didacticism, see Cuban, *How Teachers Taught;* and David Tyack and Larry Cuban, *Tinkering toward Utopia: A Century of Public School Reforms* (Harvard University Press, 1995).

58. Tyack, *The One Best System.*

59. See, among others, Richard Murnane and others, *Who Will Teach? Policies That Matter* (Harvard University Press, 1991).

60. Information about Geoff Tegnell throughout comes from personal talk with author, May 12, 2003; e-mail correspondence with author, May 16-17, 2003; and telephone conversation with author, May 18, 2003.

61. See Jennifer Rice King, *Teacher Quality: Understanding the Effectiveness of Teacher Attributes* (Washington: Economic Policy Institute, 2003); and Education Commission of the States, *Eight Questions on Teacher Preparation: What Does the Research Say?* (Washington: 2003).

62. Graduates of Teach for America and other alternative certification programs may not stay in teaching long because they tend to be placed in underserved schools with difficult students, where there is also high turnover of graduates of regular teacher certification programs.

63. For different views, see Diane Ravitch and Maris A. Vinovskis, *Learning from the Past: What History Teaches Us about School Reform* (Johns Hopkins University Press, 1995); and Maris A. Vinovskis, *History and Educational Policymaking* (Yale University Press, 1999).

64. Geoffrey Tegnell, e-mail to author, May 17, 2003.

Can a State Department of Education Increase Teacher Quality? Lessons Learned in Massachusetts

SANDRA STOTSKY *with* LISA HAVERTY

Teacher quality, however defined, is usually seen as the responsibility of schools of education. Rarely is it viewed as the responsibility of academic departments in the arts and sciences—that part of the college or university where prospective teachers study the academic content they will draw on as teachers. Only recently has teacher quality come to be seen as a major responsibility of a state department of education—and to be linked to student learning, traditionally the responsibility of the local school district. This essay sets forth the many ways in which a state department of education can enhance teacher quality and the supply of academically able teachers. I draw on my own experience in directing revisions of the major documents produced by the Massachusetts Department of Education from 1999 to 2003 and on several other major initiatives undertaken by the department to implement the education reform measures enacted and funded by the Massachusetts legislature in the 1990s. The chief documents that were the focus for my own work consisted of the preK–12 curriculum frameworks in all basic subjects, the regulations for licensing teachers and teacher-training programs, and the teacher tests required for licensure.[1]

I want to express my deep appreciation to Margaret Cassidy, Orin Gutlerner, Kathe Kirkman, Mark McQuillan, and Eileen Murphy at the Massachusetts Department of Education for their comments on earlier drafts of this essay.

131

Background

Teacher quality is a vague concept susceptible to many definitions. Few can agree on what an effective or quality teacher is unless the teacher's work is related to student academic achievement (objective measures of which are invariably controversial). Teacher quality designates some degree of disciplinary knowledge combined with some degree of professional skill at helping students learn to think with ideas from the teacher's discipline. But disagreement exists on the relative importance of each of these two components and on the extent to which each contributes to teacher quality. What is the optimal degree of disciplinary knowledge for a teacher at the primary or secondary level of education? And how would one assess the quality of the teacher's pedagogical skill in the absence of objective measures of student achievement? Although the answers to these questions are unclear, national statistics on the undergraduate majors of the elementary and secondary teaching force have long indicated that large numbers of teachers in public schools, especially in key middle school subjects, are minimally qualified if not academically unqualified for the subjects they teach. It is in this context that a comprehensive set of educational reform measures was passed and funded by the Massachusetts state legislature in the 1990s, to be implemented by the Massachusetts Department of Education. The legislature sought three goals relating specifically to teacher quality and the supply of teachers: to attract more high-achieving undergraduate majors, college graduates, and academically able midcareer changers to teaching as a career; to increase the academic qualifications of teachers entering the profession; and to increase the academic knowledge of the current teaching force.

What is the role of a state department of education in defining, maintaining, or increasing teacher quality? A traditional function in Massachusetts and in most other states, often dating back to the nineteenth century, is the licensing (certifying) of public school teachers (in some states, all K–12 teachers). In a few states, licensing is done by a different agency governed by a separate publicly appointed or elected body. It is a function that usually entails regular inspection and approval of teacher-training programs based on whatever requirements are set by state law. Until recent years, student achievement was not a typical responsibility of a state department of education. Student achievement became more prominent in the minds of department of education staff when it was linked to their role in distributing and monitoring federal funds to school districts, particularly

Title I funds and the funds provided by the Elementary and Secondary Education Act, both post-1960s phenomena that entailed the regular use of norm-referenced tests to determine the benefits of these federal funds. However, student achievement was not at the time linked by legislation to licensing requirements for preservice teachers or to efforts to increase the quality of preservice and in-service teachers. Today the provisions of No Child Left Behind explicitly link the responsibility for increasing student achievement to improving teacher quality through state standards and state assessments.

Of the three major goals for improving teacher quality in Massachusetts, only one (increasing the academic qualifications for becoming a teacher) can be considered traditional, although the use of teacher tests as the means to assure a minimal level of academic competence in new teachers is a relatively new phenomenon. Until 1994, a teaching license in Massachusetts was valid for the rest of one's life; thus no state-mandated professional development requirements existed before 1994. Nor were there state mandates requiring the Department of Education to devise ways to attract new teachers.

The Massachusetts Education Reform Act of 1993–94 (MERA) changed almost everything. Supported by leaders in business and high-technology industries, by the major teacher unions, and by the public at large, the Massachusetts legislature mandated the development of a comprehensive and far-reaching system of standards and accountability measures to improve student learning. For students, this system was to take the form of preK–12 standards (called curriculum frameworks) and accountability measures (the Massachusetts Comprehensive Assessment System, MCAS). For teachers, this system was to take the form of five-year cycles for license renewal and the requirement of individual professional development plans. For school districts, this system was to take the form of school and district standards, accountability measures applied through an established schedule of inspections, and ratings based on the inspections and student assessment results.

MERA also mandated the development of new standards and accountability measures to improve teacher training. From 1994 on, to become initially licensed, a prospective teacher would have to hold a bachelor's degree from an accredited institution of higher education, with a major in the arts or sciences appropriate to the instructional field. Henceforth prospective teachers could have an education major as a second major, which some colleges in Massachusetts still require of undergraduates seeking a teaching license, but by law their primary major had to be in the arts or sciences.[2] As soon as the tests could be developed, prospective teachers would also have to pass a test of reading and writing skills and a test of the subject matter knowledge for the license sought. MERA did not require a test of pedagogical knowledge or a performance assessment. However, accountability for pedagogical knowledge and performance was expected to take place through program approval of teacher-training institutions, a process that involves determination of the quality of the pedagogical coursework and student teaching assignments provided to prospective teachers in their training programs.

Thus MERA provided for four major reform initiatives that would heavily influence if not shape the definition of teacher quality in Massachusetts: (1) preK–12 standards for all major subjects, (2) statewide assessments based on the standards to be given annually in basic subjects at the elementary, middle, and high school levels, (3) two types of written tests for those seeking licensure as a preK–12 teacher, and (4) a two-stage licensure process followed by license renewal every five years. License renewal would depend upon the accumulation of a required number of professional development points for each five-year teaching cycle. (MERA also provided for other reform initiatives, such as financial aid to the schools that included a specific amount of money per student for professional development for teachers, but these only indirectly influenced teacher quality.)

In addition to the responsibilities of implementing the provisions of MERA, the department was asked to undertake initiatives designed to recruit "the best and the brightest" and to promote teaching as a career using an endowment fund appropriated by the legislature in 1996. The "12 to 62 Plan" included a signing bonus program for new teachers, support for accelerated routes for initial licensure, and a variety of other recruitment programs. The plan also sought to develop a career ladder for current teachers by providing them with an incentive to achieve master teacher status. Part of the endowment fund was to be used for a program that would subsidize experienced teachers who sought certification by the National Board for Professional Teaching Standards (NBPTS) and provide them with a bonus for ten years if they successfully completed NBPTS certification and were willing to undertake mentoring training and responsibilities, thereby earning the designation of master teacher by the department. These initiatives were explicitly intended to increase the number of highly qualified teachers—to some extent by bypassing traditional teacher-training programs.

The department began the implementation of MERA with the development of the teacher tests and the curriculum frameworks, or standards documents. Frameworks were developed in all major subjects: mathematics (1995), science and technology/engineering (1995), English language arts and reading (1997), history and social science (1997), and foreign language (1998). The standards in these frameworks were intended to form the basis for the student assessments and part of the basis for the teacher tests.

Student assessments were developed in the first four subject areas for grades four, eight, and ten and were first administered in 1998. The results of the first three years of student assessment (1998 to 2000) were sobering and had clear implications for teacher training. Although there was a small increase from the 1998 to the 2000 tests in the percentage of students performing at a higher level, large numbers of students failed the tests at all grade levels and in all subjects. There are many reasons for low or less-than-desired academic achievement, among them such obvious factors as erratic school attendance, limited reading ability, lack of motivation, limited fluency in English, and no consequences for failure. But the evidence from a small but consistent body of research is clear: Teacher verbal ability or knowledge of subject matter or both are also related to student achievement.[3] Teachers without an adequate academic background cannot teach to the high standards in the Massachusetts curriculum frameworks, especially in science, mathematics, and history.

In 1998 the first cohort of prospective teachers took the teacher tests—a test of reading and writing skills and a subject matter knowledge test, available in about forty areas. The results of these tests were also sobering: A large number of candidates failed the first tests. Although it had not been clear to the test takers and their program providers that these first results would count for more than a pilot test, the poor results motivated the Massachusetts Board of Education (the appointed body governing the department of education) to formulate a policy that allows the department to put on probation any institution whose teacher-training programs have less than an 80 percent pass rate on the teacher tests in several successive years. The Massachusetts scores even gave impetus to the U.S. Congress to establish an accountability system for higher education (in Title II of the Higher Education Act), based on state pass rates.

The Massachusetts teacher tests and the 80 percent pass rate threshold did provide an incentive to Massachusetts colleges and universities to strengthen their teacher-training programs and to upgrade the criteria used for admission to them. However, these tests were not the only means or necessarily the chief means the department could use to ensure that prospective teachers had stronger academic backgrounds than the legislature believed they had at the time it passed MERA. Teacher licensing regulations specifying the academic content and academic requirements for teacher licenses were another means. Many elementary and middle school teachers had weak academic backgrounds because they had not been required in their undergraduate programs to take coursework in each of the arts and sciences subjects they typically teach in the elementary and middle school. With the development of the preK–12 curriculum frameworks, licensure regulations (the official basis for the teacher tests) could now be revised to increase academic content requirements for all teacher licenses and, hence, all teacher-training programs.

I began work in the Department of Education in May 1999 with an explicit charge to monitor or enhance the academic quality of all department documents touching upon the academic content for preK–12. Thus part of my work was to find ways to increase teacher quality and supply through the revisions of any documents voted upon by the board of education. Between 1999 and 2002, in addition to the revision of the licensing regulations, I directed revisions (also required on a regular basis by MERA) of the preK–12 curriculum frameworks in all basic subjects: English language arts, reading, mathematics, history, geography, economics, civics or government, science, and technology/engineering. If designed adequately, these frameworks can be the most fundamental mechanisms for reform available to a state department of education.

Designing High-Quality Academic Standards for PreK–12

The academic content of the standards in the preK–12 curriculum frameworks heavily influences, if not determines, the academic quality of all other subject matter documents produced by a state department of education. The standards in the Massachusetts curriculum frameworks serve to guide not only annual statewide student assessments in basic subjects (as mandated by MERA) and early childhood (preschool) curricula, English as a Second Language curricula, and instructional technology programs, but also professional development activities for teachers sponsored by the department, regulations for licensing teachers and approving teacher-

Figure 1. Central Role of PreK–12 State Standards in the PreK–12 Curriculum and in Teacher Training and Retention

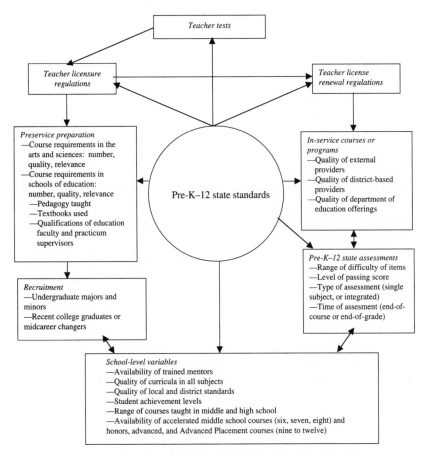

training programs, and the content of the teacher tests required for licensing (also mandated by MERA). The standards also strongly influence the form and content of district curricula as well as classroom organization, even though a state department of education cannot mandate curriculum and instruction, in theory the province of the local school board. See figure 1 for a diagrammatic illustration of the central role of preK–12 standards in all aspects of preK–12 education and teacher training.

For these reasons, my specific objectives for the framework documents were

—To restore disciplinary learning to the central place in each subject area,

—To provide intellectually coherent standards at each grade level or each span of two grades as the basis for the required state assessments at each educational level,

—To make the organization of the content of high school standards compatible with the normal disciplinary training of current and prospective teachers of that subject,

—To make explicit the content to be taught by teachers in each subject area, grade by grade or by spans of two grades,

—To lay the academic groundwork in the middle and high school grades for advanced coursework in grades eleven and twelve,

—To broaden the range of recommended or acceptable pedagogical strategies to include teacher-directed as well as student-centered ones, and

—To provide school districts with options for curricular sequences wherever possible.

What more specifically did the first (and most important) objective mean in the context of each of the major disciplines taught in preK–12? For the English language arts, it meant distinguishing more clearly the reading of literary works from the reading of informational or expository texts, creating lists of recommended core authors or literary works at all educational levels, and embedding the goals of beginning reading and writing in a distinct group of standards set off by themselves. For science and technology/engineering, it meant creating adequate sets of preK–12 standards for the life sciences, earth and space science, the physical sciences, and technology/engineering and then making these four sets of standards the only content strands in the revised document. This was to be achieved by eliminating one of the original content strands titled "Science, Technology, and Human Affairs" and putting the slender academic content in its standards into an appendix; eliminating another one of the original content strands titled "Inquiry" and delineating the substance of its content-free standards in a short introductory section as skills to be learned with the study of scientific content; and distinguishing physics from chemistry at the high school level so that high school science teachers may teach each of the four disciplines of science as well as technology/engineering independently of each other in courses devoted to each discipline and assessed by an end-of-course test in that discipline, not by (as was the original test) an integrated test covering all five areas. Most high school science teachers strongly favor discipline-specific, end-of-course science tests. For history and social science, a complete reorganization and rewriting of its content was necessary to provide, at most grade levels, one set of chiefly narrative history standards addressing the particular historical period(s) to be covered at that grade level; to integrate relevant geography, civics, and economics content with these history standards; and to indicate where a number of seminal primary documents should be studied in high school courses in U.S. history and government. Finally, for mathematics, it chiefly meant creating and providing sets of standards for the subject areas of mathematics taught in most secondary schools (algebra I, algebra II, geometry, and precalculus), in addition to more academically demanding sets of integrated standards for each two-year grade span from prekindergarten and kindergarten to grades eleven and twelve. The department sought to increase the academic level of its mathematics standards in preK–8 because international comparisons suggested that American public schools tend to expect less in mathematics from their students than many other countries. For example, the mathematics curriculum used in many Asian countries such as Singapore expects students to learn as much mathematical content by grade six as most mathematics curricula used in the United States expect students to learn by grade eight.

Another objective sought to address the mismatch between the kind of disciplinary training that high school history and science teachers have typically received in their undergraduate coursework in the arts and sciences and the current effort by education faculty to promote the construction (and assessment) of high school courses in these two disciplines that integrate all the subareas in each discipline (or associated with it). Although it may sound educationally desirable for high school students to take a sequence of science courses from grade nine through grade twelve, each of which integrates concepts in earth science, biology, chemistry, and physics around a presumably engaging series of topics, a science major is unlikely to obtain a strong background in all these sciences and be able to teach all four subareas equally effectively at any high school grade level. Similarly, although it may sound educationally desirable for high school students to take a series of history courses, each of which integrates standards for world history, American history, civics or government, geography, psychology, sociology, anthropology, and economics, a history major is unlikely to obtain a strong background in all the social sciences as well as in both world history and American history and be able to teach all areas of world and American history as well as the social sciences equally effectively. Moreover, undergraduate courses in the social sciences and the sciences (or mathematics for that matter) are unlikely to be taught in an integrated way and thus provide a model for what is promoted by the pedagogical faculty. For these reasons, my goal was to organize high school standards in each subject area to promote the construction of courses that would enable teachers in these areas to draw most effectively from their academic training.

Using Licensing Regulations to Increase Teacher Quality

A major goal of both the Massachusetts Board of Education and the commissioner of education was to make sure that prospective teachers would be prepared to teach to the learning standards in the curriculum frameworks. Redesigning the licensure regulations to accomplish this goal required, among other things, anticipating unintended interpretations or undesirable effects of whatever was redesigned. The devil is always in the details. This task would have been daunting under any circumstances because of the need to work within (and around) statutory requirements that might not be academically helpful but could not be removed without creating a political firestorm. (For example, at present, teachers can and do get professional status, or tenure, by their fourth year of teaching, which is often before they complete their second stage of licensure because they can work under their initial license for five years.) The task was especially daunting because pedagogical content knowledge (the professional skills and knowledge needed to teach a particular subject at a particular educational level) has often been conflated with academic content knowledge (the subject matter knowledge acquired by those interested in a discipline, whether or not they choose to become teachers of that discipline in K–12).

Clarifying the Distinction between Pedagogy and Content Knowledge

Often the distinction between what teachers should know about the subjects they teach and how they should or might best teach those subjects to particular students at particular grade levels is ignored. Some argue, on the basis of research, for the value of graduate degrees and make no distinction between a master's degree in education and one in the arts and sciences when examining the relationship between student learning and the amount of graduate-level coursework a teacher has taken. However, it is necessary to differentiate between an increase in the teacher's academic knowledge and an increase in a teacher's pedagogical knowledge when accounting for a correlation between graduate-level work and increased student learning. This distinction has sometimes been denied by those who seek to decrease the amount of mathematical or scientific content needed by prospective teachers of mathematics and the sciences. They make the argument that what you teach is (or should be) determined by how you teach and that how you teach is more important. This argument is commonly made by supporters of reform mathematics and science who reconstruct mathematics and science as disciplines in ways that make them less substantively demanding for both prospective teachers and low-achieving students to learn (that is, making these disciplines more accessible, to use current parlance).

In some instances the contributions of courses in the arts and sciences and of courses in schools of education are simply merged for purposes of evaluating teacher-training programs. The blurring of the distinctive contribution to teaching quality made by coursework in pedagogical theory versus academic content can be seen in the standards or principles for accrediting teacher-training programs recommended by the National Council for Accreditation of Teacher Education (NCATE), the Teacher Education Accreditation Council (TEAC), and the Interstate New Teacher Assessment and Support Consortium (INTASC).

Spelling Out Required Academic Topics

In the revision of the licensure regulations, the Massachusetts Department of Education delineated the subject matter knowledge required for each license as clearly, distinctly, and succinctly as possible. These lists for each license identify, to the extent possible, those topics that candidates for a particular teaching license should study in their arts and sciences major and in other arts and sciences courses. They reflect as comprehensively as possible the relevant academic background for the preK–12 content standards the prospective teacher will be expected to teach to, at the educational level for which the candidate seeks licensure. To obtain program approval, teacher-training programs must demonstrate how students in their programs can cover these topics in arts and sciences coursework. The list of topics for each license excludes, to the extent possible, professional or pedagogical skills and knowledge and, as such, serves as the basis for revisions of the original subject matter teacher tests, which formerly combined questions about pedagogy with questions about academic content. Although the department was accused by higher education critics of downplaying or even eliminating pedagogical training because of its emphasis on increasing subject matter knowledge requirements, the regulations do cover pedagogical knowledge and skills, but in a generic set of professional standards for all prospective teachers. Preparation programs are held responsible for this aspect of teacher training.

Why didn't the department simply require a particular major, a choice from a restricted set of majors, or a specific number of credit hours in a discipline, to ensure that a prospective teacher of a particular subject would be academically prepared to teach the relevant subject matter? These methods had been used in earlier regulations. These academic shortcuts no longer work for most licenses for three reasons. First, they no longer necessarily signify that the person completing a major or the required credit hours in, for example, the humanities has addressed the academic content that is relevant to teaching K–12 students. Second, both training programs and interested candidates need to know what specific coursework is deemed useful for precollege teaching; they need some guidance in constructing their course of study. Third, licensure tests for public school teachers need external validity, and the state provides the legal basis for the content with its determination of the academic content needed for a teaching license.

Requiring a Specific Amount of Academic Time on Task

In addition to spelling out the specific academic topics to be studied by a prospective teacher, the department requires a specific number of semester hours in the academic subject(s) taught by a teacher. At first glance, this sounds counterintuitive: How does increasing subject matter requirements attract more people to a profession instead of decreasing their number? The psychology of this works in the right way today for a profession that, in general, neither enjoys a reputation in the academic world for intellectual rigor nor is accorded much intellectual respect in the public's (or legislator's) eye. If teachers are ever to be seen again as professionals with intellectual and moral stature, their training programs must be perceived as having serious academic demands. These higher standards for teachers would presumably lead to increased attractiveness of the field for highly qualified individuals. Only a modest beginning has been made in this, but it is at least a beginning.

All prospective teachers of elementary and special education students are now required to take thirty-six hours of arts and sciences coursework in the major subjects they teach in the elementary schools (composition; American, British, and other literature; mathematics; science; U.S., European, and world history; geography; economics; and U.S. government) and to take a general test covering these subjects as well as a test covering the fundamentals of the reading process and beginning reading pedagogy. Here, an exception was made to the decision that the new regulations would not spell out a required amount of coursework because of what was discovered in exploring what elementary teachers tend to choose, or are given, as their arts and sciences major. When the department first proposed this modest set of academic requirements for prospective teachers of elementary students, one teacher educator opposing this requirement charged that it would violate her undergraduate students' academic freedom.

Finally, and this remains the most contentious change in the new regulations, the master's degree in education that all teachers may use to achieve the second stage of licensure must now include for middle and high school teachers arts and sciences coursework. At least half of the courses must be related to the subject area of the license. Content-based pedagogical courses are acceptable for teachers of elementary and special education students, but the content must relate to the basic subjects taught in the school curriculum. A master's degree program in creative movement can no longer count for the second stage of licensure for anyone except the teacher of dance. And even for the second stage of licensure in this area, half of the courses in such a program must have academic content related to the art form.

Changing Grade Levels Covered by a License

The number of grades covered by a license, that is, the scope of a license, is a far more important feature of a license than most people outside of preK–12 education realize. The particular grades covered by a license not only determine the educational level of the student teaching experience but also influence how many and what kind of academic courses students take. Moreover, the scope of a particular license as well as its content requirements may vary considerably from state to state and within a state as regulations change over time. In one state or in one decade in a state an elementary license may cover grades K–8, in another state or in a later decade only grades one through six. A license encompassing a broad range of grades is desired by school administrators because it provides them with flexibility in staffing assignments from year to year. However, unless the preK–12 content standards for the highest grades (and for the most able students at these grades) in the span of grades covered by a license are supported by appropriate arts and sciences requirements, prospective teachers in undergraduate licensure programs may not have an adequate academic background for teaching to the high end of the range of grades covered by the license they seek. This may well be the case for prospective teachers of the upper elementary grades. Nor is it clear that prospective teachers choose to do their student teaching as often at the highest grade covered by the license they seek as at lower grades so that they are as well prepared to teach the most academically advanced students they may encounter as they are to teach the others.

To ensure, to the furthest feasible extent, stronger academic backgrounds for teachers at specific grade levels, the department made some changes in the grades covered by a license. The range of grades allowable for the early childhood license was reduced from preK–3 to preK–2, making grade three teachable by only a teacher with an elementary license. The range of grades allowable for middle school licenses was reduced from five through nine to five through eight, making grade nine teachable by only a teacher with a high school license. Correspondingly, the range of grades covered by a high school license was broadened from nine through twelve to eight through twelve, so that teachers with the strongest academic background requirements (those licensed to teach grade twelve) can teach grade eight if need be. In addition, grades nine through twelve were eliminated from the general science license, which now addresses only grades five through eight. All prospective high school science teachers in undergraduate licensure programs must take enough coursework in a particular science so that they can pass a discipline-specific test for licensure and teach that particular science with adequate depth through grade twelve.

Creating New Licenses

In preK–12 education, as probably in most other professions, the licenses, as well as the requirements for those licenses, that candidates must obtain from a state agency or an accredited professional organization shape the entire profession, from recruitment and training programs to hiring policies and professional practices. As part of the Massachusetts Department of Education's efforts to attract a larger number of academically able arts and sciences majors to teaching, it created several new teaching licenses in subjects of potential interest to such candidates and in areas of great need. This mechanism will work only if it stimulates the establishment of new programs in the state to prepare prospective teachers for these licenses. One new license is designed to remedy weak academic preparation for teaching a particular subject area at the high school level. A second new license is designed to address the teaching of English to students whose first language is not English. Several other licenses are designed to attract able arts and sciences majors to a teaching career in the elementary school. A final group of licenses is designed to address the academic weaknesses of current middle school teachers—the educational level where it is most urgent to upgrade the teaching force. In all cases new programs to prepare prospective teachers for these licenses would not be difficult to develop in a college or university, whether or not a teacher education program exists. Most could easily be developed under the auspices of the academic department whose content they reflect.

The new license for the high school level is for political science and political philosophy and is designed to attract undergraduate or graduate students in political philosophy or political science to high school teaching. In previous regulations in Massachusetts, the high school government or civics teacher was licensed as a social studies teacher. This new license spells out much stronger requirements in political science and political philosophy. The social studies license was eliminated altogether, leaving those interested in teaching social studies with two clear discipline-based alternatives: a history license or a political science and political philosophy license, each of which addresses geography and some economics as well.

To guide the development of sound training programs for teachers of students whose first language is not English and to respond to the educational requirements in an initiative petition passed by almost 70 percent of the voters in the November 2002 general election in Massachusetts, a license was created in 2003 for the teacher of English language learners that highlights English immersion and the sheltered teaching of academic content as well as of English language and literacy skills. This license, basically a stronger version of the existing license for teachers of English as a Second

Language, will enable the department to eliminate transitional bilingual education licenses for nine different languages because the initiative petition replaces existing legislation mandating transitional bilingual education for non-English-speaking students. Transitional bilingual education is an idea that is as flawed in theory as it has been in practice, as are the so-called two-way bilingual programs now being promoted in Massachusetts by political groups seeking to bypass and undermine the voters' intentions. Both types of programs are based on the false assumption (among others) that teachers who have learned in American schools of education what children's litera- ture, games, and songs composed in English their students should learn to read, sing, or play (and how) will automatically be familiar with the chil- dren's literature, games, and songs their students should learn to read, sing, or play (and how) in a foreign language without any coursework in the lan- guage arts of that foreign language. What is needed in the United States for academically sound second language programs to flourish from the ele- mentary grades on are foreign language teachers who have learned the elementary language arts content of the foreign language they seek to teach and how to teach it in that foreign language. That was the major purpose of another new license the department created: the teacher of a foreign lan- guage for preK–6.

To attract individuals with strong content backgrounds to elementary school teaching, the department created new licenses for mathematics, sci- ence, foreign languages, and history for the elementary grades. They are simply subject matter licenses for the elementary level instead of, as is usual, for the middle or high school level. Hiring teachers with these licenses will allow elementary schools to organize their middle to upper elementary grades around subject-divided days (with each major subject taught by a teacher of that subject) instead of as self-contained classrooms taught by a generalist elementary teacher with weak academic knowledge in most if not all of the many subjects he or she is typically expected to teach. Preparation programs leading to these licenses may attract academically able undergraduates or graduates with majors in other areas but with sufficient coursework in one of these areas and sufficient interest in teaching children to enable them to pass a teacher test assessing the level of academic content needed for teaching the subject in the elementary school. Prospective teachers completing programs in elementary mathematics may be especially attractive to schools seeking much less expensive and possibly more effective alternatives to the use of mathematics coaches for grades one through six.

To address the peculiar needs of the middle school, the department created another set of licenses. The middle school is the educational level where teachers without majors or minors in the academic disciplines they are expected to teach are most apt to be found. One reason for this sad state of affairs is the nature of the license created for this level in many states, including Massachusetts. The middle school generalist license, as it was called in Massachusetts, came into being as a way to address what many educators perceived as the special needs of the young adolescent. The preparation programs developed to lead to this license typically required little more than a smattering of academic coursework across all the subjects taught in a typical middle school. The license was designed to allow a person to teach all subjects in a self-contained classroom in grades five through eight. But self-contained classrooms rarely exist in grades seven and eight, and the license has been grossly misused by desperate administrators to allow underqualified teachers to teach twelve- and thirteen-year-olds demanding subject matter in those grades. The history of the middle school contributed to this situation.

The traditional junior high school (grades seven, eight, and nine) generally had teachers with majors or at least minors in the subjects they taught in a subject-divided day. As the middle school concept was translated into a reality—because it was proposed as a reform of the problematic junior high school concept—most of the academically strong junior high school teachers moved up to the high school level to continue teaching, while many elementary teachers added a middle school license enabling them to teach grades seven and eight as well as grades five and six. The net result of this reform was the eventual replacement over time of academically stronger teachers by academically weaker teachers in grades seven and eight. Only three junior high schools are left in Massachusetts today. Whether young adolescents have been well served by this reform is a question unanswered by focused research, although enough commentary has been written on the general academic weaknesses of middle school students and their teachers to suggest that if the middle school concept did solve a social problem, it did not solve the academic one and may have exacerbated it.

The department eliminated the middle school generalist license altogether and, using the same rationale as for the subject matter licenses for the elementary school, created a number of new licenses for prospective middle school teachers: a combined English and history license and a combined mathematics and science license, each requiring at least thirty-six hours of coursework; a separate middle school mathematics license; and a separate middle school general science license, with teacher tests for each license that are less demanding than those for high school teachers of these subjects. At first blush, one might wonder whether standards were being lowered. But the department faces a Hobson's choice here. If it required a major in mathematics or a science for teaching middle school today, it would probably get few candidates. By requiring a reasonable amount of academic coursework in one or two disciplines, the department hopes to attract and keep teachers who have an adequate academic background to address the academic content that should be taught in the middle school. Box 1 shows the topics required for study (and for the teacher tests) for the three different educational levels of the mathematics license in the Massachusetts regulations.

One final addition to the department's menu of licenses is a specialist license for a teacher of academically advanced students in preK–8. This license requires an academically strong teacher whose main task is to find ways to provide accelerated learning for high academic achievers in the elementary and middle school. Similar in many respects to licenses other states have for teachers of gifted and talented students, this license is intended as the counterpart of the various licenses for teachers of students with learning disabilities or physical handicaps. Although Massachusetts has many training programs for different kinds of special education teachers, it has no preparation programs for teachers of academically advanced students in K–8. The department hopes this license will stimulate the development of appropriate training programs and encourage schools to hire their graduates.

Upgrading the Licensure Tests for Teachers

As a consequence of making these changes to the content standards of the licensure regulations, the Massachusetts Department of Education then had to revise the existing subject matter knowledge tests for licensure. These tests are arguably the most important mechanism provided by MERA for upgrading teacher quality. All subject matter tests originally developed by 1998–99 are now in the process of being revised, and tests for new licenses are being created. All must address the academic content teachers need to teach the revised preK–12 standards. Pedagogy is no longer tested on these tests, and question types have been changed to promote abstract or deductive thinking. The revised or new tests are generally much more demanding

Box 1. Topics for the Elementary, Middle, and High School Mathematics License

The following topics will be addressed on a subject matter knowledge test for the first- through sixth-grade level:

—Basic principles and concepts related to elementary school mathematics in the areas of number sense and numeration, patterns and functions, geometry and measurement, and data analysis
—Algebra
—Euclidean geometry

The following topics will be addressed on a subject matter knowledge test for the fifth- through eighth-grade level:
—Algebra
—Euclidean geometry
—Trigonometry
—Discrete and finite mathematics
—Introductory calculus through integration
—History of mathematics

The topics set forth for the fifth- through eighth-grade level and the following topics will be addressed on a subject matter knowledge test for the eighth- through twelfth-grade level:
—Abstract algebra
—Number theory
—Calculus through differential equations
—Probability and statistics
—Non-Euclidean and transformational geometries
—Applied mathematics or mathematics modeling

than the original tests. In addition, the department has attempted to involve more arts and sciences faculty for the volunteer committees charged with reviewing test objectives and test items.

Apart from their actual content, the two most important qualities of good teacher tests are the appropriateness of their overall level of difficulty and the meaningfulness of their passing scores. Both qualities need much more attention than they have received. Surprisingly, a volume of essays on the role of licensure tests in improving teacher quality published by the National Research Council in 2001 does not address either the difficulty level of current teacher tests or the level of the cut scores established by the various states using them.[4] Most current teacher tests may be deficient in these respects. According to Education Trust's study of a number of teacher tests produced by the Educational Testing Service and National Evaluation Systems (the two companies that have been producing teacher tests), most have content that is at a high school level.[5] Anecdotal accounts by journalists and others corroborate this judgment.[6] In a caustic commentary on the first Title II report on the quality of teacher preparation in the fifty states, put out by the U.S. Department of Education in June 2002, Education Trust noted that most state cut scores are set at or below the 25th percentile.[7]

Easy teacher tests are an insult to an academically strong candidate for licensure. And if a teacher test can in theory be passed by a good high school student in grade eleven, the profession is also intellectually diminished in the public's eye. The original Massachusetts teacher tests developed an instant national reputation for being relatively demanding when the 1998 fiasco occurred, and despite the dire mutterings of critics (mainly in the state's schools of education) that the teacher tests would drive prospective teachers away from teaching in Massachusetts or cause a decline in the numbers of students enrolling in their licensure programs, the opposite seems to have occurred. Every year an increasing number of candidates for licensure have taken the tests and passed them, and enrollment in teacher-training programs has increased, not decreased. Table 1 shows the total number and percentage of communication and literacy skills tests taken and passed from 1998 to 2002. As table 1 indicates, the number of tests taken has steadily increased from 6,301 to almost 24,000 over the five-year period, while the percentage of tests passed has ranged from 57 percent to 64 percent, with a yearly average of 59 percent. Given that this test must be taken by all those seeking an educator license, the numbers include administrators and professional support personnel, such as school psychologists, as well as teachers. As examples of these trends in specific subject areas, tables 2 and 3 indicate the total number and percentage of prospective teachers of elementary school and secondary mathematics who have taken and passed both the communication and literacy skills test and either the elementary or mathematics test in the same time period. As these tables

Table 1. Communication and Literacy Skills Tests Taken and Passed, 1998–2002

Year	Number of tests administered	Number of tests passed (percent)
1998	6,301	3,735 (59)
1999	16,598	10,637 (64)
2000	19,471	11,080 (57)
2001	23,223	13,270 (57)
2002	23,744	13,889 (58)

Source: Massachusetts Department of Education.

Table 2. Number and Percentage of Prospective Teachers Taking and Passing Both the Elementary Licensure Test and the Communication and Literacy Skills Licensure Test, 1998–2002

Year (A)	Number who took elementary test (B)	Number who passed elementary test (C)	Elementary test pass rate (C/B) (D)	Number of elementary passers who also passed communication and literacy skills test between 1998 and 2003 (E)	Percentage of E/B (F)	Percentage of E/C (G)
1998	1,701	1,207	71	1,165	68	97
1999	3,023	2,297	76	2,256	75	98
2000	3,253	2,403	74	2,339	72	97
2001	3,789	2,834	75	2,785	74	98
2002	4,017	2,999	75	2,901	72	97

Source: Massachusetts Department of Education.

Table 3. Number and Percentage of Prospective Teachers Taking and Passing Both the Mathematics Licensure Test and the Communication and Literacy Skills Licensure Test, 1998–2002

Year (A)	Number who took mathematics test (B)	Number who passed mathematics test (C)	Mathematics test pass rate (C/B) (D)	Number of mathematics passers who also passed communication and literacy skills test between 1998 and 2003 (E)	Percentage of E/B (F)	Percentage of E/C (G)
1998	283	111	39	109	39	98
1999	530	250	47	244	46	98
2000	683	296	43	288	42	97
2001	978	404	41	392	40	97
2002	1,547	685	44	637	41	93

Source: Massachusetts Department of Education.

show, the number of prospective teachers taking the elementary school test or the secondary mathematics test has steadily risen since 1998, while the percentage of those passing ranges from 71 percent to 76 percent for the elementary school test, and from 39 percent to 47 percent for the secondary mathematics test. About the same percentage of those who pass the subject matter test also pass the communication and literacy skills test. The department's program approval staff have even found anecdotal evidence that other states have been aggressively recruiting graduating students who have passed Massachusetts's teacher tests, a phenomenon that, if widespread, suggests that teacher tests with an aura of difficulty surrounding them may be appealing to prospective employers even if they have little appeal to the candidates' training institutions.

Providing Accelerated Training Programs for Academically Strong Prospective Teachers

As the department was incorporating strong content requirements into the state's teacher licensing regulations, it also was addressing the problem of recruiting candidates with strong content backgrounds. The new regulations for licensing teachers and training programs provide for the development of accelerated programs (often called alternative programs) by school districts or other entities such as educational cooperatives and charter schools. These alternative programs enable college graduates or midcareer changers to bypass traditional postbaccalaureate programs in schools of education for their training (although some districts collaborate with a nearby institution of higher education to provide instructors and supervisory personnel for the district's program). Box 2 shows the requirements for the two accelerated routes to initial licensure that were developed. Route 3 is for someone learning to become a teacher through an apprenticeship in the schools, while Route 4, designed to facilitate the Massachusetts Institutes for New Teachers (MINT) initiative, enables the person accepted into the MINT program to work in the fall as teacher of record after summer coursework and a summer practicum. In addition to providing for accelerated training programs that must meet the same standards as traditional programs for the first stage of licensure, the new licensing regulations provide explicit alternatives to a master's degree in education for achieving the second stage of licensure (alternatives required by MERA but not spelled out in previous licensing regulations).

These new routes for the initial stage of licensure facilitated the growth of innovative recruitment initiatives. Using funds from an endowment fund established by the Massachusetts legislature, the department began the Massachusetts Institutes for New Teachers in 1999 as a way to attract recent college graduates and midcareer changers with demonstrated high academic or professional achievement. Prioritizing applicants with mathematics and science backgrounds, the program has openly sought to increase the supply of academically strong teachers for the middle and high school by enticing prospective candidates with an accelerated summer training program and the certainty of being hired immediately as teacher of record in the fall (together with bonuses for a limited number of candidates). A limited amount of pedagogical coursework, a short and inexpensive training period, and guaranteed placement in a teaching position are major conditions for increasing the number of academically strong teachers in schools. Although this new initiative has not been warmly welcomed by institutions of higher education offering traditional teacher-training programs (or by districts whose staff agreed with the critics in institutions of higher education or resented the bonuses given the MINT graduates or both), the results of the program are promising. What is of growing significance is the much higher proportion of males applying for this program than for admission to traditional programs in institutions of higher education. From 1999 to 2003, 1,453 women and 1,115 males have applied, and 309 women and 252 males have been accepted. By contrast, women are the overwhelming majority of those in traditional programs.

Since the inception of this initiative through 2002, 444 recent college graduates and midcareer changers have completed the department's accelerated training program and obtained a teaching position, about one-third in high-needs districts. One higher education critic has claimed that the overall pass scores of the MINT graduates are not much higher than those of teachers who have completed traditional training programs. Even if true, the criticism is irrelevant because a majority of the MINT-trained teachers replying to a survey conducted by the Center for Education Policy at the University of Massachusetts–Amherst for the Massachusetts Department of Education said they would not have considered teaching if it had meant going through a traditional training program.[8]

Moreover, the fact that a large number (perhaps a majority) of the state's new mathematics and science teachers in recent years have come through MINT reflects the very reason for the MINT initiative, or the deeper prob-

Box 2. Alternative Routes to Initial Licensure Allowing Accelerated Training Programs

(3) Route Three is for teacher candidates who hold a Preliminary license, serve in a school but are not hired as teachers of record, have not completed a practicum or practicum equivalent and related pedagogical coursework, and will receive their preparation in approved programs for apprentices. Such candidates shall serve an apprenticeship in a classroom under the direct supervision of a teacher who holds an appropriate license. Candidates seeking licensure under Route Three shall meet the following requirements:

   (a) Possession of a Preliminary license in the field of the license sought.

   (b) Early field-based experience together with seminars or courses that address the Professional Standards for Teachers.

   (c) Successful completion of an apprenticeship of at least one half year, with a supervising classroom teacher present, during the school year in the field and at the educational level for the license sought, including a practicum equivalent.

(4) Route Four is for teacher candidates who hold a Preliminary license, are hired as teachers of record, have not completed a practicum and related pedagogical study, are assigned to a mentor, and will receive their preparation in approved programs except as

lem the legislature sought to address through the endowment fund—that is, traditional training programs are producing few new mathematics and science teachers.

Upgrading Requirements and Professional Development Activities for License Renewal

Finally, the department turned its attention to the teachers already in the field. The department has tried to strengthen professional development for the current teaching force in a number of ways. First, to implement one of the reform measures in MERA, the Massachusetts Board of Education voted provided in (d). Candidates seeking licensure under Route Four shall meet the following requirements:

(a) Possession of a Preliminary license in the field of the license sought.

(b) Early field-based experience together with seminars or courses that address the Professional Standards for Teachers.

(c) Successful completion of a practicum equivalent.

(d) If the school district does not have an approved program, candidates seeking an Initial license in a core academic subject at any level may demonstrate that they meet (4) through a Panel Review providing they meet the following requirements:

1. Possession of a Preliminary license in a core academic subject.

2. At least three full years of employment in the role of the Preliminary license.

3. Documentation of seminars, courses, and experience relevant to the license sought.

4. A recommendation from the principal of each school where the candidate was employed under the Preliminary license.

Source: *Regulations for Educator Licensure and Preparation Program Approval* (Massachusetts Department of Education, 2003).

in 1999 that most of the professional development points (PDPs) required for renewal of a license in a five-year cycle must have academic content. Guidelines for high-quality professional development and criteria for determining the number of PDPs that can be awarded for various professional development activities were then hammered out by department staff. These guidelines included the use of pretests and posttests, visible products, and ten-hour minimums as criteria for judging worthwhile professional development. Nevertheless, formulating these guidelines was a thankless task because the variations on such activities are myriad, the number of points awarded is ultimately arbitrary, and the vast bulk of in-service professional development is arranged by school districts themselves (typically using their own teaching force or education school faculty) and must be accepted as worthwhile. Unless there is a small list of approved providers (an unlikely situation in a country filled with educational entrepreneurs), a department of education is unlikely to have the capacity to screen all professional development providers and monitor all locally sponsored professional development activities. Professional development not only is costly, but it also is a bottomless can of worms. Often a combination of insult and entertainment for an intelligent teacher, it is usually remedial in nature—attempting to fill in gaps in a teacher's professional skill and academic knowledge that should have been addressed in preservice training.

The department has been able, with federal funds such as those provided by Goals 2000, to sponsor and manage some professional development initiatives to address specific areas of the curriculum. These have included academic institutes, one to two weeks in duration, designed to help teachers learn how to teach to preK–12 standards in mathematics, science, history, foreign languages, the arts, and English. In addition, for ten years (1992 to 2002), supported by grants from the National Science Foundation (NSF) and the Noyce Foundation to a state systemic initiative (SSI) in Massachusetts known as PALMS (Partnerships Advancing Learning in Mathematics and Science), millions of dollars were spent on professional development in mathematics and science (through workshops, consultants, conferences, regional curriculum centers, and development of teacher leaders) to upgrade teachers' knowledge in these areas, to support the purchase and implementation of NSF-endorsed or -funded mathematics and science programs for K–12, to align these curricular materials with state standards, and to teach teachers the specific pedagogical strategies required for teaching these programs. This huge investment did not seem to have paid off if one is to judge by MCAS scores in mathematics and science in the elementary and middle grades.

One major professional development initiative undertaken by the department in a large number of low-performing middle schools served as the basis for a research project. Called the Middle School Mathematics Initiative, this two-year intervention was completed in 2002 and involved about fifty teachers and six mathematics specialists employed full time by the department. This initiative sought to determine if coaching teachers with a focus on lesson planning, together with mathematics coursework for the teachers in these schools, could improve the mathematical learning of their students. This initiative did have statistically significant results, although they could not be judged as having practical significance.

A second major professional development initiative, also in mathematics, began on a statewide basis in the summer of 2003. Called the Singapore Mathematics Initiative, this project provided about forty volunteer K–8 teachers in eight school districts throughout the state with relevant mathematics coursework and guidance in how to understand and use the Singapore Mathematics Curriculum in their classrooms during the 2003–04 academic year, together with follow-up support during the school year. Originally planned and directed by a mathematician at Worcester State College, the Singapore Mathematics Curriculum was piloted in one Massachusetts school district for three years and grew dramatically from year to year in that district on a voluntary basis. From a modest beginning in 2000 with volunteer teachers in six classrooms, over half of all the district's K–8 teachers were planning to use the Singapore Mathematics Curriculum in the 2003–04 school year (about sixty-five classrooms). The project has expanded rapidly in this school district from year to year because nonparticipating teachers have been able to talk freely to colleagues and to students who had already begun to use the curriculum, because district administrators strongly supported the project and because MCAS scores in mathematics for grade four have risen for students using that curriculum, from the learning disabled to the academically able.

The department also sponsored a large number of institutes for retraining teachers of reading. Some were for the state-funded Bay State Readers Program (the appropriation for which has just been eliminated because of the state budget deficit). An even larger number were for the Reading Excellence program, a multiyear federally funded project. The department is planning an equally large number of institutes to retrain teachers in kindergarten to grade three, as part of a major initiative funded by the U.S. Department of Education known as the Reading First program. One might ask why it is necessary to retrain, at great cost, most of the elementary teaching force, and in the one subject area one might reasonably expect them to be able to teach after completing their original teacher-training programs. Unfortunately, today, one cannot necessarily expect newly minted teachers to be able to teach any of the basic subjects typically taught in the elementary school. Several years ago, I asked a principal of a highly reputable suburban school what she thought new teachers were prepared to do as a result of their training programs. Her answer: "They come in with a very good understanding of children's needs." But she was candid and added: "However, as soon as we hire them, we have to start training them how to teach reading and mathematics."

Providing for a Career Ladder to Retain Quality Teachers

The program subsidizing the application of experienced teachers for certification from the National Board for Professional Teaching Standards produced 358 certified teachers by the end of 2002, with the largest group in elementary education. However, because no criteria were established in the statute or in the regulations for this program requiring a link between the applicant's performance in the classroom and student learning for eligibility for subsidization, these teachers have all been self-selected so far, needing only a principal's recommendation to receive the application subsidy of $2,300.

Results

So far, the results of all these initiatives to enhance teacher quality and the supply of academically able teachers are chiefly positive. It will take many years of data gathering for more definitive evaluations.

Teacher-Training Programs

A number of changes have been made in teacher preparation programs in response to the changes in the licensing regulations. These changes have been made for at least two reasons. First, teacher-training programs have to demonstrate that they have made these changes to get department approval to continue preparing prospective teachers for initial licensure and practicing teachers for the second stage of licensure. Second, they are not unaware of the mounting nationwide criticism of teachers' academic preparation and Massachusetts's schools of education, as well as the new federal laws spelling out what it means to be a highly qualified teacher.

According to department staff responsible for approving all teacher-training programs, most undergraduate programs in Massachusetts have worked out ways to ensure the thirty-six hours of academic coursework required for prospective elementary (and special education) teachers. These staff suggested the following as some of the clues they noted in the materials prepared by the training programs for their site visits: the identification of specific courses in the arts and sciences as addressing the Massachusetts curriculum frameworks; the integration and use of the Massachusetts curriculum frameworks in education methods courses; better lessons in the portfolios that prospective teachers create as part of the assessment of their student teaching; more joint appointments of arts and sciences faculty in education schools and the involvement of arts and sciences faculty in the design of methods courses in their discipline; and greater use of arts and sciences faculty in supervising student teachers.

In addition, many education schools are providing test preparation workshops or seminars for students preparing to take the basic teacher test of reading and writing skills. After the 1998 debacle, education schools began to offer these workshops or seminars, and consequently the overall failure rate on this test has steadily declined. However, extremely few test preparation workshops address the subject matter tests. This is clearly a hard nut for the education schools to crack; they need the cooperation if not the leadership of their arts and sciences colleagues if they are to provide assistance to the students enrolled in their licensure programs who are weak in required content knowledge.

Teacher Tests

The situation in Massachusetts has vastly improved since 1998. In 2001 about 60 percent of the test takers passed all the tests required for initial licensing—the communication and literacy skills test and the test of subject matter knowledge. Moreover, the overall number of test takers has not declined, even though many teacher-training programs in the state are now requiring a passing grade on the communication and literacy skills test before a prospective teacher is admitted into an education program or allowed to do practice teaching. The overall number of test takers has increased from year to year, as have the mean pass rates for each quartile of the state's fifty-eight institutions with approved teacher licensure programs, a ranking system required for Title II reports beginning with the 1999–2000 cohort of prospective teachers. For example, as table 4 shows, the mean pass rate for the lowest quartile in academic content was 64.8 for the 1999–2000

Table 4. Mean and Range of Pass Rates for All Fifty-eight Massachusetts Teacher-Training Institutions by Quartile Ranking

Percent

Cohort and quartile ranking	Communication and literacy skills test	Subject matter knowledge tests
1999–2000 cohort		
Q1 mean (range)	98.8 (97–100)	96.1 (91–100)
Q2 mean (range)	92.8 (90–96)	87.2 (85–90)
Q3 mean (range)	85.2 (82–89)	81.1 (77–84)
Q4 mean (range)	70.2 (47–81)	64.8 (50–76)
2000–01 cohort		
Q1 mean (range)	99.8 (99–100)	99.2 (97–100)
Q2 mean (range)	95.9 (94–98)	93.2 (90–96)
Q3 mean (range)	90.7 (87–93)	86.5 (84–89)
Q4 mean (range)	77.4 (70–86)	70.7 (53–83)
2001–02 cohort		
Q1 mean (range)	100 (100)	99.9 (97–100)
Q2 mean (range)	98.0 (97–99)	95.5 (93–98)
Q3 mean (range)	93.6 (90–96)	89.4 (86–92)
Q4 mean (range)	74.5 (36–89)	68.2 (36–85)

Source: Massachusetts Department of Education.
Note: Based on the pass rate for each institution for all its program completers for that cohort year.

cohort and 68.2 for the 2001–02 cohort; the mean pass rate for the highest quartile in academic content was 96.1 for the 1999–2000 cohort and 99.9 for the 2001–02 cohort.

Nevertheless the Massachusetts teacher tests have eliminated a large number of academically unqualified candidates. As the right-hand column in table 5 shows, varying percentages of prospective teachers across the different subject areas have not passed the subject matter knowledge test required for their license, such as 18 percent in English and in general science, 30 percent in chemistry, 38 percent in mathematics, and 51 percent in earth science. A large number of those who eventually did pass took the test more than once; some more than six or seven times.

The value of one of the newly created licenses is also already apparent. The new middle school mathematics test for prospective mathematics teachers for grades five through eight became available in September 2002 and in its first three administrations was taken by a large number of candidates (652). (This test contains some items on calculus but addresses mainly alge-

Table 5. Cumulative Pass Rates on Massachusetts Tests for Educator Licensure from April 1998 to November 2002

Test	Number of test takers	Number of passers	Number kept from licensure by the test (percent)
Communication and literacy skills test	62,718	52,593	10,125 (16)
Biology	1,562	1,176	386 (25)
Business	704	565	139 (20)
Chemistry	463	323	140 (30)
Chinese	27	23	4 (15)
Dance	37	35	2 (5)
Early childhood	4,415	3,630	785 (18)
Earth science	326	159	167 (51)
Elementary	13,948	11,740	2,208 (16)
English	4,370	3,598	772 (18)
English as a Second Language	536	398	138 (26)
Foundations of reading	146	137	9 (6)
French	483	327	156 (32)
General science	861	706	155 (18)
German	70	61	9 (13)
Health education	584	456	128 (22)
History	2,385	1,876	509 (21)
Home economics	64	52	12 (19)
Italian	52	47	5 (10)
Latin	121	91	30 (25)
Mathematics	2,802	1,746	1,056 (38)
Middle school generalist	1,388	1,145	243 (18)
Middle school mathematics	292	177	115 (39)
Moderate disabilities	4,578	4,154	424 (9)
Music	1,044	776	268 (26)
Physical education	1,189	985	204 (17)
Physics	286	207	79 (28)
Portuguese	38	34	4 (11)
Reading specialist	775	650	125 (16)
Russian	13	11	2 (15)
Social studies	2,043	1,489	554 (27)
Spanish	1,420	1,147	273 (19)
Speech	63	31	32 (51)
TBE Cape Verdean	13	12	1 (8)
TBE Chinese	16	12	4 (25)
TBE Haitian–Creole	11	6	5 (45)
TBE Portuguese	63	56	7 (11)
TBE Russian	10	9	1 (10)
TBE Spanish	270	217	53 (20)
Technology education	171	103	68 (40)
Theater	228	221	7 (3)
Visual art	1,252	1,081	171 (14)

Source: Massachusetts Department of Education.
Note: TBE = Transitional Bilingual Education.

bra and geometry.) To judge whether it was serving its intended purpose, the department determined the number of test takers who had already failed the more difficult mathematics test before September 2002 (the test for grades five through twelve) and who took the new middle school mathematics test in September 2002, November 2002, or February 2003 and passed. The pass rate on the new middle school mathematics test for those who had already failed the more difficult test was 70 percent. The good news is that the state now has ninety-eight more teachers qualified to teach middle school mathematics than it would likely have had without the test. The bad news is that, overall, 43 percent of the prospective teachers who believed they could pass the middle school mathematics test (those taking a mathematics test for the first time as well as those who had failed the more difficult test at least once) failed it.

Recruitment

With respect to the results of the new recruitment initiatives, the evaluation by the Center for Education Policy at the University of Massachusetts–Amherst found that the college graduates and midcareer changers prepared through an accelerated training program were obtaining jobs and being judged positively by their principals (although it remains unknown how much of their enthusiasm reflects the dire straits in which the schools find themselves in their efforts to locate qualified mathematics and science teachers). Moreover, the accelerated training programs sponsored and run by the department are now providing a model for many of the district-based programs coming into being, as well as providing a much-needed group of male teachers for secondary schools.

Master Teacher Status and the Career Ladder

This initiative turned out to be more expensive than anticipated and not sustainable in the face of serious state budget cuts. Moreover, the selection process was too open-ended, and the demands on teachers receiving the bonus not rewarding enough to the state. Of the 358 Massachusetts teachers who achieved NBPTS certification since 1996, approximately 275 are mentoring in their districts and are eligible for master teacher status and the planned $5,000 annual bonus for ten years. The original target was one thousand master teachers. However, to address the state's budget problems in 2003, legislators decided to use the principal in the endowment fund to help reduce the state budget deficit. Thus continuation of this initiative is not possible at present. If there is renewed funding for it in the future, the department will strengthen criteria for the application subsidy, receipt of the bonus, and the amount of the bonus, as well as spell out acceptable pathways for achieving master teacher status that would include NBPTS certification but not depend on it alone. Of the 645 subsidized applications for NBPTS certification between 1998 and 2001 (at $2,300 per application), only 333 applicants (52 percent) passed. Despite partial subsidization of these 645 applications by NBPTS itself since 1998, this has been a costly program for the state to fund and there is no evidence yet that NBPTS-certified teachers have been more successful in their classrooms or increased their students' scores on MCAS more than have noncertified teachers with similar students either before or after NBPTS certification.

Professional Development

With respect to the Middle School Mathematics Initiative, the results were positive, and the teachers highly valued the specialists and the work they did on lesson planning. However, although the gain scores on posttests were higher in the treatment groups than in comparison classes, reaching statistical significance, the practical importance of these modest gains (twenty was the maximum number of points that could be obtained on the test, with items mostly at a grade six level of difficulty) raises questions about the use of coaching as the strategy of choice for improving mathematics learning for very low-performing students (see table 6). Perhaps these very low achievers would benefit more from improved attendance rates and special classes providing intensive help. It is difficult to determine how useful coaching is, in general, or with what populations, because there seem to be no peer-reviewed, published research studies using comparison groups addressing its efficacy at any educational level. Moreover, the department spent about $2 million on this project (the chief costs, as one might expect, were the six full-time specialists or coaches working with forty to fifty classroom teachers), making this a very expensive strategy to use on a large scale, even if the results had been of greater practical significance.

Table 6. Mean Scores and Mean Change Scores of MSMI Students versus Each Comparison Group

Group	Pretest	Posttest	Change
MSMI (*N* = 1,756)			
Mean	7.81	10.58	2.77[a]
Standard deviation	3.81	4.53	3.27
Specialist only (*N* = 263)			
Mean	8.71	11.46	2.75[a]
Standard deviation	3.97	4.89	3.26
Course only (*N* = 98)			
Mean	8.26	11.79	3.53[a]
Standard deviation	3.31	4.42	3.04
No intervention (*N* = 749)			
Mean	8.97	10.96	1.99
Standard deviation	4.04	4.51	3.30

Source: University of Massachusetts, Donahue Institute, *Analysis of Student Outcomes: Evaluation of the DOE Middle School Mathematics Initiative* (December 2002).

Note: MSMI = Middle School Mathematics Initiative.

a. Difference from no-intervention mean change score is statistically significant.

Lessons Learned

The Massachusetts Department of Education learned a number of important lessons from its efforts to enhance teacher quality and supply. All can be useful to other state departments of education and to legislators at both the state and federal levels.

Capacity for Data Collection and Analysis Is a Major Priority

One of the most important lessons I have learned is that a state department of education cannot determine the results of most of its policies if it does not have the necessary technology in place and the capacity to collect and analyze the right information. With respect to the revised preK–12 standards, all Massachusetts teacher-training programs know they must make sure that student teachers are familiar with the standards and can create and implement lesson plans oriented to them. So far, according to the department's program approval staff, they are doing so. But whether a reference to the preK–12 standards in educational methods courses is increasing prospective teachers' knowledge of the academic content behind each standard is difficult to determine. They could be doing so; the relevant empirical evidence simply cannot be gathered in the context of a licensure program. The department does find out whether prospective teachers in a licensure program pass the relevant subject matter knowledge teacher test, but that test reflects their arts and sciences coursework, not their methods courses. The best qualitative sources of information on the effects of preK–12 standards on preservice teacher training might be the evaluations of first-year teachers by their principals or supervisors. Unfortunately, the department has no capacity to locate and interview newly licensed teachers in their first year of teaching. Nor do most state departments of education have the necessary technology and research capacity to do so, especially in states such as Massachusetts where many private institutions of higher education produce many teachers who teach elsewhere. Likewise, most school districts do not have the necessary technology and personnel to provide such information to a state department of education, and certainly not on a relatively effortless and routine basis.

Because of the lack of capacity and technology in a typical department of education, external evaluations can be useful. Commissioned by the Massachusetts Department of Education to evaluate its various initiatives to attract able college graduates and midcareer changers to teaching, especially in mathematics and science, the Center for Education Policy at the University of Massachusetts–Amherst gathered a great deal of valuable information on the quality and results of these programs between 1999 and 2001. The report containing the center's findings, the department's proposed plans and policies based on these findings, and the current fiscal situation was released by the department in March 2003. Although such evaluations in a time of shrinking budgets cannot be funded on a regular basis, this report demonstrates that research on the results of public policy initiatives is worth doing.

Cooperation from the Board of Higher Education Is Vital

Cooperation from a board of higher education is vital if a state's public colleges and universities are to support the efforts of schools or departments of education to strengthen the academic background of prospective teachers. Depending on its statutory powers, a board of higher education can encourage if not require arts and sciences faculties to strengthen coursework in disciplines taught in K–12, to put into place more rigorous general core requirements, to revamp existing courses, to aim for consistent disciplinary content across constituent members in those courses most likely to be taken by prospective teachers, and to create special courses in mathematics and science for prospective elementary or middle school teachers. An understaffed board of higher education with little statutory power cannot provide the necessary leadership or the work to support a department of education in realizing the benefits of strong preK–12 standards and teacher licensing regulations.

Arts and Sciences Faculty Cooperation Is Critical

Perhaps the chief lesson I learned in my work with the department is that the quality of prospective teachers may not be upgraded in any appreciable way unless arts and science faculties can be held accountable for the quality of their undergraduate teaching and the content they provide in courses that prospective teachers are apt to take, regardless of whether the students in these courses go on to teaching or to other careers. It is ironic that the education schools took all of the blame for the poor showing of their students in the 1998 Massachusetts teacher test fiasco. Who was really responsible for the debacle? In my eyes, both education school faculty and their counterparts in the arts and sciences were to blame. No pedagogical test had been mandated by the legislature and given to these prospective teachers, so there was no way to judge the influence of their education courses per se. One could point a finger only to the admission and exit criteria used by the schools of education, criteria that are often subject to review by university presidents, provosts, and other deans. Those responsible for the level of subject matter knowledge attained by the 1998 cohort of test takers were those who had taught them that content, presumably in the arts and sciences.

The irony in this situation cannot be blinked away. Many scholars and citizens believe that little is learned in pedagogical coursework and that most of it is unnecessary. But here was a situation wherein the deficiencies these test takers exhibited reflected course taking and learning chiefly in the arts and sciences. Teacher educators on the whole did not complain that the arts and sciences people were not doing their job. Nor were they about to say that teachers do not need knowledge about the subjects they teach. Instead, their complaint boiled down to the claim that the tests were psychometrically flawed and that subject matter knowledge was being overvalued. I suspect that a major reason for the lack of complaints about the quality of the academic preparation of those candidates who failed the 1998 teacher tests was a desire by teacher educators not to see greater academic demands put on prospective students or on those students already in teacher-training programs. After an extensive review of the research literature published in February 2001, only grudgingly did three well-known education faculty members at Michigan State University conclude that "research has shown that subject matter preparation is important and that the current results of subject matter preparation are disappointing."[9] They do not go so far as to say that knowledge of the subject matter being taught is indispensable; it is merely "important."

Given rampant grade inflation, it is not hard to sympathize with education departments that try to establish meaningful admissions standards for students who decide at the end of their freshman or sophomore year to become a K–12 teacher and apply for admission to their college's teacher-training program. Requiring more, or more difficult, content courses may lead not to an increase in their students' academic knowledge but simply to an increase in their students' grades.

While the quality of a single course is an individual and departmental responsibility, arts and sciences faculty members as a body are responsible for a much deeper problem I discovered: what constitutes an arts and sciences major itself—and an appropriate major. Many years ago, the prospective elementary teacher typically majored in education, an intellectually flat major (because there was little academic content after the sophomore year), but they nevertheless fulfilled common, academically meaningful distribution requirements at public universities and colleges. The increase in choices in distribution requirements, or the total elimination of these requirements, came about in the 1960s as a revolt against the requirement of a common core of knowledge for all liberal arts students, or against the possibility that one could even exist. From my perspective, the abolition of a demanding set of introductory (often broad survey) courses distributed across major subject areas had disastrous consequences for that large group of students at public colleges and universities who became the next wave of teachers in K–12. In reducing or eliminating what all students should have in common, and what was most intellectually demanding, and in allowing the construction and proliferation of artificially constructed majors for practical or political purposes, universities ended up damaging the quality of the academic education needed by a very important group of students—not those able students, male and female, who went on to serious graduate study in the arts and sciences, but those students who became the next generation of K–12 teachers, many of whom had much lower academic achievement. All undergraduates should be taking courses that advance their understanding of the disciplines being taught, especially courses in their major. All should be capable of passing a subject matter teacher test in their major area by the time they graduate.

The quality of prospective elementary teachers in particular (and perhaps middle school teachers as well) probably will not be upgraded if the arts and sciences faculties in public colleges and universities do not address the academic quality and relevance of the arts and sciences majors they approve for elementary (and possibly middle school) teachers. I understand a major to consist of a sequence of courses (perhaps thirty-six to forty hours) in a recognized academic discipline or in an area with a focused or circumscribed body of knowledge. Moreover, to complete a major means that a student has undertaken upper-level as well as lower-level courses, achieving some intellectual depth in the area by graduation. At the time I was revising the teacher licensing regulations, I had originally suggested restricting the majors of prospective elementary teachers to those subject areas that are typically taught in the elementary school. The storm raised by that idea across education schools in Massachusetts almost blew me out to sea. I then asked a staff member to obtain some information on what these prospective teachers were choosing as their majors.

The first kind of problem with majors is what I call the respectable but irrelevant major. It is respectable because it is a traditional and legitimate undergraduate major. It is irrelevant because it has no direct connection to what a K–12 teacher is expected to teach. The irrelevant major is what a large number if not a majority of prospective elementary school teachers are taking, for one of two reasons. First, if an arts and sciences major is required of prospective elementary teachers, in addition to or in place of an education major, then weak students are apt to choose what they perceive as a relatively undemanding major—not mathematics, science, English, history, geography, or political science, but psychology, child development, or sociology. Second, prospective elementary teachers, whether or not they are weak students, may choose on the basis of interest alone one of the many other majors now available at universities, as the National Association of Scholars found in a study of the situation at the University of Colorado–Boulder. There is nothing wrong with French, religious studies, marketing, business, dance, or theater as majors; they are simply not instructionally relevant ones for the prospective elementary school teacher, who is unlikely to have to teach any of these subjects. Students completing an irrelevant major are likely to obtain the intellectual experience a major should provide, but they do not take courses that give them the background knowledge they need for the subjects taught in the typical elementary school. As a result of a report by the National Association of Scholars, the Colorado Board of Education now limits prospective elementary school teachers to the following majors: anthropology, distributed studies in biology or chemistry, communication, economics, English, geography, history, humanities, linguistics, and mathematics. Forty-four others were deemed unacceptable as majors for these prospective teachers.[10]

The second kind of problem is what I call the grievance major. Such a major is usually described as interdisciplinary and has such titles as "Politics, Culture, and Society," "Perspectives on the Hispanic Experience," "American Heritages," "Environmental Studies," and "Multicultural Studies." It is unclear from my reading of the college catalogues in which these titles appear just what these majors consist of from an academic perspective. They seem to be tendentious in orientation and without academic depth or breadth. To judge from their titles, they most likely come about because of particular faculty or student interests.

The third type of problem is what I call the composite major, an artificially constructed major that varies from college to college. It has many good things in it—a little of everything—but not much of any one thing. It is not one of the traditional majors at a college and probably results from collaboration between education faculty and arts and sciences faculty. In a well-intentioned attempt to provide prospective elementary (and sometimes middle) school teachers with some academic preparation in all the subject areas they teach, members of both faculties cobble together a few arts and sciences courses in each of the major subject areas taught in the elementary and middle school, join them to some education courses, and approve the camel as an arts and science major. This kind of major has legitimate breadth but no intellectual depth. It is given a variety of names, including liberal studies major, liberal arts major, educational studies, and interdisciplinary studies major for elementary education. It is unclear how many courses are upper level in this conglomeration. Across institutions, it assumes a variety of forms, encompasses a wide range of different credit hours, often includes a large number of education courses, and may add up to almost three-fourths of the number of credit hours needed for graduation. It is an honest but mis-guided attempt to address the needs of those teachers (usually early childhood, elementary, and special education) who teach children in self-contained classrooms in kindergarten through grade six or eight. Some variations are for prospective middle school teachers who may be little more than glorified elementary school teachers as the result of the development of the generalist middle school license.

The arts and sciences faculties in universities or colleges with teacher education departments or schools need to engage in a dialogue through their respective deans about the kind of academic majors prospective K–6 or K–8 teachers should be taking. Then more serious discussions need to take place about the content of the courses prospective teachers (and perhaps others) should take in the various disciplines informing the subject matter they will teach in the typical elementary and middle school.

High-Quality Teacher Tests Are Not the Whole Answer

The content of most teacher tests is still not equivalent in difficulty level to upper-level college work. Most could not serve as the equivalent of department-based examinations for undergraduates completing a major in a particular discipline, no matter what cut score is used. Nevertheless, education or educational research faculty at Massachusetts institutions of higher education continue to criticize the Massachusetts teacher tests on psychometric grounds, despite a positive technical review by an advisory committee composed of nationally prominent experts on large-scale assessment and licensing procedures. This committee, hired by the department in the fall of 2001 to examine all aspects of the department's teaching testing procedures, concluded in a report presented to the department in January 2002 that the Massachusetts teacher testing system was psychometrically sound and of high quality. Nevertheless, the higher education critics continue to dwell on the supposed psychometric deficiencies of the Massachusetts tests, presumably because, if they cannot eliminate teacher tests altogether, they would like the state to switch to the Educational Testing Service's Praxis tests. This desire may stem from the impression that the Massachusetts tests are generally harder than most of the Praxis tests, an impression supported by the results of a study reported in the spring 1999 issue of Education Trust's quarterly journal.[11]

The higher education critics also sidestep the question of the relevance of a state's own preK–12 academic standards to the state's teacher tests, an issue of high importance to the department. Immense value exists in having teacher tests tailored to a state's own standards (especially if the standards are high and good, as the Massachusetts frameworks have been independently judged to be) and in using local educators (both those in the schools and those in institutions of higher education) in test development.[12] Local educators can see that they are playing a major role in determining the quality and content of both the multiple-choice test items and the prompts for the open-response test items and in ensuring that the items are relevant to the academic standards that prospective teachers must teach to at the educational level of their license.

In revising the subject matter tests (and creating new ones) to fit the new licensure regulations, the National Evaluation Systems staff has worked diligently with the department as it sought to raise the level of difficulty (and appropriateness) of the original Massachusetts teacher tests to ensure that prospective teachers could teach to the newly revised preK–12 standards. The revised tests have better as well as more difficult questions on them and are more appropriate for undergraduates completing a bachelor's degree program, regardless of the educator licensure program they may also have completed. But, the department found that even more difficult teacher tests tailored to demanding preK–12 academic standards are not the whole answer to the problem of how to increase teacher quality.

They are not the whole answer because of three unforeseen problems, two of which are related to the political dynamics underlying the Title II accountability for institutions of higher education. The first problem is that most of the cut scores (before scaling) for the first batch of revised or new teacher tests are now much lower than those for the original tests (that is, a smaller proportion of correct answers on the multiple-choice test items is needed for passing). Possibly both the education school faculty and the arts and sciences faculty on the standard-setting committees feel threatened by the 80 percent pass rate requirement for schools of education. It is not illogical for them to predict that if education schools or departments are placed on probation or lose state approval to provide teacher-training programs, then the number of students seeking admission to their institution as a whole (especially to a state college) may decline. Despite these proportionally lower cut scores, with the exception of three tests with unusually high pass rates, the difference in pass rates between the original tests and the revised tests is not great. Possibly the members of the standard-setting committees (the majority of whose members must be licensed teachers) have low expectations for what new teachers are apt to know. Possibly faculty in higher education institutions are judging on the basis of the students in their own institutions. Possibly school teachers are judging on the basis of what they themselves know and on what they observe in novice teachers. (In setting a cut score, they are asked to consider the minimum knowledge that entry-level teachers would have, not what level of knowledge the beginning teacher should have.) Possibly the general hostility to testing that has been expressed openly by education school faculty and conveyed in their courses throughout the country has increasingly influenced K–12 teachers, and coming in with a lower cut score is one way school teachers may demonstrate this influence. Possibly resentment by higher education faculty at being held responsible for their students' academic achievement, their slighting of the importance of academic knowledge in determining teacher quality, their opinion that tests of academic achievement are detrimental to efforts to get more minority students into teaching (with all that implies about their view of minority students), and their claim that pedagogical knowledge is much more important than academic knowledge also account for lower cut scores on the revised teacher tests.

The second problem is that many education schools have nullified the intent of the 80 percent pass rate by requiring their undergraduate students to pass the communication and literacy skills test before enrolling them into their licensure programs. This ensures a higher quality of students in these programs but relieves the faculty of any responsibility to strengthen these programs. Many programs also misuse the licensure tests by requiring enrolled students to take and pass the subject matter knowledge test before admitting them to student teaching. For these students, this may mean in effect that if they pass the subject matter knowledge test for their license by the beginning of their senior year, they will not take any more upper-level courses in their major, or in the arts and sciences altogether, if they have already fulfilled the requisite number of credit hours for the major or in the arts and sciences. For undergraduates simultaneously completing a licensure program and the requirements for a bachelor's degree, it is unclear how the taking of the subject matter knowledge test by the end of the junior year may affect the quality of the intellectual experience they should obtain from their major or the quality of the arts and sciences courses they may be required to take in their junior year.

The third problem is related to the fact that the education schools offer few test preparation seminars or workshops for the subject matter knowledge test. This is not surprising because education schools are not responsible for the content taught in the arts and sciences. But the more basic problem is the low level of involvement by arts and sciences faculty in developing, reviewing, and setting a standard for the teacher test in their own discipline, in the construction of pedagogical courses for their discipline with colleagues in the education school, and in the supervision of student teaching in classes in their discipline. The department and National Education Systems have made strenuous efforts to involve arts and sciences faculty in the state's many private and public institutions of higher education in the development of the teacher tests, but it seems that the more prestigious the higher education institution, the less likely that faculty are interested. Until more arts and sciences faculty have a better knowledge of what is required on a teacher test (or unless they have children of their own in the public schools), they are unlikely to realize the importance of providing the course content that prospective teachers of K–12 need and of expecting them as well as the others to meet high academic standards in their own courses.

Professional Development May Be No More Than a Band-Aid

Large numbers of teachers, especially those teaching in the elementary and middle grades, whether the mainstream or the special education student, need extensive coursework in the subjects they are licensed to teach. It is not clear to me, based on descriptions that have come across my desk of what constitutes professional development in the form of either in-service activities or graduate-level courses taken by teachers in schools of education, that professional development for teachers does much to increase the academic knowledge teachers need. Instead of offering serious study of the academic base underlying what teachers teach, professional development presenters tend to be pedagogues who show teachers how to teach whatever are deemed the best practices du jour, strategies such as differentiated instruction that almost never have research evidence to support their efficacy in improving student learning and that are unrelated to conceptual issues in specific subjects.

In 1996 the department began funding summer content institutes that provide serious study of the content required for teaching to the state's preK–12 standards. The institutes have been based on proposals submitted to the department by local school districts in collaboration with higher education faculty or educational nonprofit organizations following department guidelines. Each year the department has taken greater and greater pains in the request for responses it sends out to explain what academic concepts are and how to organize five to ten days of work to help teachers acquire them. Most of the proposals for institutes in mathematics and science that the department now receives are oriented chiefly to the study of mathematical or science content (the message in these subject areas finally got through), but sound, academically oriented proposals in the humanities are still not the general rule. However, the more basic problem is trying, in one or two weeks, to teach teachers the subject matter knowledge they should have acquired in their four undergraduate years, especially when there may be a deeper interest in pedagogy than in content on the part of the presenters.

For example, despite the millions in National Science Foundation funds that the department spent on a variety of professional development activities in mathematics from 1992 to 2002 (including the summer content institutes), no meaningful evidence has yet emerged from MCAS scores in mathematics in the elementary and middle grades that these activities, the bulk of which were designed to help teachers learn how to understand and use NSF-endorsed curriculum materials to address state standards, improved students' mathematical learning. In both grade four and grade eight, little increase is evident from 1998 to 2003 in the percentage of students in the top two categories on the MCAS mathematics tests. The lack of high stakes at these two grade levels could have left students unmotivated to do better (although the lack of high stakes does not usually dampen the motivation of fourth-grade students to do their best). But the slight increase does raise questions about the worth of the pedagogical goals that dominated professional development activities in mathematics until recently. It is not known whether these activities increased the mathematical knowledge of current teachers beyond the life of the professional development activity itself, even if these activities do not seem to have improved student learning in mathematics in K–8 very much, to judge from MCAS scores.

Concluding Remarks

Can a state department of education enhance teacher quality and supply? Yes, it can try to do so in many ways, and it clearly can do so, as some of the results in Massachusetts so far suggest. Depending on their state law, other departments of education may be able to benefit from the lessons learned in Massachusetts after it began to implement the policies and programs described in this paper. However, at a time of shrinking budgets for both state agencies and the public schools, the extent to which departments of education can increase teacher quality and supply in the future may also depend on whether they are given mandates and sufficient appropriations by their state legislatures, beyond the funds they receive from No Child Left Behind, to help their public schools address the academic needs of the entire range of students in them, not just those of low-achieving students, the chief beneficiaries of No Child Left Behind and most other federal funding. MERA had a broad vision of the public schools and sought to upgrade achievement by all students, providing for a certificate of mastery and other incentives for high achievers in high school, in addition to an accountability system that would compel schools with large numbers of low-performing students to improve their educational performance. No Child Left Behind has a more limited vision, seeking through its accountability provisions to move all students up to a proficient level of achievement in reading and mathematics over the next decade, using National Assessment of Educational Progress results as the common yardstick by which to judge state efforts and differences in definition. It contains no monetary (or other) incentives to encourage, never mind compel, the schools to try to move large numbers of students already at a proficient level to more advanced levels of academic achievement (for example, by mandating the availability of accelerated, honors, or Advanced Placement courses and teachers academically qualified to teach them). In the current fiscal climate, No Child Left Behind may have unintended negative consequences for the higher-performing students in U.S. schools (who nonetheless do not achieve as highly as do their counterparts in other countries). These students need teachers who can challenge them intellectually with texts, textbooks, and curricula that are much more demanding than the texts, textbooks, and curricula that can move low-performing students to the proficient level. He who pays the piper calls the tune. Departments of education with few or no state funds for programs that might counterbalance No Child Left Behind's emphasis on the academic progress of low-performing students may inadvertently encourage cash-starved school districts (especially school districts with large numbers of low-performing students) to ignore the academic needs of their higher-performing students and to concentrate all their efforts on their low-performing students to continue receiving No Child Left Behind funds. And, with no state or federal mandates and funds to provide for the academic needs of higher-performing students, departments of education may determine the adequacy of their state's teacher tests, their teachers' academic qualifications (so long as they have passed the state's teacher tests), and the curricula they use chiefly by the academic needs and academic progress of the low-performing students they teach. This view of the qualified teacher has been endemic in schools of education, and it would be ironic if No Child Left Behind unintentionally reinforces it.

Whether or not No Child Left Behind continues in its present form, I do not see wholesale improvement in teacher quality on a nationwide basis in the future without a reconceptualization of the way in which prospective teachers are trained in the United States. The Massachusetts Department of Education has clearly increased teacher quality and the supply of quality teachers in Massachusetts by means of the policies and initiatives it has pursued in the past decade in response to MERA and by means of the revisions that have been made to its basic documents. But much more could be done if teacher training as a whole was dramatically changed. My ideas stem, first, from the belief that the public is unlikely to abandon the licensing of teachers in the public schools to rely on a free market approach, especially for elementary and special education students. My ideas also stem from the belief that the current training of preK–12 teachers suffers from two kinds of cultural or intellectual divides. The first was described many years ago by C. P. Snow, a physicist and author who served in several government positions in Great Britain during and after World War II. In a 1959 lecture that aroused a great deal of controversy, he called attention to what he saw as a growing division between literary intellectuals, or those in the humanities, and scientists, or those in the world of science and technology. This division still exists. But, in addition to this division, an even more profound one exists today—the general isolation of teacher educators and teachers themselves (and, as an unfortunate consequence, educational publishers) from the scholars and researchers in the arts and sciences who should ground and orient pedagogy in the disciplines taught in K–12. Training programs for teachers must be integrated with the arts and sciences if academic goals are to regain priority in the public schools and teacher quality enhanced. In addition, many things must be done to upgrade teachers' working conditions, including increases in teachers' salaries and differential pay for mathematics and science teachers and possibly other specialties, if the professional dignity that teachers once had in their own eyes and in the public's eye is to be restored.

A few departments of education in some institutions of higher education, I have discovered, have some of the components I mention below in place. But I know of no undergraduate college with the first one (except for one small private college in South Carolina that abandoned the practice in 2003).

First, faculty in each academic discipline in the arts and sciences across all public colleges and universities in a state need to develop and use common exit exams and reduce the pressure on teacher tests of subject matter knowledge, if not their very existence. At present, the public cannot gauge or compare the substantive value of a major in any discipline within or across universities. Even better would be the development and use of a common exit exam for obtaining a bachelor of arts or science degree across public institutions.

Second, all licensure programs for grade four or above should consist of no more than a one-year postbaccalaureate program but not a master's degree program. The postbaccalaureate program could precede or succeed a master of arts or sciences degree program. If candidates in public institutions of higher education applying to the program have not passed a common exit exam in the subject, the requirements for admission for prospective high school teachers would be a major in or related to the subject; for prospective middle school teachers, at least a minor in or related to the subject(s) they will teach; and for prospective teachers of grades four and five, at least a minor in or related to one of the subjects taught in the elementary school, with subject matter knowledge topics spelled out in a state's licensing regulations and assessed on a required subject matter test for admission. Teacher licensure tests would also be required. For midcareer changers, evidence of some relevant coursework or professional work or both would be necessary, as well as the licensure test.

At least three compelling reasons exist for eliminating teacher licensure programs at the undergraduate level. First, they tend to attract the weakest undergraduate students into teaching careers. Second, they may consume up to one-half or more of all the credits needed for graduation with a bachelor of arts degree in institutions that do not allow education majors. Third, they deprive these students of the full complement of upper-level courses a graduate of the arts and sciences should have taken. In a survey of undergraduate licensure programs in Massachusetts in 2002, the department found that the percentage of total credits required in education coursework (including the practicum) as part of the total credits required for a bachelor's degree ranged from 16 percent to 39 percent in foreign languages, from 13 percent to 39 percent in science, from 13 percent to 42 percent in mathematics, from 22 percent to 51 percent in elementary education, and from 25 percent to 59 percent in special education, with over two-thirds of the institutions that offer programs in these areas responding. Although some potential teachers might be lost to other careers that could be pursued right out of college or to a lack of interest in adding another year of study, schools might gain an academically stronger and more motivated corps of teachers in return, especially if a higher beginning salary could be instituted for all subject area (that is, middle and high school) teachers, together with differentiated pay among these subject areas depending on supply and higher salaries at the other end of the salary schedule.

Third, academic departments need to be responsible for the preparation of all subject matter teachers from grade four on. Mathematics, science, computer science, and engineering departments should be responsible for the preparation of all teachers of mathematics, the sciences, technology education, pre-engineering, and instructional technology in these postbaccalaureate programs.[13] These departments should hire and oversee pedagogical adjunct faculty who would collaborate with them in the design of the pedagogical coursework and in the supervision of student teaching. Similarly, medical- or health-oriented professional schools or departments should be responsible for the preparation of all special education and health teachers. These schools or departments should hire and oversee pedagogical adjunct faculty who would collaborate with them in the design of the pedagogical coursework and in the supervision of student teaching. Similarly, art, music, and dance departments or schools, in collaboration with the relevant academic disciplines in the arts and sciences (for example, art history or musicology), should be responsible for the preparation of all teachers in the arts (music, art, dance). These schools or departments should hire and oversee pedagogical adjunct faculty who would collaborate with them in the design of the pedagogical coursework and in the supervision of student teaching. Teachers in the arts now tend to be prepared in this manner but not necessarily in postbaccalaureate programs. Similarly, humanities and social sciences departments in the arts and sciences should be responsible for the preparation of all teachers in the humanities and social sciences (from history, political science, geography, English, and theater to foreign languages) in postbaccalaureate programs. These departments should hire and oversee pedagogical adjunct faculty who would collaborate with them in the design of the pedagogical coursework and in the supervision of student teaching.

Fourth, undergraduate licensure programs should be available only for prospective physical education teachers, for preschool and kindergarten teachers, and for primary grade teachers, grades one through three. Teachers for preschool through grade three could even be prepared in three-year programs (as in most other countries), not in four-year programs requiring an arts and sciences major and a bachelor's degree.

Fifth, the second stage of licensure should be eliminated wherever it is in place. After three years of satisfactory teaching on an initial license, as determined by an evaluation every year by a school supervisor, teachers should be able to receive partial tenure, renewable on a five-year basis after completion of specific coursework requirements for their license in the arts and sciences (or in the pedagogical institutes for preschool to third-grade teachers), to be undertaken during the summer and paid for by school district, state, or federal funds. No coursework would be expected or allowed during the first three years of teaching so that beginning teachers could concentrate on developing their pedagogical and classroom organization skills.

Sixth, the requirement of a master's degree in education for a second stage of licensure or for an increase in salary should be eliminated. Salary increases should be related to course taking for credit in the arts and sciences, supplemented by pedagogical work under the direction of the academic or professional department or school, and possibly tied to a master's degree in the appropriate arts and sciences discipline.[14] The Massachusetts Joint Commission on Educator Preparation, which was appointed in 1999 after the teacher test debacle in 1998, proposed, among other things in a report to the legislation in 2000, the elimination of the requirement in MERA that teachers earn a master's degree (or its equivalent) for the second level of licensure on the grounds that it was a barrier to licensure. However, as of mid-2003 nothing has come out of any of the commission's recommendations to boost teacher quality.

Finally, each state department of education should have an educator database that could link measurements of student achievement with information on the students' schools, school inspections, teachers' licenses, teachers' academic majors and minors and undergraduate institutions, teachers' training programs and institutions, teachers' teaching experiences, and teachers' college admission test scores. Such a database would enable a department of education to undertake the kind of detailed research that is needed for understanding the connections between teaching and learning on a statewide as well as a national level.

Comment by Margaret Raymond

Sandra Stotsky provides an in-depth case study of policymaking at the state level. To improve the quality of teaching and enhance student performance, Massachusetts has undertaken a number of initiatives in recent years. The state carefully integrated teacher preparation reforms with other efforts to define content requirements for students through standards and curricular frameworks, aligned with student testing and school accountability programs. Stotsky reviews the steps taken and the reaction to them and then draws a few conclusions about the experience. The focus of these comments is on the rational formulation of policy.

The United States is in a brave new world with No Child Left Behind, where the focus is squarely on creating positive impacts on student outcomes. Stotsky correctly characterizes a primary focus of No Child Left Behind as seeking to raise the floor for low-performing students. Additional elements of the law recognize the critical role of teachers in that process. States then must focus on teacher quality as a driver of improved student achievement.

Stotsky's paper is important in part because of the role that Massachusetts has taken on in the evolution of school reform. Massachusetts has been first among states to initiate a number of new policies. Its efforts have received considerable attention from education reform leaders, researchers, and the media over the last few years. Other states, for a variety of reasons, are waiting and seeing what happens in Massachusetts.

Policy concerns the choices that states make. The large number of proposals for new programs or refinements to existing programs amounts to a menu of alternatives that states can contemplate. Eventually, state education

Figure 1. Useful Analysis for Policy

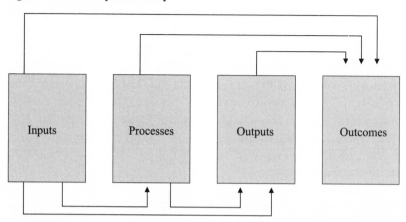

departments and state legislatures narrow down the range of policy possi-bilities, and they make specific choices. And at that point, they have a particular policy or program to put in place, which presumably strives to be a good steward of the public trust.

The programs resulting from the combined efforts of the Massachusetts legislature, the board of education, and the Department of Education reflect their choices. In most cases, the choices represent best guesses as to the wisest course of action, the best investment of scarce resources aimed at an educational objective. The primary objectives for Massachusetts were to attract more high-achieving undergraduate majors, graduates, and academically able midcareer changers to teaching; increase the academic qualifications of new teachers entering the field; and increase the academic knowledge of the current teaching force.

All these objectives focus on the factors of production in education. While the focus is entirely reasonable, it is important to set out the larger context: Superior teaching is the goal because positive impacts on student performance are expected from good teaching. So the ultimate question for policymaking ought to be, How do state policies, not the near-term effects of improving teachers, affect student performance in the long run?

A framework for both the proximate and ultimate impacts of state education policies is captured in figure 1. The framework provides a simple structure for thinking about evaluating policies in the area of teacher quality. Teachers—measured both by number and by quality—are important inputs. Their presence in classrooms is influenced by the policies and programs described by Stotsky.

Each choice has a mix of inputs, or specific processes, either that the policies and programs are seeking to change or that they rely on to create better teaching, which is the output of these initiatives. But Massachusetts needs to couple its choices with rigorous attempts to figure out whether those choices lead to the student academic performance outcomes that they expected. While Stotsky examines the output effects of several of the policies, she acknowledges that outcome or impact evaluations are not the general practice in her state.

That deficiency has broad ramifications. If Massachusetts knew more about the effectiveness of policies that were put in place, some of the debate could be put to bed. Policymaking is always a political process, but it might be possible to at least narrow the domain of the debate if better information could be collected about some of these (and other) attempts to improve teacher quality.

All states are in a better position to conduct such evaluative work than before. From all the state accountability and state testing programs, outcome data finally are available about students and schools. So it is or will soon be possible to relate program efforts and outcomes in a systematic way. The results would be a good source of information for policymakers.

One could potentially argue that Massachusetts is doing too much at the same time, making it difficult to parse all the effects to determine whether achievement is improving. This is possibly less problematic if the programs were rolled out in a way as to create viable—if not randomly selected—control groups for comparison of results. However, this has not happened in Massachusetts—all policies have been implemented universally. This leaves Massachusetts in the position of needing to use trend data to make its case on outcomes. Such an uncontrolled analysis leaves the state to take responsibility for results that could be influenced by a far wider set of factors than just the programmatic ones of interest to the state.

Stotsky provides an example in her paper. She discusses the fact that the initial teacher test, which led to the 80 percent rule for teacher-training programs, had bad results in the first year. Additional data about the trends over time were offered to build the case that the policy was having a desirable effect.

While more teachers are taking the test and proportionally more teachers then come out the other end, the pass rate has not changed much. It seems unlikely that the prospect of a teacher's test is motivating more students to pursue teaching. Other factors, such as a weakening economy, seem more salient. The mix of teacher candidates could differ over time, creating the flat trend. Without better information, after five years of fairly low performance, one might be prompted to take a look at whether or not the policy of teacher testing (or this particular test) needs to be revisited.

The primary point of these comments is that states do not do much to evaluate whether these policy choices work. Across all of the ideas that Stotsky described, only one has been evaluated against student performance. No one knows which of the remaining programs work and which ones do not. One need not be a statistician to know that the probability that 100 percent of them are working is zero. And so which ones should the state perpetuate and which ones should it eliminate? States need more information to inform future decisions. Given that the stakes are politically high for states, state education departments need to embrace program evaluation as seriously as they embrace new initiatives.

By way of conclusion, consider a brief list of useful evaluation topics. First, states must measure the impact of teachers, not just their output. It took fifteen years to figure out the efficacy of individual doctors in their medical practice. It will not take that long in education.

A second topic is the impact of a variety of teacher compensation schemes on teacher and student performance.

And, finally, given the central role of professional development in the federal legislation and state plans, it will be important to assess the impact of the various forms of professional development not just on teacher knowledge, but also on classroom practice and student academic impacts.

Comment by John T. Wenders

Teachers, when asked about what in their college experience contributed most to their teaching competence, invariably say practice teaching. Few suggest that pedagogy is very useful. This evidence, together with the evidence that shows a few years of experience are important in determining teacher quality, strongly suggests that an apprentice program that attracts bright students, with a strong mentor and supervision, could replace the entire certification and licensing process now in place in Massachusetts and elsewhere. That is how it works in many private schools. This is also how it works in almost all colleges, although college teaching is clearly not always comparable to that in lower education, especially at the elementary level.

In a broader sense, learning by doing—experience—is how most productivity is acquired in a market economy, and free entry is one of the main features of such an economy. Much of the high productivity of the U.S. economy comes about when workers face real-world problems and learn how to solve them. Out there, mistakes are penalized and successes are rewarded, and what emerges seems to be fairly good. Because of this, the U.S. economy immediately doubles or triples the productivity of many immigrants the moment they step across the border. The drive to determine competence by any ex ante, top-down credentialing process, such as traditional teacher training, seems inconsistent with these observations.

What Teacher Characteristics Matter?

Presumably teacher licensing has the objective of assuring good student performance. Thus the evidence on what makes an effective teacher as measured by student performance goes to the heart of the relationship between teachers and students and to finding "the teachers we need."

An extensive literature exists on teacher quality as measured by student performance.[15] The results show two general aspects of the connection between effective teachers and students: what matters (verbal cognitive ability, subject matter knowledge, and some experience) and what does not (traditional pedagogy and teacher training, certification, and licensure).

The process described by Sandra Stotsky does not make a serious gesture at attracting smarter teachers. It continues to rely on the colleges of education, where the worst college students gravitate.[16] And it relies on the traditional certification and licensing process that is notorious for discouraging the better college students. If the objective is "to attract a larger number of academically able arts and sciences majors to teaching," then "creat[ing] several new teaching licenses in subjects of potential interest to such candidates" is a perverse way of doing it. All such licensing does is create another barrier to entry for the kind of noneducation college graduate the state wants to attract.

The efforts described by Stotsky focus on improving the academic, as opposed to pedagogic, qualifications of teachers within the context of Massachusetts's existing teacher training. (She quickly finds out that nonpedagogy—academic—training is not the same thing as training in relevant subject matter because many arts and science majors are irrelevant to that end.) Thus Massachusetts presumably tries to effect improved teacher subject matter qualifications, which research shows to be important at the secondary level, via a process that has been conclusively demonstrated not to produce that kind of teacher. As Stotsky shows, while the reform had the intent of reducing the number of undergraduate education courses taken by prospective teachers, it failed to do so, and enrollment and credits taken in the education colleges continued to increase.

While Stotsky confidently asserts that "the Massachusetts Department of Education has clearly increased teacher quality and the supply of quality teachers," she presents almost no evidence on student achievement to support this statement. This assertion, again, falls back on the common mistake of substituting the measurement of teacher characteristics (inputs) for the measurement of student performance (outputs). As Stotsky states, "The first three years of student assessment . . . were sobering and had clear implications for teacher training." And, "although there was a small increase from the 1998 to 2000 tests in the percentage of students performing at a higher level, large numbers of students failed the tests at all grade levels and in all subjects." These results are even more depressing in the light of Stotsky's discussion of the inability of the Massachusetts Department of Education to collect and assess data relevant to the effectiveness of its policies. Further, much of Stotsky's paper describes how the existing teacher credentialing program in Massachusetts has made this task very difficult, if not impossible.

Stotsky does not address the fact that the research also shows that traditional teacher training, certification, and licensing do not matter. Most of her paper discusses ways in which teachers can purportedly be improved by tinkering with the failed traditional process. If one were to use the evidence on what makes an effective teacher, it is just as important to abolish what does not work as it is to promote what does.

Top-Down versus Bottom-Up Market Determination of Teacher Quality

Existing research also has something to say about the top-down, credentialed approach to teacher quality determination as compared with bottom-up, market approaches. In her study of how school choice affects the kind of teachers demanded, Caroline Hoxby found that

> school choice would change the teaching profession by raising the demand for teachers with high quality college education, raising the demand for teachers with math and science skills, and raising the demand for teachers who make extra effort and assume responsibility. Keep in mind that school choice raises the demand for teacher characteristics that attract parents. The evidence suggests, therefore, that parents value teachers' college quality, teachers' effort, and teachers' subject area knowledge (math and science are fields with chronic shortages of subject area knowledge). All of the characteristics apparently valued by parents are characteristics likely to improve student achievement. . . . The evidence suggests that school choice would reduce the demand for credentials that are not valued by the broader labor market, such as master's degrees in education (many of which are low quality) and teachers' certification.[17]

Thus the teacher quality characteristics that improve student performance are also the same characteristics that parents want, but they are not what the present teacher-training process provides.

In a larger sense, these findings of Hoxby, as well as those of Dale Ballou and Michael Podgursky, are remarkable.[18] It turns out that effective teacher characteristics are also the very ones that are emphasized by private schools. In other words, private schools, driven by parental choice in the marketplace, emphasize the same characteristics that independent research has found to be most important in student performance. As an economist, I find that a remarkable noncoincidence. It also shows that market mechanisms do a better job of effecting teacher quality than do the top-down, credentialed approaches preferred by the education establishment.

False Positives and False Negatives in Occupational Licensing

In the light of the characteristics of effective teachers, it is useful to assess some of the pitfalls of any ex ante licensing system.

Any occupational licensing scheme runs the risk of causing two kinds of damages, false positives and false negatives. False positives result when the licensing criteria fail to screen out incompetent performers. False negatives result when these criteria screen out potentially competent performers.

What is worse about occupational licensing is not so much the common and observable false positives that result from present teacher training, mistakes that are difficult and costly to correct because of early tenure and onerous dismissal procedures, but the unobservable false negatives that exclude effective ways of finding and producing effective teachers. Cognitively superior college graduates are automatically excluded from the profession and denied the opportunity to acquire the experience that research shows to be effective in producing good teachers.

This latter kind of damage becomes more likely as time passes, and new opportunities and technology open up. Yet licensing requirements are cast in stone and difficult to change, often because they acquire entrenched incumbent defenders. This kind of damage from licensing is more likely to appear whenever those who control the licensing qualifications use this control to protect themselves from alternative providers. Every licensing criterion will acquire a constituency. The damage from false negatives is also more likely to appear when productive talent is something likely to be developed by learning by doing than from ex ante formal training. Teaching is just this kind of profession, and therefore any occupational licensing requirement is highly likely to produce false negatives by preventing potentially competent teachers from entering the profession at the same time it does not, and cannot, assure the competence of those licensed.

The Fundamental Fallacy of Top-Down Approaches

Stotsky's paper describes the tradition of well-intentioned, top-down public education management. With a credential-oriented determination of teacher quality, this tradition turns the real source of information about teacher quality on its head. This approach is flatly inconsistent with the way labor quality is determined and assessed in a market economy where products succeed or fail on the basis of how well they satisfy consumers. In a larger sense, this approach is a poignant example of why government enterprises—from the U.S. Postal Service to the Union of Soviet Socialist Republics—always fail compared with private institutions operating in a market environment.

At the end of her paper, Stotsky fantasizes about reconceptualizing the institutional framework for teacher training in the United States. It is a fantasy because no real-world choice mechanism exists by which it could happen. But fantasies can be useful teaching metaphors.

One of my recurring fantasies is that I wake up some morning and find the whole superstructure of public education gone. Poof. No school districts, no state departments of education, no U.S. Department of Education. Furthermore, suppose the National Council for the Accreditation of Teacher

Education (NCATE), the National Board for Professional Teaching Standards, and the National Commission on Teaching and America's Future went poof, too. (This is a fantasy.) If this were to happen, aside from a blip in the unemployment rate as those idled found productive employment, few would notice. Down at the bottom of the present public school outhouse—at the schools—teaching and learning would largely go on as usual, for better or for worse.

While this might seem like a fantasy, in private education it is not. Private schools have almost no administration above the individual school level, and no state department of education periodically drops mandates on them. There, a much cheaper and arguably better education system proceeds without any top-down direction whatsoever. Yes, there is the exception of Catholic education, which does have some nominal school district-type structure and administration, but these schools operate with only a tiny fraction of the bureaucracy of the public schools.[19]

The point of this fantasy is that all of the information relevant to education production is way down at the bottom of the education establishment, whether public or private, and not up where Stotsky sits in a state department of education. Teachers are in the best position to evaluate students. First-line administrators, usually principals but sometimes department heads, are in the best position to evaluate teachers. And their judgments about teacher quality should be made by looking at the demand for education output, from their customers—the parents, who unfortunately are even further down in the present public education outhouse. Those who think they can assure and evaluate teacher quality by a supply-side certification and licensing process emanating like Papal Bulls from on high miss this obvious point. While the information is all down at the bottom, that does not mean that under present public school institutional arrangements there is an incentive to use it well. When you possess vast monopoly power, as the public schools do, it is easy to abrogate your evaluation responsibilities. Where else are the customers going to go?

You Cannot Do Merely One Thing

In the title of her paper, Stotsky asks, Can a state department of education increase teacher quality? In my view this is an irrelevant question. The relevant question is not what such a department can do in some hypothetical, perfect, unconstrained world controlled by well-intentioned, omnipotent, omniscient public servants. The relevant question is, What will such a department be able to do in a world filled with the constraints of real institutions and stakeholders—rent-seekers, to use the jargon of economists? The relevant task is how to get existing, political, public choice and market mechanisms to address the teacher quality issue. In the real world, this is a formidable task.

The public schools are the ultimate regulated industry. They have all the bad characteristics of public utility regulation plus a few more. This industry is even more insulated from efficiency-producing market forces than utilities. What goes on is primarily a political, redistributive process among stakeholders. Production enters the game only because it satisfies the needed host, the public treasury, the source of funds for redistribution.

In an environment isolated from market forces, it should be no surprise that since World War II real per pupil spending in public education has increased by a factor of six. Public school per pupil costs are now at least 50 percent greater than comparable private and foreign schools. And, as a result of massive consolidation and unionization, average student performance took a massive plunge in the 1960s and 1970s and has remained largely flat ever since.[20]

Under these conditions, the possibility of improving general teacher quality is slight. The real-world education establishment will take Stotsky's proposals; chew them up; retain what, if anything, is in the various stakeholders' self-interest; spit out the rest; and continue business as usual. This is what has happened to every other reform proposal that has hit public education in the last fifty years. And much of what Stotsky describes reveals just that. Some proposals do improve matters, marginally, in some dimensions, but to make it through the education public choice process they usually pay a high price, often making it not worthwhile.

Her proposal is naive because she implicitly assumes that there is some mechanism by which the existing political actors and the present institutional arrangements in the public education establishment will embrace her proposals. She never addresses the issue of how her proposals will work their way through the existing establishment, either in Massachusetts or elsewhere, although she frequently describes and laments the inertia there. The observed features of the present public education system, such as teacher quality, are the result of a complex political interaction among various stakeholders. The resulting quasi equilibrium of these political forces has embedded in it potent defenses that make the system largely immune to the exogenous changes she proposes.

The mere fact that the Massachusetts Education Reform Act of 1993–94 (MERA) had the widespread support of all the stakeholders in the Massachusetts education establishment, including the powerful teachers unions, meant that each thought there was something in it for them. Specifically, in the face of a perennial general glut of teachers, I would bet the teachers unions looked at MERA as a way of reducing the supply of qualified teachers, thereby making it easier to argue and bargain for increasing teachers' pay. (The 40 percent failure rate apparently does just that.) The teacher testing process applied only to initial teachers and therefore was of little threat to existing union members. And the second stage of licensing that applied to existing teachers amounted to a less threatening accumulation of development points, which Stotsky aptly characterizes as often "a combination of insult and entertainment for an intelligent teacher."

As an example of how stakeholders behave, it is worth ruminating about how Stotsky's proposals to inject more subject matter into teacher training will be greeted at the university level.

Most teacher education is in public universities, and the fiction is that these public universities are eleemosynary institutions interested only in upholding academic standards. While this is certainly part of public universities' motivation, these universities must survive in a largely political world. There, teacher education is a cash cow, which attracts many marginal students, and any attempt to minimize it will not be warmly received. With tuition, fees, and, most important, state aid determined on a flat per student basis, public universities have the incentive to maximize enrollment, especially in low-cost colleges, such as education schools. Warm bodies produce cold cash. Colleges of education are important to any public university because they are an alternative for many students who would, and do, flunk elsewhere or would not go to college at all. For this reason they are often the only colleges in public universities that produce more graduates than they initially enroll as freshmen, most of whom never darken a classroom. As such they are highly valued by university central administrations where recruitment and retention of any warm body are rewarded, and on average only some 50–60 percent of entering freshmen graduate in six years. Low admissions standards, fluff courses and majors, and grade inflation are everywhere symptoms of these incentives, not just in the colleges of education. Stotsky's description, and lament, of what has happened to core curricula in most public universities, and the appearance of academically light majors there, is right on the mark. What she does not appreciate is that what she describes was the inevitable result of the incentives faced by university administrators, incentives that are still there and which will determine the outcome of any proposals she makes. Universities in general will be relieved that Stotsky's proposals retain a role for their colleges of education, instead of calling for the abolition of teacher licensing altogether. But her suggestion for the elimination of some undergraduate teacher licensing will be fought tooth and nail because of its effect on profitable undergraduate enrollments. Likewise, they will be nervous about her suggestions for more rigorous courses in math and science, fields in which marginal operating costs are much higher. The education schools will likewise be wary of more academic rigor, unless they can capture these courses and enrollments within their own colleges.

Consider, in Stotsky's own words, the fate of the various ways the traditional teacher training, certification, and licensing process greets attempts to upgrade teachers.

TEACHER TESTING

—"Most have content that is at a high school level."

—"Based on [a reporter's] examination of sample test items, . . . Praxis I was not even at the high school level of difficulty."

—"Most state cut scores are set at or below the 25th percentile."

—"Easy teacher tests are an insult to an academically strong candidate for licensure. And if a teacher test can in theory be passed by a good high school student in grade eleven, the profession is also intellectually diminished in the public's eye."

PROFESSIONAL DEVELOPMENT AND IN-SERVICE TRAINING

—"Professional development not only is costly, but it also is a bottomless can of worms. . . . It is usually remedial in nature—attempting to fill in gaps in a teacher's professional skill and academic knowledge that should have been addressed in preservice training."

—"It is not clear to me, based on descriptions that have come across my desk of what constitutes professional development in the form of either in-service activities or graduate-level courses taken by teachers in schools of education, that professional development for teachers does much to increase the academic knowledge teachers need."

—"The more basic problem is trying, in one or two weeks, to teach teachers the subject matter knowledge they should have acquired in their four undergraduate years, especially when there may be a deeper interest in pedagogy than in content on the part of the presenters."

PRESERVICE SUBJECT MATTER TRAINING

Stotsky goes into great detail on how general academic education has been dumbed down outside the colleges of education by the elimination of core academic requirements and the introduction of shallow or irrelevant academic majors.

Thus an existing political system, with extensive inertia and strong constituencies in the status quo, can defeat even the best top-down intentions. All this is an example of one of Mancur Olson's laws: Every rule, or law, no matter how stupid, silly, or inefficient, will acquire a narrow, self-interested, constituency that will benefit and therefore will fight to keep it in place. The damage to those hurt will be individually small and dispersed. Hence the United States still has a helium reserve for dirigibles. As the *Economist* noted in Olson's obituary:

> As parochial lobbies form . . . each gains, then fiercely defends, some benefit for its members, usually with government help. Subsidies, trade protections and other economic distortions accumulate, and resources increasingly flow to a specialised class of lawyers, bureaucrats and lobbyists who know how to work the system. Redistributive struggles displace productive ones.[21]

Like Chinese culture, wave after wave of Mongol public education reformers, from James Coleman to James Conant to Terrel H. Bell and now Rod Paige, have been absorbed into the public education system without significant effect.

How the Salary Grid Thwarts Reform

One central feature of the public education system makes reforms, such as those suggested by Stotsky, virtually impossible.[22] That feature is the ubiquitous teachers salary grid. Other actors in the public education drama will support or oppose her suggestions, but the most effective negating influence, intended or not, will come through the salary grid in which many have a stake. Unless Stotsky can change that, all of her top-down, excellent, and informed, ceteris paribus, suggestions for improving teacher quality will be for naught. Good intentions are not enough.

The teachers salary grid is a method for determining teacher pay based solely on years of service and education credentials. The grid is usually codified in the local union's contract with the school board, and my conjecture is that such a grid is part of every teachers union contract in Massachusetts. The state wants to improve teacher performance and subject matter competence, but neither of these is rewarded by the typical salary grid. So, down at the level of the individual teacher, compensation incentives are in direct contradiction with what Massachusetts wants to accomplish. The salary grid will therefore largely nullify every performance and subject matter standard proposed.

The salary grid did not spring full-blown from Zeus's head. It came about because it served a purpose in the complex political interactions of the education establishment. It has strong constituencies.

Early in the second half of the twentieth century, a vast consolidation of schools and school districts increased their monopoly power in their product market and effectively weakened the public schools' accountability to parents and taxpayers. This consolidation at the same time produced homogeneity among schools and diversity within them, both of which negatively affected student performance.

Teacher pay and employment determination are good examples of how consolidation has produced homogeneity, inflexibility, and sclerosis in public education. Teachers unions bargain at the district, not the school, level. Teacher salaries generally are the product of a political, not a market, process. Those on both sides of the negotiations are far removed from the details and knowledge relevant to individual teachers, subject matter, and schools, all way down at the bottom of the education establishment. The broad currency of the negotiations necessarily forces disparate details into the same mold. The results are then spread homogeneously over all the schools and teachers below, regardless of differing education and market conditions. Physical education teachers get paid the same as physics teachers, and dolts the same as brilliant teachers. Pay in the inner-city schools is often the same as or less than pay in the suburbs, so good teachers quickly move from the former to the latter. The result is a rigid, ubiquitous, top-heavy, bloated salary schedule that locks in and rewards the worst teachers and drives out the best. In addition, a fulcrum for union power is largely responsible for public school per pupil costs that are about 50 percent higher than comparable private and foreign schools. All this is much different than in other managerial and professional situations—even universities—where salaries are usually decided at the department level where relevant market conditions for different individuals are taken into account.

As irrational as it is from a market standpoint, the inflexible salary grid is popular because it has something for all the actors in the political pay-determination process. For teachers, it gives many of them an automatic, stealth, annual salary increase no matter how they perform—no performance review, no salary negotiations, and no newspaper headlines showing increased teacher pay. The grid also gives them a convenient lever for raising all salaries by focusing on one element of the grid and then generalizing it to the whole grid. For union leaders and school administrators, the grid is easy to administer and makes their lives easier. It gives both something to hide behind as it relieves them of the burden of having to make, justify, and adjudicate, via grievance procedures, salary differentials based on such performance factors as merit and subject taught. And for school boards, which are generally composed of naive, well-intentioned advocates for public education, and whose members are playing with taxpayers' money, the grid allows them to give automatic, low-profile salary increases without specific negotiations that might get the public's and media's attention. Unlike in the marketplace, the taxpayers who are paying the bill and the parents whose children are being educated are out of the loop. This is in sharp contrast to what would happen in a market environment where parents had a choice between schools where cost and product quality determined which schools and teachers survived.

The grid is a powerful inoculation against outside changes, such as Stotsky proposes. In my view, the salary grid is responsible for much of the sclerosis in the whole lower public education system, a condition so bad that it makes piecemeal reform virtually impossible. Given the present players and features of the present education system, it is doubtful that the elimination of this grid is remotely possible.

Suppose you want to improve teaching, as measured by student performance. Because the evidence is that better teachers are smarter, and smarter people always have more opportunities outside the teaching profession, you are going to have to pay new teachers more. But the only way to do this within the confines of the salary grid is to bring these teachers in at the bottom of the grid and raise the whole grid. This, in turn, reduces the already low teacher attrition and turnover rates. When combined with ironclad, early, and ubiquitous teacher tenure, this locks in place many of the teachers you are trying to upgrade. Lower turnover rates also mean less demand for new hires, which in turn will eventually have a depressing effect on the supply of those training for teaching because of reduced prospects of gaining employment. And this depressing effect will hit most those smarter potential teachers who have better employment opportunities outside of teaching. This reduces the relative quality of potential new hires. Aside from the wasteful aspect of simply paying windfalls to existing teachers—those you wanted to upgrade—the induced reduced turnover rates also mean that it will take a long time before the new, higher-quality hires arrive in sufficient numbers to make a difference. The net result is that, even assuming the administrators want and find better-quality teachers as measured by improved student performance, a general upgrade of the faculty will take a long time and waste a considerable amount of money paying lower-quality faculty to hang on until retirement. This is not simply an academic exercise. The analysis of Ballou and Podgursky shows that this is what happened in public education in the 1980s—when teachers' real pay increased significantly.[23]

In the face of the salary grid, and the general lack of incentives to hire better teachers even when given the chance, the prospects for improving public school student performance by hiring better-quality teachers, as proposed in this paper, seem both wasteful and hopeless. Aside from a passing reference that, somehow, differential pay for math and science teachers would be useful, Stotsky says that "salary increases should be related to course taking for credit in the arts and sciences, supplemented by pedagogical work under the direction of the academic or professional department or school, and possibly tied to a master's degree in the appropriate arts and sciences discipline." This is simply more of the same: salary tied to credentialization, not student performance.

Stotsky describes an alternative teacher licensing program, called the Massachusetts Institutes for New Teachers (MINT), which is designed to bring superior noneducation majors into public school teaching. "A limited amount of pedagogical coursework, a short and inexpensive training period, and guaranteed placement in a teaching position are major conditions for increasing the number of academically strong teachers in schools." MINT is similar to a New Jersey alternative program and to the Teach for America (TFA) program, which is aimed at recruiting top graduates from selective colleges who do not major in education but are the kind of teachers that research has found to be the best at increasing student performance.[24]

But superior performance is exactly what the ubiquitous salary grid is designed not to recognize.

Consider the following from Jane Liebbrand, vice president for communications at NCATE, an organization that advocates further raising the barriers into public school teaching by increasing the pedagogy requirements for certification and licensing.

During the past decade, TFA has placed 7,000 recruits in classrooms—but only 2,000 to 3,000 of these are still in the classroom. Retention is lower than among regularly trained teachers, creating constant turnover in those schools that choose TFA recruits. . . .

However, TFA is not the answer to the teacher shortage in America. . . . The select group of top college graduates that includes TFA members will not stay for long in jobs that are at the bottom of the pay and perk scale. . . . The vast majority did not attend Ivy League schools to earn less in a year than it costs for nine months of their undergraduate education. . . .

If the salaries and working conditions of teachers were raised to a level commensurate with those of other college graduates, the profession would begin to attract more of the best and the brightest into teacher preparation programs.[25]

Liebbrand spins this evidence to argue for higher pay for everyone. But what her statement really shows is how the salary grid, by bringing smart teachers in "at the bottom of the pay and perk scale," systematically wrings superior teachers out of public school teaching by failing to reward academic subject matter and superior performance.

The response of the public school establishment and NCATE is not to do the obvious; that is, abolish the grid, or at least make it much more flexible. The strategy is to use the problem created by the grid—the failure of the public schools to retain the best teachers—as a lever to argue for higher salaries for all. This would result in rewarding lower-quality teachers and further entrenching them in public school teaching.

Given the lack of competition for students in the retail market, Liebbrand's and NCATE's suggestion that all salaries be raised will be fruitless, as it has been in the past. It will mostly transfer more money from taxpayers to entrenched, incumbent teachers. No incentive will be created to improve hiring in the monopolistic public school retail market where most parents and students are trapped. Contrast this with Hoxby's finding, which shows that private schools hire better teachers because their retail market requires them to compete for students by doing so.

Whether teacher turnover is good or bad depends on the filtering criteria. And an issue exists as to whether or not teaching should be a career occupation. However, with the salary grid, the best teachers are filtered out, and the worst filtered in. In a market-oriented world, where administrators have incentives to hire and keep the best teachers by adopting a reward system consistent with this objective, the best teachers are filtered in and the worst out. This scenario is impossible with the current rigid salary grid.

In the context of a monopolistic public school system at the retail level, the teachers salary grid has an insidious ability to wring competence out of the public schools. It will similarly dispose of Massachusetts's well-intentioned proposals.

Like most economists, I believe, based on considerable evidence, that product quality should be determined from the bottom up by consumers' preferences. As Adam Smith said, the goal of all production is consumption. The demand for consumption, in turn, creates a derived demand for those inputs, such as teachers, that best contribute to the product quality preferred in the market. Exactly how this good input quality comes about is immaterial as long as it produces the best final product. Credentialization is meaningless unless it produces the best product, and the evidence is that the existing teacher credentials, as well as those proposed in this paper, have little or no connection to student performance.

Notes

1. All documents produced by or for the Massachusetts Department of Education can be located on its website (www.doe.mass.edu).

2. The requirement of an arts and sciences major was intended to ensure that prospective teachers take some demanding upper-level courses in the arts and sciences, in addition to arts and sciences electives or distribution requirements. By means of this requirement, reformers also hoped to curb the number of education courses undergraduates would take to satisfy degree requirements. However, no evidence suggests that the requirement of an arts and sciences major has had this effect on undergraduates who enroll in a licensure program as part of their undergraduate program.

3. D. Monk, "Subject Area Preparation of Secondary Mathematics and Science Teachers and Student Achievement," *Economics of Education Review*, vol. 13, no. 2 (1994), pp. 125–45; R. Ehrenberg and D. Brewer, "Do School and Teacher Characteristics Matter?" *Economics of Education Review*, vol. 13, no. 1 (1994), pp. 78–99; R. Ehrenberg and D. Brewer, "Did Teachers' Verbal Ability and Race Matter in the 1960s? *Coleman* Revisited," *Economics of Education Review*, vol. 7, no. 3 (June 1995), pp. 1–21; R. Ferguson, "Paying for Public Education: New Evidence on How and Why Money Matters," *Harvard Journal on Legislation,* vol. 28, no. 465 (1991), pp. 465–98; R. Ferguson and H. Ladd, "How and Why Money Matters: An Analysis of Alabama Schools," in H. Ladd, ed., *Holding Schools Accountable: Performance-Based Reform in Education* (Brookings, 1996), pp. 265–98; D. Goldhaber and D. Brewer, "Why Don't Schools and Education Seem to Matter?" *Journal of Human Resources,* vol. 32, no. 3 (1997); K. Haycock, "Good Teaching Matters," *Thinking K–16,* vol. 3 (1998); and H. Wenglinsky, *How Teaching Matters: Bringing the Classroom Back into Discussions of Teacher Quality* (Princeton, N.J.: Educational Testing Service, Policy Information Center, October 2000).

4. National Research Council, Committee on Assessment and Teacher Quality, *Testing Teacher Candidates: The Role of Licensure Tests in Improving Teacher Quality* (Washington: National Academy Press, 2001).

5. Ruth Mitchell and Patte Barthe, "How Teacher Licensing Tests Fall Short," *Thinking K–16* (Spring 1999), pp. 3–19. See also Education Trust, *Not Good Enough: A Content Analysis of Teacher Licensing Exams* (Washington: Summer 1999).

6. See, for example, Melanie Scarborough, "More Than Money for Teachers," *Washington Post,* July 17, 2001, p. A17 (www.washingtonpost.com/ac2wp-dyn/A6399-2001jul16?language-printer [July 17, 2001]). This reporter's judgment, based on her examination of sample test items, was that Praxis I was not even at a high school level of difficulty.

7. Sandra Huang, Yun Yi, and Kati Haycock, *Interpret with Caution: The First State Title II Reports on the Quality of Teacher Preparation* (Washington: Education Trust, June 2002).

8. Massachusetts Department of Education, *An Analysis and Evaluation of the 12-to-62 Plan for Recruiting and Retaining Teachers in Massachusetts* (March 2003) (www.doe.mass.edu/news/news.asp?id=1497 [May 3, 2003]).

9. Suzanne M. Wilson, Robert E. Floden, and Joan Ferrini-Mundy, *Teacher Preparation Research: Current Knowledge, Gaps, and Recommendations* (University of Washington, Center for the Study of Teaching and Policy, February 2001), p. 35.

10. Dave Curtin, "State Refocuses Teachers' Studies: Elementary Education at CU Faces New Limits," *Denver Post,* May 3, 2001 (www.denverpost.com/Stories/0,1002,11%7E29378,00.html [May 3, 2001]). See also Julie Poppen, "Certain Majors Axed from Elementary Teaching Program: Colorado Links Rules to Its K–12 Standards for State CSAP Tests," *Rocky Mountain News,* May 3, 2001 (www.rockymountainnews.com/drmn/local/article/0,1299,DRMN_15_405534,00.html [May 3, 2001]).

11. Ruth Mitchell and Patte Barth, "How Teacher Licensing Tests Fall Short," *Thinking K–16* (Spring 1999), pp. 3–19.

12. Achieve Inc. conducted an evaluation of the state's K–12 mathematics standards and the tenth-grade Massachusetts Comprehensive Assessment System tests in English language arts and mathematics during the spring and summer of 2001. According to the report issued by Achieve in the fall of 2001, *Measuring Up: A Report on Education Standards and Assessments for Massachusetts,* the "state's English language arts standards were not analyzed because Achieve believes these are already among the best standards in the nation and uses them as 'exemplary standards' against which other states' standards are compared" (p. 5). Achieve's evaluation found that "overall, Massachusetts' standards and high school tests are of high quality and are aligned, providing a solid foundation on which to build state education policy" (p. 5).

13. This is not an original idea in Massachusetts. As I understand their structure, the preparation programs for secondary subjects at Northeastern University are under the auspices of the relevant academic departments in the arts and sciences.

14. Expecting teachers of secondary school subjects to have a master of arts or sciences in the subject they teach would not be too high an expectation. According to an employee of the Spanish government located at the Massachusetts Department of Education and in charge of a visiting teacher program for teachers in Spain who wish to teach in American schools for two or three years, most middle and high school teachers in Spain have the equivalent of a master's degree in their discipline before they take a one-year course in pedagogy that makes them eligible for teaching in the Spanish public schools. This requirement, he told me, is not uncommon in other European countries.

15. A good summary can be found in Kate Walsh, *Teacher Certification Reconsidered: Stumbling for Quality* (Baltimore, Md.: Abell Foundation, 2001) (www.abell.org/pubsitems/ed_cert_1101.pdf [September 10, 2003]). Additional summaries of the research findings can be found in Dale Ballou and Michael Podgursky, *Teacher Pay and Teacher Quality* (Kalamazoo, Mich.: W. E. Upjohn Institute for Employment Research, 1997); Eric A. Hanushek,

"The Economics of Schooling: Production and Efficiency in Public Schools," *Journal of Economic Literature*, vol. 24, no. 3 (September 1986), pp. 1141–77; Lewis Solomon's remarks in Harold Wenglinsky, *How Teaching Matters* (Princeton, N.J.: Educational Testing Service and Milken Family Trust, 2000); Jeff Archer, "Focusing In on Teachers." *Education Week,* vol. 21, no. 29 (April 3, 2002), pp. 36–39; and Kirk A. Johnson, *The Effects of Advanced Teacher Training in Education on Student Achievement,* CDA00–09 (Washington: Heritage Foundation, 2000).

16. National Center for Education Statistics, *The Condition of Education 2002.* NCES 2002–025 (Government Printing Office, 2002), p. 91.

17. Caroline M. Hoxby, "Would School Choice Change the Teaching Profession?" (Harvard University, January 2002) (post.economics.harvard.edu/faculty/hoxby/papers/schoolcho.pdf [September 10, 2003]).

18. Ballou and Podgursky, *Teacher Pay and Teacher Quality*, chap. 6.

19. Casey Banas, "Enrollment's Down, Central Office Workers Up," *Chicago Tribune,* September 29, 1987, and Archdiocese of Chicago, *Chicago Catholic Schools, 1987–88 Report* are both cited in Herbert J. Walberg and others, *We Can Rescue Our Children* (Chicago: Heartland Institute, 1988), p. 12; John Chubb, *Making Schools Better* (Manhattan Institute, Center for Educational Innovation, 1989), pp. 10–11; Dana Wochsler, "Parkinson's Law 101," *Forbes,* June 25, 1990, pp. 52–56; and Mike Bowler, "Catholic Schools: More for Less," *Baltimore Sun,* October 8, 1995, p. 2C.

20. John T. Wenders, "The Relative Efficiency of U.S. Public Schools," paper presented at the twenty-eighth annual conference of the Association of Private Enterprise Education, Las Vegas, Nevada, April 6-8, 2003 (www.uidaho.edu/~jwenders/Essays%20In%20Persuasion/New2/Public_School_Ineff_(APEE-MSW).pdf [September 10, 2003]).

21. "Mancur Lloyd Olson, Scourge of Special Interests, Died on February 19, Aged 66," *Economist*, March 7, 1998, p. 91 (www.economist.com/displaystory.cfm?story_id=115687 [September 10, 2003]).

22. This section summarizes John T. Wenders, "The Economic Effects of the Teachers' Unified Salary Schedule," *Government Union Review*, vol. 20, no. 3 (Summer 2002), pp. 11–26 (www.webpages.uidaho.edu/~jwenders/Essays%20In%20Persuasion/New2/The_GridUnion_Review.htm [September 10, 2003]).

23. Ballou and Podgursky, *Teacher Pay and Teacher Quality*.

24. After a finding that "most undergraduate education courses are not useful" and that they displace academic courses, New Jersey reduced the required education courses to three and "gave all candidates with degrees in academic subjects the option of taking the three courses during their initial year of employment." See Leo Klagholz, "No Alternative," *Education Next*, vol. 2, no. 3 (Summer 2002), pp. 6–7.

25. Jane Liebbrand, "Quick Fix," *Education Next*, vol. 2, no. 3 (Summer 2002), p. 6.

How Within-District
Spending Inequities Help
Some Schools to Fail

MARGUERITE ROZA *and* PAUL T. HILL

School district budgets are in the news. In the past year, super-intendents in Seattle, Rochester, and Baltimore have all left their jobs under pressure because of unexpected deficits, and as of summer 2003 Oakland's superintendent was in similar trouble because of a $50 million deficit for the year.

The bad economy is partly responsible. These and thousands of other districts have suffered simultaneous declines in local, state, and federal revenue. But in these cases, district actions made the worst of a tough situation. Instead of adjusting expenditures as revenues declined, these districts continued spending, with some plugging their budgets (that is, inventing revenues to make the books look balanced) in the hope that things would work out in the end.[1] Such plugging is neither new nor limited to Seattle, Rochester, Baltimore, and Oakland. As a former superintendent involved in an earlier financial meltdown elsewhere explained to one of us, "You can always find money if you are committed to doing something. You just spend it now and cover it next year when the budget goes up."

Another justification for budget plugging is uncertainty. Few districts know precisely how much money they have, and surprise surpluses are also possible. Even in these recent recessionary times, the Philadelphia public schools found $8 million it did not know it had—enough, according to the *Philadelphia Inquirer*, to employ 180 teachers.[2]

Funding for this research was provided in part by grants from the Annie E. Casey Foundation and Atlantic Philanthropies.

Tracking money is a huge challenge for school districts for many reasons: Their revenues come from many sources (state, local, federal, and philanthropic) at different times. Funders require separate record-keeping for each program, and their rules about cost accounting differ. Districts therefore maintain separate accounting systems for funds from different sources, and information is often kept on separate computer systems, bought and programmed at different times, so they cannot talk to one another.

Expenditure systems are also fragmented and isolated from one another. After five years of trying, Washington, D.C., schools still cannot say how many people they have on the payroll. Philadelphia's surplus became apparent only when the district linked up its separate systems for paying employees and funding benefits, to reveal that some employees were covered by insurance multiple times.

No wonder, then, as business analyst Larry Miller has commented, a superintendent can ask five different district budget managers the same question and get five different answers.[3]

With that as background, it should be no surprise that districts do not know what they spend on particular functions. San Diego superintendent Alan Bersin has tried for two years to find out what different central office services cost and he still cannot say for sure. And determining how much has been spent at any one school is even more difficult. Schools are not cost centers, so districts do not track the dollar value of resources (teachers, services, and equipment) that flow into them. District budgeting processes create big and hidden differences in school budgets. The fact that districts do not know how much is spent at one school versus another allows for serious inequities that often hurt the schools most in need of resources.

This paper focuses on one aspect of district spending ambiguity, namely, differences in per pupil spending masked by teacher salary cost averaging. It shows how an often-discussed phenomenon—that schools serving poor children get less qualified teachers than schools in the same district serving more advantaged children—is hard-wired into district policy.[4] It profiles the budget layering that is then created in attempts to remedy these unacceptable consequences. It also shows how more open funding and accounting practices can help re-sort the most capable teachers so that schools serving poor students can become better staffed.

Research Study

This paper is the result of five years' study of school district budgets. We did not rely, as most researchers do, on published district budgets but assembled real-dollar budgets for schools from the ground up. This involved identifying the schools to which personnel (administrators and teachers) were assigned and calculating the true dollar cost of employing those individuals, based on their actual salaries and benefit rates. This approach gets results that differ strongly from published district budgets, which assume that all staff members of a given type (for example, teachers, principals) cost the same. The data presented here reflect the actual salary costs of certificated teachers at schools in four districts that cooperated with our research: Baltimore City schools, Baltimore County schools, Cincinnati public schools, and Seattle public schools.

Baltimore City and Baltimore County data were from the 2001–02 school year. Additional figures on the demographics of each school were assembled from district websites, the Common Core of Data from the National Center for Education Statistics, Maryland State's website, and information reported by the *Baltimore Sun*. Cincinnati salary data were from the 2000–01 school year with additional demographic data assembled from district reports and the Common Core of Data. Seattle's salary and benefit data were from the 1999–2000 school year with additional student and school demographics assembled from the district's own school and student reports.

Analysis for each district was conducted separately. In each district, comparisons were made between the true costs of each school and its allotted expenditures assigned by the district. Patterns were then identified among groups of schools identified as low performing, high performing, low poverty, and high poverty. Other factors that distinguished schools and student populations (such as school size, school level, percent minorities, and concentration of Limited English Proficient students) were also considered.[5]

Focus on Teachers

Though we are now studying many aspects of district budgeting, we started with the distribution of teachers. Good teaching matters in determining the learning gains of students.[6] However, research shows that teacher qualifications are not spread evenly throughout schools in larger urban districts.[7]

Several forces work together to create this imbalance of teachers. Teaching jobs vary substantially from school to school. A high-performing school in a wealthy suburb offers a very different work environment than a chronically low-performing inner-city, high-poverty school. In the former, a teacher may be more likely to have students whose parents read to them at night, emphasize education, enforce homework completion, and come to parent nights. In the latter, a teacher may experience a student population with less parental involvement, greater health needs, increased student mobility, and behavioral problems as well as heavy scrutiny from the district central office and increased staff turnover. These kinds of schools create more difficult jobs for teachers.

Under union contracts, teachers with even one or two years' experience have some say over where they teach, and many teachers with any choices avoid the most challenging schools. In our research, we have seen over and over that schools in wealthier neighborhoods can receive more than a hundred applications for a teacher vacancy, while schools in poor neighborhoods might receive only two or three. For schools serving the poorest children, this means that they have little choice of whom they employ, and their teachers are disproportionately inexperienced.

Historically, experienced teachers have had no incentive to work in challenging schools. Teacher salaries reflect seniority and years of graduate study, not a teacher's productivity or the difficulty of the job done. Within a district's fixed salary scale, a teacher with five years of teaching experience and a teaching certificate makes no more money if he or she chooses a challenging position in a high-poverty school over a less demanding position in a high-performing school.

Therefore, not surprisingly, teachers with enough seniority to make choices seek the positions in the more advantaged schools. Struggling schools are left with no means to lure the most experienced teachers, particularly those with good reputations who can readily find jobs elsewhere in the district. Poor schools are often left with the low-paid rookies, many of whom will transfer to other schools once they have gained experience.

HOW DISTRICTS COUNT TEACHER SALARIES. School districts divide up their entire budgets into portions that can be assigned readily to schools (in the form of school allotments) and portions that remain under central office control.[8] Expenditures for teachers and principals are assigned to the schools where they work and typically make up more than 80 percent of each school's allotment.

Published school budgets do not, however, reflect the actual cost of salaries and benefits. Urban districts calculate school budgets using average teacher costs. Thus, in a district where teacher salaries range from $25,000 to $65,000 annually, all teachers are assumed to earn some average amount, say $45,000. This averaging would not distort school budgets if all schools had the same mix of teachers, some with high salaries and some with low.

However, not all schools have the same staffing patterns. Some have disproportionately higher paid staff and others the opposite. But school districts go with the averages. They do not charge the extra costs of all-senior staffs to the schools that employ them, and they do not reimburse schools with low-paid staffs for the difference between districtwide average teacher salaries and the actual salaries paid. This practice creates a transfer of funds from the less to the more advantaged schools. The only way districts can afford to pay more expensive teachers who congregate in certain schools is by drawing on the dollars saved on the low-cost teachers in the schools with the most junior staffs. As a result, when actual salaries vary from school to school, the real cost of each school is not reflected in the school allotment and is not even transparent to district budget personnel.

WHETHER TEACHER SALARIES MATTER. Some argue that teacher salary is not an accurate indicator of teacher quality, and therefore variations in teacher salary should not be a matter of concern. Certainly the characteristics that predict teacher effectiveness are hotly debated. Researchers generally agree that teacher effectiveness increases during the first five to seven years of teaching and then tends to level off.[9] Other characteristics of teachers linked to larger student gains are not captured at all in the salary scale. For instance, some studies have correlated teachers' high scores on college entrance exams and verbal assessments with larger student gains.[10] Others show a link between deep content area knowledge and student achievement.[11]

In sum, given the research, at best a weak link exists between salary and teacher effectiveness, based on the link between salary and those first five to seven years of teacher experience. But for any individual teacher, his or her effectiveness cannot be accurately judged by his or her salary.

However, when aggregating salaries to the school level, there is good reason to believe that schools with higher average salaries have more capable teachers. Some schools have many more applicants per opening than others and thus have the luxury of many choices when hiring. On average, given that each school can hire the best talent available, schools with more applicants get more talent. And our research shows that schools with the most applicants employ higher-salaried teachers.[12] Those with much smaller applicant pools have fewer hiring choices and end up with lower-salaried teachers. In sum, the average salary for all teachers at a given school reflects the school's ability to hire teachers and thus can be related to teacher quality.

Findings

Our analysis of personnel salary data from four districts quantifies the extent to which personnel costs are unevenly distributed among schools and profiles the kinds of students and schools that lose out most because of salary averaging.

Salaries Vary among Schools within Each District

At the outset of this study, one of us informally phoned more than twenty urban districts (including those in this study) to ask if any used real salaries in their budgets. In every instance, a district official (usually from the budgeting office) claimed that while his or her district did use average salaries in accounting for expenditures, he or she felt that real teacher salaries were evenly distributed in that district. Nearly every respondent went on to say that expenditures in that particular district would not change if average salaries were replaced with real salaries.

Analysis of teacher salaries in the Cincinnati, Seattle, Baltimore City, and Baltimore County districts shows that the opposite is true. In all four districts, some schools were staffed heavily with teachers at the high end of the pay scale and other schools were staffed predominantly with more junior, lower-paid teachers. As a result, from school to school in each district, significant differences were evident in actual salary costs.

The graphs in figure 1 show the distribution of salary costs for all schools in each district. One graph, for example, shows the true average teacher salary for each school in Baltimore City, where the districtwide average is $47,178. At one elementary school, the average teacher is paid $37,618, well below the district average. At another school, the teachers average over

Figure 1. Distribution of Teacher Salaries (School Averages) among Public Schools in Baltimore City, Baltimore County, Cincinnati, and Seattle

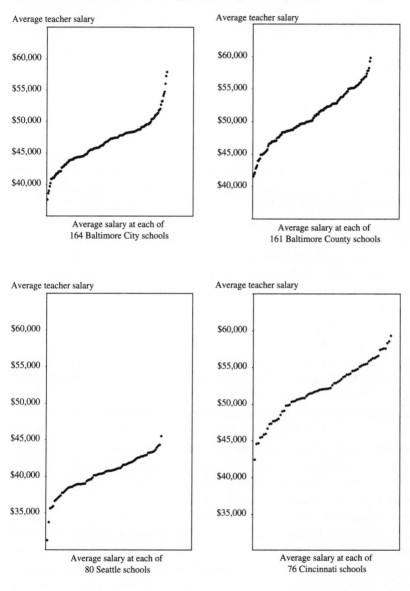

$57,000. Yet in these schools, as in all other Baltimore City schools, the district uses the districtwide average in its school budgets.

In Baltimore County, the districtwide average was $50,830. Again, some schools have average salaries that deviate substantially from the district average. Teachers at one elementary school are paid an average of only $41,520. Similar salary patterns existed in Seattle and Cincinnati.

Uneven Salaries Impact Spending Patterns

Under current budgeting practices, variations in teacher salaries create uneven spending patterns in ways that do not show up in official budget documents. For each school, we determined the difference between the real salary costs and the average salary figure used for accounting and budgeting purposes by the districts. In other words, for a school with a majority of highly paid teachers, this calculation determined how much the total of real teacher salaries paid exceeded the amount that would have been paid if the school were constrained to spend no more on teachers than the district average. For a school with lower-salaried teachers, the analysis shows how much less was spent at the school than if it were allowed to spend at the district average.

Table 1 summarizes the implications of teacher salary variations on school expenditures. The average Baltimore City school stands to gain or lose 5.9 percent of its school budget as a result of salary averaging, which impacts the average school's bottom line by over $100,000. In Baltimore County, the variations are even greater (most likely because the county demographics represent greater variations in student body ethnic makeup and family income). Here the average school's budget is impacted by 6.5 percent, which means that the average school gains or loses over $120,000. Seattle's school allotments were impacted by a lesser amount, $72,576. For the four districts, salary averaging introduced an error between 4.9 percent and 6.5 percent in the average school's allotment.

It is important to examine the extremes. In each district, there were some schools for which salary averaging meant gains or losses of much greater magnitude. In Baltimore City, one school spends more than half a million dollars over its average teacher salary allocation (22 percent of its budget), while another effectively loses $379,489. In one Cincinnati school with much lower than average salaries, the district's budget documents showed expenditures totaling $959,730 more than was actually spent at the school,

Table 1. The Impact of Salary Averaging on School Expenditures in Four Districts

	Baltimore City	Baltimore County	Cincinnati	Seattle
Average gain or loss				
In school budget as a result of salary averaging	± 101,786	± 120,612	± 106,974	± 72,576
Per pupil dollars	± 246	± 232	± 189	± 144
Average percent of impact on each school's budget	5.9	6.5	5.9	4.9
Maximum benefit				
As a percent of the school's budget	21.8	17.7	15.6	11.0
In real dollars	553,138	411,052	522,495	238,539
Per pupil dollars	2,322	1,917	497	322
Maximum loss				
As a percent of the school's budget	-20.8	-18.4	-19.2	-21.8
In real dollars	-379,489	-470,436	-959,730	-263,622
Per pupil dollars	-521	-544	-613	-637

based on real teacher salaries. That school had no way to recoup the million dollars that was transferred elsewhere to pay for other schools' higher teacher salaries.

Some Schools Win, Some Lose

In each district, specific types of schools routinely received fewer teacher salary dollars than the official district budget claimed. In each city, high-poverty, low-performing schools were staffed with teachers whose salaries were lower than average (see figure 2).[13] In Baltimore City, teachers in high-poverty schools earn an average of nearly $2,000 less than the average across the whole district (and some $4,000 less per year than those in the lowest-poverty schools). And teachers in the low-performing schools are paid even less. The salary differences in Baltimore County are even greater. The difference between the average salaries districtwide and those at high-poverty schools was over $2,400. And again, teachers at low-performing schools were paid even less. The same patterns existed in Seattle and Cincinnati with lower-paid teachers congregating in high-poverty and low-performing schools.

Figure 2. Average Teacher Salaries in Baltimore City, Baltimore County, Cincinnati, and Seattle

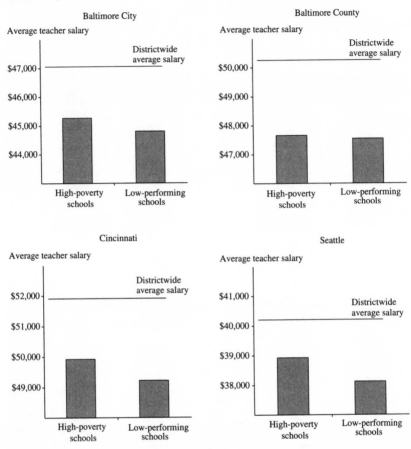

In Seattle, salary differences also showed up when comparing schools in different parts of the district (see figure 3). Teachers in elementary schools in the district's wealthier Northeast zone averaged salaries over $41,000, while teachers in the Southeast zone earned an average of $37,670. These kinds of deviations show that dollars are being diverted from schools in Seattle's Southeast zone to schools in the Northeast.

Figure 3. Seattle Salaries Vary across the District

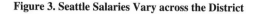

Average teacher salary

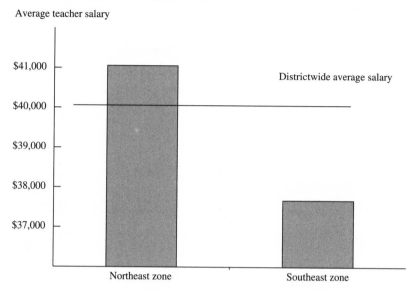

Budget Layering Works Counter to Salary-Averaging Policies

Education leaders have long recognized the patterns of chronic low performance in high-poverty schools. Yet leaders in large urban districts continue to ignore the very budgeting practices that systematically funnel
resources away from poor and low-performing schools. Instead of fixing the
budgeting problem, the policy response has been to layer on additional
funds to counteract the inequities.

In a prominent example, the federal government has stepped in to help
high-poverty schools. The now $11.7 billion Title I program for disadvan-
taged students was designed to provide high-poverty schools with extra
resources above and beyond what the district spends in state and local dollars. These and other programs insist that the extra federal dollars supplement funds from state and local sources. Federal dollars are supposed to be
added only after poverty schools get at least an equal share of state and
local funds.

Figure 4. Salary Averaging Diverts Resources Allotted to High-Poverty Schools to Low-Poverty Schools

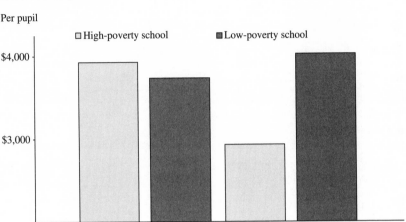

However, current Title I legislation allows districts to use average salary figures when comparing expenditures among schools.[14] As a result, high-poverty schools appear to receive the same basic education resources as do low-poverty schools, when, in fact, as the data demonstrate, they do not.

Programs such as the federal Title I grants serve to add a layer of funds for certain (mainly high-poverty) schools. While these funds do help equalize total spending, not all federal dollars make it to the children they were designed to help. When federal Title I dollars are used to purchase the services of lower-salaried teachers, some of those dollars are diverted to higher-salaried teachers at other schools. In effect, the salary averaging provision enables districts to divert some of the federal grant dollars away from the very children they are designed to reach.

The effect of salary averaging on both the base funding level and the Title I allotments is displayed in figure 4. Figure 4 shows the difference between the real and budgeted figures for a high-poverty and low-poverty school in Seattle. In this instance, the high-poverty school is supposed to get more per pupil resources (in part because of Title I and other compensatory funds) as indicated by a higher allotment. When actual expenditures are computed using real salaries, the opposite is true. The low-poverty school actually receives fewer real-dollar resources than the high-poverty one.

Teacher Incentives Can Miss the Mark

Another layering of funds can take the form of salary incentives. With increased pressure to improve teacher quality in some schools, thirty-four states now offer retention bonuses to veteran or accomplished teachers.[15] Yet, when these dollars are directed to teachers in higher-performing, wealthier schools (where veteran teachers are more likely to serve), the policy serves as another budgeting layer that misses the mark. Education resources never reach the schools most in need of teaching resources and the dollars essentially increase the already large disparities between high- and low-poverty schools.

Five states offer salary incentives or retention bonuses specifically for teachers in high-poverty, high-minority, or low-achieving schools.[16] While these dollars more appropriately target the students that need them, they, too, serve as a budget layer added on to correct the inequities created by the districts' budgeting policies.

An analysis of Maryland's salary incentives clarifies the impact of the state's $2 million investment in this program in Baltimore City alone. Maryland offers a $2,000 stipend for teachers holding an advanced professional certificate and working in a low-performing (deemed "reconstitution eligible") school. More than one thousand Baltimore City teachers received bonuses. Figure 5 shows the distribution of salaries before and after adding on the bonuses. The distribution of salaries with bonuses among schools looks very similar to the distribution without bonuses.

A comparison of average salaries in low-performing schools both with and without the bonuses shows that directing bonuses at low-performing schools did mitigate some of the disparity by raising salaries slightly (see figure 6). The salary difference between low-performing schools and the district average narrowed by 20 percent with the state-paid bonuses.

Yet, as the graph shows, the incentives were not nearly sufficient to fully remedy the disparities in salary. In one sense, they served as another funding layer in a budgeting system wrought with problems.

Implications

Opaque and unaccountable budgeting threatens more than the financial stability of school districts. It renders many urban districts unable to serve

Figure 5. Distribution of Teacher Salaries (School Averages) among Baltimore City Public Schools with and without Incentive Bonuses

Average teacher salary

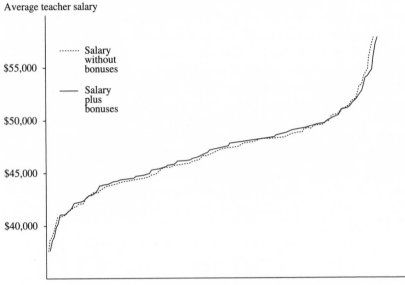

Average salary at each of 164 Baltimore City schools

the poor and minority students who depend most on district-provided education. Their schools have the greenest teachers, and they experience the highest rates of teacher turnover, ensuring that whatever teachers learn on the job will move elsewhere with them. Schools that consistently lose in the market for experienced teachers often have annual teacher turnover rates above 50 percent. Such schools are turbulent and difficult to lead. They are also impenetrable for parents, who cannot build stable and mutually confident working relationships with teachers and principals. In the absence of financial incentives to attract teachers, and without freedom from regulation to allow improvements in working conditions, the poorest schools will always get the teachers with the fewest options and lose those teachers as soon as they gain seniority.

Strong though the case for change may be, changing the budgeting and teacher allocation practices will not be easy. They are deeply embedded in school district operations, as a result of collective bargaining agreements and

Figure 6. Impact of Bonus on Teacher Salaries in Low-Performing Baltimore City Schools

Average teacher salary

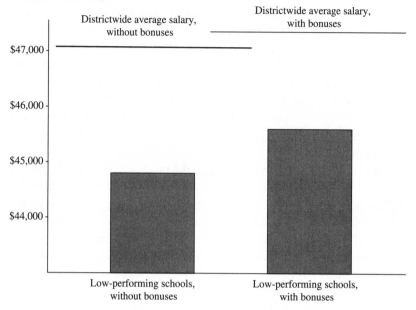

state laws and federal regulations written expressly to allow such practices. New laws such as No Child Left Behind put pressure on practices that systematically shortchange schools serving disadvantaged children. New competition from charter schools and voucher programs will also lead some districts to question whether they can continue resource allocation methods that virtually guarantee that their lowest-performing schools are also their most weakly staffed.

These practices are so deeply embedded that many districts will defend them even in the face of evidence that they hurt schools in the poorest neighborhoods.[17] In an earlier study several respondents from urban districts echoed one official who said, "I just don't want to force principals to choose teachers on the basis of cost. That would mean that only junior teachers could get access to some good jobs." Arguments that extra funds spent in one school must come from somewhere else, or that letting a few schools corner the market in experienced teachers leaves others with only green recruits, have little effect in district environments where linkages and trade-offs are invisible.

State and federal laws also enable spending and staffing inequities. At the state level, collective bargaining laws permit senior teachers to make personnel choices that distort the allocation of funds within school districts. State funding schemes for schools are also blind to within-district spending inequities, allocating dollars on a programmatic, instead of per pupil, basis. Washington State, for example, pays districts on a weighted per teacher basis, providing more money for senior teachers than for junior ones, but requires nothing in terms of how districts distribute teachers among schools. Thus students, who are the intended beneficiaries of state funds, can still be treated inequitably.

Even federal law has accommodated the practice of teacher-driven district funding policies. The Elementary and Secondary Education Act (ESEA) has long included provisions that require district funds to be distributed equitably before federal program funds are distributed (the "comparability" and "nonsupplanting" provisions). However, in the early 1980s, these provisions were amended to allow averaging of teacher salaries. Districts were henceforth allowed to maintain major inequities in school funding, as long as these were driven by teacher allocation. Thus (apparently in most cases unwittingly) members of Congress eviscerated the provisions generally thought to guarantee the promise that federal funds were going to be something extra for disadvantaged children.

Even in the current policy environment, district leaders can take steps toward making resource allocations transparent and improving poor schools' access to good teachers. So can many others, including state and local officials, and groups of parents who know that their children have been short-changed.

What Districts Can Do

Districts that want to reverse inequities in school funding and teacher quality will have battles to fight. Teachers unions will not easily give up hard-won privileges for senior teachers that allow them to work in the nicest schools. Parents in neighborhoods that have the most and best of everything will also resist transfers of dollars and people to other schools.

Districts can, however, take a first step by making resource allocation transparent. That requires, at a minimum, tracking real-dollar spending on a per pupil basis, using real teacher salaries, not averages. Though few districts have developed the capacity to do this, the necessary data management and computational methods are well known and not technically challenging.[18]

An annual report of real-dollar expenditures would not be politically neutral—families in schools with low real spending would surely demand an explanation. But it would also strengthen the district's position in contract negotiations and against demands for even more spending in already high-spending schools.

What States Can Do

State agencies overseeing collective bargaining could require that salary and benefit agreements hold students harmless against distortions in spending. State laws could also clarify the expectation that collective bargaining agreements not violate the principle of horizontal equity among the children in a school district.

The best remedy, however, is the most direct one. States could fund children, not teachers or other goods and services. If states made it clear that dollars were generated by children and should follow children to the schools in which they enroll, they could then demand that districts report real-dollar per pupil funding and be expected to explain any situations in which dollars intended for poor or disadvantaged students are spent instead on others.

What the Federal Government Can Do

The long-standing comparability and nonsupplanting principles of federal education programs provide great leverage over state and local spending practices. Though this leverage was undercut a few years after ESEA Title I was written, it could be established simply by requiring districts to calculate spending based on real-dollar cost, including actual, not average, teacher salaries.

This idea was proposed in the 2001 reauthorization cycle for ESEA by a bipartisan coalition including House Democrat George Miller of California, Senate Democrat Joseph I. Lieberman of Connecticut, House Republican John A. Boehner of Ohio, the Bush administration, and the Democratic Leadership Council. However, horse trading with union interests (and civil rights groups that apparently thought it best to keep this issue under wraps) led to its being quietly shelved. The same amendments could be offered, more publicly and with greater political force, in the next reauthorization cycle.

What Parent Groups Can Do

The patterns of spending clearly violate the principles of horizontal equity established by the Fourteenth Amendment. Courts have struck down school financing schemes in virtually every state, finding that variations in state funding for districts constitute denials of equal protection of the laws. As our studies have found, variations of per pupil funding within districts are often greater than the within-state variations that have been found unconstitutional.

Parent groups have standing to complain if districts systematically short-change particular students, especially if those children are poor or are from ethnic minority groups. Within-district spending data of the kind we have illustrated, whether provided by government agencies or privately funded researchers, can support a strong claim of discrimination, which could move courts to order sweeping remedies.

Parent groups might prefer to avoid litigation, using the threat of it to enter serious negotiations with their school districts. School districts will almost surely prefer negotiated remedies to unpredictable and possibly draconian court orders.

Conclusion

Equalizing per pupil spending within districts is necessary, but probably not sufficient. Districts that equalized real-dollar spending among their schools would still find that schools serving poor students had trouble attracting their share of the best-trained and most productive teachers. While these schools might benefit from having extra funds to spend on smaller class sizes or better technology, they might still be short of teachers who can set the tone for a school and help younger teachers learn their trade. Districts should monitor the distribution of teacher talent within the district and add financial incentives to influence the distribution if need be. These policy changes, coupled with efforts to improve school climate and leadership, would go far toward addressing the core problems facing poor schools.

Comment by Susan Sclafani

Marguerite Roza and Paul T. Hill raise an issue that should be on the front page of newspapers across the country. Those of us serving with Rod Paige, when he was superintendent of schools of the Houston Independent School District, had considered the issue of the implications of teacher salary cost averaging. (I was his chief of staff.) We started the planning for actual teacher salary costs, not just weighting for pupil funding, which we had already done. We recognized that great differences existed in actual teacher salaries when we looked carefully at high school budgets. We compared teacher salaries at a premier high school that produced fifty-five to sixty National Merit scholars every year and an inner-city high school that was 98 percent Hispanic and had a much lower rate of college-bound students. The difference in actual teacher salaries was $1 million a year.

Having seen that, and having seen the differential outcomes of those two institutions, we recognized that the lower-funded school could have done many things with that money to attract the kinds of teachers who would be able to help those students improve their skills and knowledge and prepare for college.

We made the argument to the board of education. The board accepted it. We agreed to phase in the move to actual teacher salary costs over time, because clearly such movement is an issue of staff management. Principals had to start using the natural attrition within their schools, if they had a highly experienced, high-salaried faculty, to begin evening out the disparity with other schools. We expected that when one of the high-priced teachers left, the school would bring in a new, less-experienced person.

What better way to mentor new people coming into the profession, we argued, than to put them in schools with high expectations for students, with high achievement levels, and with highly skilled teachers? Doing this, we suggested, would offer opportunities at the school level to bring in new ideas, to get people to think differently about what they were doing—so as to change the status quo thinking that kept a high-powered high school from being a high-powered high school for all kids.

And the board agreed. The plan stipulated 10 percent the first year, 30 percent the second year, and so on, for a total of seven years to full use of actual salaries. Each year, the school would be responsible for paying a progressively larger percent of the actual cost of the salaries of the teachers at that school. Over time, the school would pay the full salary costs of the teachers. This would have happened. We knew the retirement rates in the district would enable the plan to work, without having to have principals cast off great teachers because suddenly they were too expensive.

We heard all of the arguments on the other side—that principals were going to have to hire people by what they cost, that principals would no longer be able to consider quality. We countered that principals could find high-quality young people to bring into the profession and into their schools.

Paige left Houston in 2001 to become U.S. secretary of education. In the spring of 2003, the board of education voted to table the proposal and to come back to it at a later time. It was not that the board did not want to follow through on it, but the time was not right. And I can tell you what happened in between.

Principals of the high-powered schools said: "How are we going to explain this to our parents? How are we going to tell them that we can't hire the best any more?" They talked to their school board members and said: "We're going to see white flight. We're going to see a decline in the achievement levels of our schools. And all of this will be for somebody's theory about the good this will do for other schools." The principals continued: "There's no proof; there's no one else doing this"—and this part is true because we had surveyed other districts. "There is no other school district in the United States" that attempted to implement such a proposal. The school administrators in Edmonton, Canada, whose system we looked to as our model in terms of changing to a weighted per pupil, decentralized move, passed on the idea—"Not even they did this"—because they knew it was not the right thing to do.

The board accepted the opponents' reasoning, member by member, with a sufficient number of them agreeing to table the proposal. The minority board members were not of sufficient numbers or interest, apparently, to overcome that view. As a result, these two high schools still have a million-dollar difference in teacher salaries; high-powered schools still have no responsibility for mentoring or entry of new people into the profession; and new teachers are still allowed to go into the less-wealthy schools, those serving children of great poverty, to learn how to be teachers and, after they are able to prove themselves over time—ten years, fifteen years—then they are considered to fill vacancies at a high-powered school. This situation is destructive for kids as well as for faculty morale. Everybody knows that when a person becomes a good teacher, he can teach in one of those good schools on the west side of Houston, and until then, he is forced to stay put. And, if he does not prove himself to the satisfaction of the principals doing the interviewing at those schools, then he is stuck in the school that he is in. The situation is thus bad for morale because now that teacher feels that he should have or could have gone elsewhere and somebody has told him that he is not good enough.

Not only did a turnover of new teachers occur among schools in the district, but the high-poverty schools also became the training grounds for suburban schools. The scenario that played out was: Go to Houston, learn how to teach, and then be hired in the suburbs.

The changes described by Roza and Hill will not happen without a sustained political campaign to make them happen. This is going to be the absolutely critical piece. Even having the information available to parents is not enough without the rallying call, without the parents' getting so exercised that they go back to the school board to say, "This should not have been postponed, this needs to happen as soon as possible, and we need to have those additional resources."

Houston went further than many school districts in terms of having gone to a weighted per pupil funding system. The state provided the dollars on a weighted per pupil basis, yet we did as every other district around us did—we allocated those dollars on an average basis. Every twenty-two kids get a teacher; five hundred kids earn a school an assistant principal. A school needs, if I remember correctly, four hundred kids before it gets a librarian. It gets a piece of a nurse—courtesy of a subsidization from Medicaid—for free; the rest of the position is paid for out of the local allocation, depending upon the number of kids in the school.

That formula, in itself, is inherently unfair. The premise behind Title I was "supplement, not supplant." The district was supposed to fund an adequate program for all children and then add Title I funds on top. Equal funding of all schools was not adequately funding some schools, most especially those with many high-poverty children.

The results of this change have been dramatic. Winners and losers emerged who were held harmless at the beginning of the process. But the schools with more affluent children understand that they can have a Parent-Teacher Association fund-raiser and collect $100,000 if things got lost in their budget.

One of the middle schools, over three years, lost $500,000 because of the weighted per pupil model. Other schools gained. A large elementary school gained $1.5 million, which was dedicated to some of the things that it wanted to do. Many schools were providing intense remediation for children who needed it. While the district had a salary schedule, schools—now that they had their own funding—were able to supplement that schedule if it helped them to attract and retain teachers.

Most districts have never looked carefully at or do not have accurate enough accounting systems to be able to know the disparate funding that is occurring at their schools. In many states, the dollars come to them on the basis of how many students they have in their districts. Given that that is just the way things have always been done, states do not look beyond it.

Now that schools will be held accountable for the performance of children in poverty, the principals and faculty in those schools are going to start calling for the additional funding that their students deserve to help meet the new expectations.

It is difficult to raise performance levels of children in poverty enough to make up for some of the resources they have not had—to give them the kind of enrichment that other children have had. If I believed it were not possible, I would not be in education. The later the intervention, the more intensive that intervention is going to have to be. Maybe high schools cannot make it all happen within a four-year time period, particularly doing what they currently do.

But, what the No Child Left Behind Act says is that, starting with four-year-olds, after twelve years of schooling they should be at high levels of achievement—providing that the way in which schools are funded and what is done with those dollars are rethought.

Perhaps the current financial crisis of the states may turn out to be the best thing that will have happened to education, especially if it forces school districts and schools to look more carefully at how they are spending their dollars.

Unfortunately, in good times, new dollars come in and new programs get piled on top of what is already there. Title I is notorious for this. Unless people start considering zero-based budgeting, determining whether their spending is effective in improving student achievement, needed changes will not be made.

But an opportunity exists now to start looking at the cost-benefit analysis on these programs, to ask which ones are providing the kind of bang for the buck that is needed to raise student achievement. It is a great time to get rid of sacred cows that people like but that do not improve student achievement—and look more clearly and more carefully at how the dollars in hand are being spent.

I think that what would be revealed is that the problem is not so much that the money is not sufficient, but that it is not being used well.

President George W. Bush is committed to putting more dollars into Title I and into the Individuals with Disabilities Education Act because he knows that the public will not believe that more money is not necessary and that much more intensive work could be done in certain areas with additional dollars. But school districts must take a good, hard look at how they are spending their dollars and see whether those funds are benefiting the children most in need, as well as maintaining comprehensive programs for all children.

School spending should not go to teaching reading and math to only some; it should deliver a full, rich core curriculum to all children. But this will not happen unless the schools are ready to do the intensive work needed to serve the children with the greatest obstacles to learning.

Comment by Sheree Speakman

Marguerite Roza and Paul T. Hill explain a core financial issue that prevents school leaders from using money effectively to improve the learning quality and outcomes of the classroom experience. The authors demonstrate the inequitable financial result that comes from using the age-old central office dictate of budgeting schools using average salaries while staffing them according to contractual bargaining norms. This practice gives the false appearance of equity, while it drives higher-priced resources—that is, better-paid teachers—to higher-performance schools. Across America, schools are exhorted to perform at the averages of their budgetary inputs, while their spending realities support relatively few options. After all, quality is not purchased by the average dollar but by the most effective application of dollars to the issue at hand.

Roza and Hill do not conclude so directly, but the practical remedy for this problem is to budget and account for school dollars using a weighted per pupil allocation factor, as discussed in the comment by Susan Sclafani. The implementation dictates of this weighted allocation method, over time, forces lower-salaried teachers into the good schools and improves the number of teachers or the salary range in the low-performing schools. Therefore the projected outcome of weighted per pupil funding, that is, moving toward equity in teacher salary assignment across all schools within a district, puts school and district leaders into the unenviable position of explaining to parents with real power within the institutional school system why their children are not skimming the best (read: the most expensive) of everything. Most district leaders would not be able to deliver this message successfully and thus most do not. The only other possible message, therefore, is a battle cry for more money, a cry that is in everyday use.

The No Child Left Behind Act (NCLB) is going to be the stimulus that forces the stakeholders of K–12 education to change the school finance debate from its decades-old emphasis on the mathematical calculation of equity to the real discussion of how spending will be used to trigger a demonstrable improvement in student learning and outcome measures. Because NCLB has, for the first time in the nation's history, changed the desired framework for K–12 education from compulsory attendance to mandatory learning, money that flows into the system should result in targeted, step increases in results. In a financial framework, this is known as the cost-benefit results of resource investments in schools and programs.

To move to cost-benefit as the framework for resource allocation and budgeting, a better understanding is needed of how much money or how many resources are at stake. Roza and Hill's analysis centers on teacher salaries in Cincinnati, Seattle, Baltimore City, and Baltimore County. Their figures 1–4 and table 1 show that the notion of using "salary averaging introduced an error between 4.9 percent and 6.5 percent in the average school's allotment." The dollars that equate to these percentages in the study created a loss to low-resource schools ranging between $400,000 and $1 million. These dollars are significant enough in value to provide an investment in resources, teachers, and supplemental education materials that might improve the learning environment. Thus Roza and Hill make the case in a compelling fashion that to think about the significance of these dollars is to invite solutions; that is, transition strategies for school districts that put teacher budgeting practices into place for resource reallocation methods and strategies, from which true equity and improved outcomes can result.

The answers to true equity and improved outcomes will be found in many places. Focusing on finance and budgeting as levers to a successful solution set, specific answers will be found in better policy, improved accounting and disclosure practices, and the use of pre- and posttesting of instructional programs. This testing must be focused specifically on producing a better understanding of student growth and the associated costs of the specific instructional programs producing the growth in learning. Further, this growth and program cost information must be gathered to calculate and study cost-benefit ratios and norms. Understanding what works, for which students and at what cost, year after year is the next most important discussion framework. Said and framed differently, this is the underlying knowledge set anticipated by the full implementation of NCLB.

The leading issue preventing effective financial analysis, budgeting, and resource allocation from becoming the norm is the relatively mediocre quality of accounting practices and systems in public education. Numerous reasons can be cited for this, but a simple collective statement will suffice: Excellent accounting and analysis have not been rewarded, and the opposite practice has not been sanctioned. Further, at the level of student performance and classroom teaching, the system moves financially to reward poor performance and poor children. But district leaders have not used these additional dollars to remediate poor performance and teaching, but instead to siphon monies away from said schools to those where performance gains are more common. The remedy is to start an incentives system where failure is rewarded with higher-quality and tangible resources. To do this, the actors in the system, that is, the principals, administrators, and teachers, must come to understand the underlying fundamentals of school finance and school budgeting as a first imperative. Little demand exists for this information, however, as the level of discretionary spending in school resources is pitifully low, often below 5 percent of dollars budgeted to a school. When someone in the system has little discretion, he spends precious little time on the issue.

So where is the largest opportunity for improvement in financial practices, leading to significant additional dollars to invest in low-resource schools? The opportunity lies in the understanding of programs, and program accounting, within school finance. In all cases, the accounting in American education now centers on a presentation of functional spending: salaries, computers, building costs, and textbooks, to name a few. In a small number of places, an emphasis is put on presenting functional costs at the school site, by location. But in a very few instances, does anyone other than the school business official have a good understanding and presentation of program accounting? Examples of program accounting include the expenditure of Title I dollars in the district and in schools, the use of dollars to buy reading and language arts programs, and the use of Safe and Drug Free Schools money. In every American school, dozens of programs are being implemented for which there is little accounting and fewer cost-benefit metrics available for review. Thus starting to identify, understand, and report the cost-benefit of literacy or Title I would be an enormous asset to the emergence of resource reallocation strategies. Dollars should be taken away from things that do not work, or work in few instances, and redeployed to people and programs that do work for improved student learning.

Roza and Hill offer solutions that point, rightly so, at policy changes that would correct inequitable distributions of teacher talent and put more tangible resources into classrooms. But the real payoff is to start to peel back the onion of decades of investment in school-based and categorical programs, including human resource programs, that do not produce the results stated in the promises made at the outset. After evaluating the endless array of school-based programs, resource investments could be narrowed to those that do work for a significant proportion of students. Where programs have proved ineffective, they are nonetheless a reason for employment and thus attractive to every person so employed. Now, with a mandate for learning, not attendance, resource reallocation practices must be undertaken that bring equity and stated performance targets into positive alignment for all students.

Notes

1. See, for example, Moss Adams LLP, *Seattle Public Schools Financial Operations and Information Systems Audit* (April 16, 2003) (www.seattleschools.org/area/finance/budget_page.html [October 22, 2003]).

2. Susan Snyder, "Schools Uncover Extra Millions," *Philadelphia Inquirer*, April 18, 2003.

3. Larry Miller, "Bad Economy Could Be Good for Struggling School Districts," *Seattle Times*, May 1, 2003.

4. See, for example, Kati Haycock, "Honor in the Boxcar, Equalizing Teacher Quality," *Thinking K-16* (Spring 2000), pp. 1–28.

5. Only analysis of those factors that presented significant trends is included here.

6. Eric A. Hanushek, J. F. Kain, and S. G. Rivkin, *Teachers, Schools, and Academic Achievement,* Working Paper 6691 (Cambridge, Mass.: National Bureau of Economic Research, August 1998); and Willliam L. Sanders and J. C. Rivers, *Cumulative and Residual Effects of Teachers on Future Academic Achievement* (University of Tennessee, Value-Added Research and Assessment Center, 1996).

7. See Haycock, "Honor in the Boxcar"; and Education Week, *Quality Counts 2003: "If I Can't Learn from You": Ensuring a Highly Qualified Teacher for Every Classroom* (Bethesda, Md.: January 9, 2003).

8. Districts allocate only some 40–60 percent of their general fund into the school budgets. The remaining portion remains centrally controlled and typically includes transportation, food services, staff development, central administration, and so on.

9. M. Fetler, "High School Staff Characteristics and Mathematics Test Results," *Education Policy Analysis Archives*, vol. 7, no. 9 (1999); R. J. Murnane and B. R. Phillips, "Learning by Doing, Vintage, and Selection: Three Pieces of the Puzzle Relating Teaching Experience and Teaching Performance," *Economics of Education Review*, vol. 1, no. 4 (1981), pp. 453–65.

10. R. P. Strauss and E. A. Sawyer, "Some New Evidence on Teacher and Student Competencies," *Economics of Education Review*, vol. 5, no. 1 (1986), pp. 41–48.

11. D. H. Monk, "Subject Matter Preparation of Secondary Mathematics and Science Teachers and Student Achievement," *Economics of Education Review*, vol. 13, no. 2 (1994), pp. 125–45.

12. Marguerite Roza, "Policy Inadvertently Robs Poor Schools to Benefit the Rich," *Seattle Post Intelligencer*, September 24, 2000, p. F1.

13. Low-poverty schools were designated relative to the student demographics in each district studied. In Baltimore County, a high-poverty school was defined as one in which more than 60 percent of the students received free or reduced-price lunch; in Baltimore City, more than 80 percent; in Seattle, more than 75 percent; and in Cincinnati, more than 90 percent. In each district, student performance data were considered from the same year as the salary data and natural cutoffs were drawn to define lowest-performing schools. In Baltimore City and Baltimore County, we examined results from the Maryland School Performance Assessment Program. In Cincinnati, low-performing schools were those that the district labeled as "under review." In Seattle, we considered Iowa Tests of Basic Skills scores in reading and math.

14. Roza, "Policy Inadvertently Robs Poor Schools to Benefit the Rich."

15. Education Week, *Quality Counts 2003*.

16. Education Week, *Quality Counts 2003*.

17. Seattle schools defended the practice of salary cost averaging even after an independent auditor claimed that it corrupted district budget oversight and had led, in recent years, to annual budget errors as great as $10 million. See Seattle Public Schools, *Management Response, Financial Operations, and Information Systems Audit* (Seattle Public Schools' Executive Management Team, May 1, 2003), p. 13.

18. The Annenberg Task Force for School Communities That Work has published a tool kit for how to analyze district data in this manner. It is available at www.schoolcommunities.org.

The Elephant
in the Living Room

KATI HAYCOCK

Each year, when national and state assessments once again reveal alarming gaps between poor and rich, minority and white, most educators are quick to blame the problem on the children themselves or their families. The common refrains are that "the children are poor," "their parents don't care," "they come to school without an adequate breakfast," and "they live in difficult neighborhoods." As a profession, education has gotten so good at pointing the finger of blame that, instead of hearing these claims as the excuses they are, much of the public has come to accept them as fact. Poor kids, in other words, perform at lower levels because they are poor. Likewise, black or Latino kids perform at lower levels because they are black or Latino (and because they are also disproportionately poor).

No wonder folks around the country are shaking their heads in disbelief at the new federal mandate to close gaps between groups over time. They simply do not believe it is possible. And education leaders are shockingly outspoken on the subject. "They may as well have decreed that pigs can fly," said the president of one state's teachers association.[1] "I have difficulty with the standards because they're so unattainable for so many of our students. . . . We just don't have the same kids they have on Long Island or Orchard Park," said a New York district superintendent.[2]

Research undoubtedly fed this view. Large-scale studies such as the Coleman Report issued in 1966 told the nation that schools contributed little to students' academic achievement as compared with families.[3]

More recent research, however, has turned these understandings upside down. Some things that schools do matter greatly in whether students learn, or whether they do not. And the thing that matters most is good teaching.

229

A 2002 analysis of Texas data put it this way: "The issue of whether or not there is significant variation in education quality has lingered, quite inappropriately, since the original Coleman Report. This analysis identifies large differences in the quality of education in a way that rules out the possibility that they are driven by family factors." According to the authors, "Teacher quality is a very important determinant of achievement. Systematic teacher differences drive substantial differences in student achievement."[4]

Although this Texas study focused on between-school differences, differences in teacher quality do not begin or end at the schoolhouse door. Even within schools, big differences in teacher quality exist from one classroom to another.[5] Moreover, in most states there are significant differences in teacher quality between school districts of different types.[6]

The core problem is that all these differences—between districts, between schools, and between classrooms—have the same primary victims: low-income children and children of color. Almost regardless of where they live, such children are taught disproportionately by the least qualified teachers.

The pattern nationally is the same no matter which indicator of teacher quality one uses—certification status, years of experience, performance on licensure exams, academic major in field, quality of undergraduate institution, or even effectiveness in producing student learning. Typically, and this is the case across the country, students who are most dependent upon their teachers for academic learning are systematically assigned to teachers with the weakest knowledge and skills.

Despite overwhelming evidence of the negative effects of the current maldistribution of teacher talent on the most vulnerable children, getting much traction on the problem has been difficult. While policymakers are often interested, the levers they have at their disposal are awfully blunt—and in many cases their close ties with teachers unions make them fearful to act. While a majority of states provide bonuses of some sort—from signing bonuses for new teachers to bonuses for board-certified veterans—only a handful have targeted those bonuses toward service in high-needs schools.[7] But education leaders are no braver. In my experience, even the most reform-minded leaders generally prefer simply to work around the problem.

The View from America's Classrooms

The problem is far more than an academic exercise for me and my colleagues at the Education Trust. We have spent considerable time in classrooms, working with teachers and principals who are trying to improve the achievement of the children that they serve. Over the past ten years, we have spent thousands of hours in schools all across the country.

In that work, we sometimes see absolutely wonderful teaching—in all kinds of schools. Even the lowest-performing schools always seem to have some terrific teachers. But we often see teaching that is dreadful, especially in the highest-poverty schools. Many of these teachers are clearly struggling with the content themselves, even as they are supposed to be teaching it to their children.

The data demonstrate the issues clearly.

Certification

In most states where reliable data are available, poor and minority children are more likely than other children to be taught by uncertified teachers.[8] In California, for example, approximately 23 percent of the teachers in high-poverty schools are uncertified, compared with only 13 percent of the teachers in low-poverty schools.[9] Children in schools where poverty rates are above 75 percent are about three times as likely to be taught by uncertified teachers as children who attend schools with poverty rates below 25 percent. The proportion in high-minority schools is five times as great as in predominantly white schools.[10] African American students in high-poverty schools are particularly vulnerable: Nearly 30 percent have an uncertified teacher.[11]

In New York, the patterns are similar. Statewide, approximately 17 percent of teachers in high-poverty schools are uncertified, compared with only 4 percent of the teachers in low-poverty schools.[12]

A similar ratio holds for nonwhite versus white children.[13]

And Maryland is no different: Uncertified teachers comprise 19 percent of the work force in high poverty schools and 11 percent in low-poverty schools. New Mexico posts 20 percent to 8 percent, respectively.[14]

Even within districts with high overall poverty rates, big differences also are found among schools. In Baltimore City, for example, the larger the percentage of low-income or minority children in a school, the larger the percentage of uncertified teachers. In the elementary grades, in particular, the schools with the lowest poverty (between 30 and 60 percent enrolled in the free or reduced-price lunch program) had between 10 percent and 22 percent of their teachers uncertified. The range in highest-poverty schools (free or reduced-price lunch enrollment above 97 percent) was about twice that.[15]

In the nation as a whole, approximately one in five core academic courses in secondary schools is taught by a teacher who is not certified to teach that course. In low-poverty schools, the number of teachers without appropriate certification is 16.9 percent, while in high-poverty schools it is 29.6 percent. The same differences hold when looking at schools by race: 18.9 percent of core academic teachers in low-minority secondary schools lack appropriate certification, compared with 27.9 percent in high-minority schools.[16]

Experience

Nationally, children who attend high-poverty or high-minority schools are also about twice as likely as other children to serve as training fodder for inexperienced teachers (approximately 20 percent versus 11 percent).[17] But even these worrisome figures understate the differences in some states.

In New York State, for example, differences are greater than in the nation as a whole. In 10 percent of the state's schools, the average number of teachers with no previous teaching experience is zero. At the other end of the spectrum are an equal number of schools with a full 17.6 percent of their teachers without experience. The biggest problem of all is in New York City, where the median school has 10 percent inexperienced teachers. In the 10 percent of schools with the most inexperienced teachers, the rates were two and one-half times higher.

Even in the same metropolitan region, the differences across communities can be stunning. For example, in 1999, about 23 percent of those teaching in New York City had fewer than three years of experience. Next door, in the Lower Hudson and Long Island districts, only about 14 percent of the teachers had less than three years of experience.[18]

As with gaps in certification—which are smaller in Texas than in most other large states—there is a small but significant gap in the proportions of Texas teachers in different types of schools who have one year or less of experience. In general, low-income students are about 20 percent more likely to be taught by such a teacher during their elementary years.[19]

Though similar demographically, the state of California is home to a much bigger gap in teacher experience. At least in part because of its massive experiment in class-size reduction, students who attend high-poverty, high-minority schools in the state are now about twice as likely as students attending predominantly white schools to be taught by a teacher with less than two years of experience.[20]

Subject Matter Expertise

Data on subject matter expertise run in the same direction. In every subject, students in high-poverty secondary schools are more likely than other students to be taught by teachers who do not have a major or minor in the subject they are teaching.

About one in four secondary courses in the core academic subjects is taught by a teacher with neither a major nor a minor in the field. In low-poverty schools, the ratio drops below one in five courses. In high-poverty schools, it climbs to more than one in three. Students in high-poverty classrooms are more than 77 percent more likely than students in low-poverty classrooms to be assigned to an out-of-field teacher.

The same differences hold for percent minority: 21 percent of the courses in low-minority schools are taught by teachers without a major or minor, compared with 29 percent of the courses in high-minority schools—and a whopping 34.6 percent in schools that are more than 90 percent black.[21]

The data for middle schools are even more troubling. In high-poverty middle schools, about 53 percent of core academic courses are taught by teachers who do not have even a minor in the subject they are teaching, compared with 38 percent in low-poverty schools. In high-minority schools, about 49 percent of the teachers in core academic subjects do not have even a minor in the subject, compared with 40 percent in low-minority schools.[22]

While out-of-field teaching is high even in subjects not characterized by any shortage in teacher supply, the problem is worst in mathematics. Nationwide, over 35 percent of secondary math classes are taught by someone without so much as a minor in mathematics or a math-related field. That figure climbs to 49 percent in high-poverty schools and 44 percent in high-minority schools. In the middle grades, about 70 percent of the students in high-poverty and high-minority schools learn mathematics from a teacher who lacks at least a minor in math or a related field.[23]

Exam Performance

Not surprisingly, minority and low-income students are more likely to be taught by teachers who performed poorly on exams themselves, including both college admissions tests and teacher licensure tests.[24]

In Illinois, for example, children in high-poverty schools are five times as likely to be taught by teachers who failed the licensure exam at least once. And they are twenty-three times as likely to be taught by teachers who failed at least five exams.[25]

Similarly, 21 percent of the teachers of nonwhite students in New York State have failed either the general knowledge or liberal arts and science certification exams, compared with 7 percent of those who teach white students. Further, more than 35 percent of the teachers in New York State's low-performing schools failed the licensure exam at least once, compared with 9 percent of the teachers in high-performing schools.

This same pattern is evident wherever analyses of teacher exam performance and student characteristics have been conducted. Researchers in Texas found that, as the percent minority of a school's student population went up, average performance on the state's teacher test declined.[26] Similarly, research in Alabama using teacher performance on the American College Test (ACT) showed that African American students there had disproportionate numbers of teachers with relatively low performance.[27]

These same patterns are also clear nationally. Of 1992 college graduates who went into teaching, 34 percent of those who ended up in high-poverty schools (free or reduced-price lunch participation over 50 percent) performed in the bottom quartile on the SAT, while only 8 percent were from the top quartile. By contrast, only 8.6 percent of those who ended up in low-poverty schools (less than 4 percent free or reduced-price lunch enrollment) were from the bottom SAT quartile, compared with 23 percent from the top quartile.[28]

Quality of Teacher's Undergraduate Institution

Given differences in performance on the admissions tests would-be teachers take to get into college and the licensure tests they take at the end, it is not surprising that available research also suggests that there are significant differences in the quality of undergraduate institutions attended by teachers in different kinds of schools. In the quartile of schools serving the fewest poor students, about 21 percent of the teachers attended minimally difficult or noncompetitive colleges. By contrast, in the quartile of schools serving the highest concentrations of low-income students, almost twice as many teachers, 39 percent, attended such institutions.[29]

Data for New York State suggest bigger differences by race than by poverty. The range in the proportions of teachers from nonselective institutions is large—an average of zero such teachers in the top decile of schools compared with an average of 30 percent in the bottom decile. However, while the proportions for poor and nonpoor students (25 percent and 23.9 percent, respectively) differ by only a little, nonwhite New York students are more than twice as likely as white students to be taught by teachers from these kinds of colleges.[30]

Teacher Differences and Classroom Effectiveness

None of these indicators is by itself damning—much less an adequate proxy for a teacher's ability to take learners to needed levels of achievement.

At least in theory, teachers could certainly be weak on one of these measures, but strong on the others. Unfortunately, though, available research suggests just the opposite. "Even though it is feasible that some schools have less skilled teachers as measured in one dimension, while others have less skilled teachers as measured by another dimension, this is generally not the case," say Hamilton Lankford, Susanna Loeb, and James Wyckoff of their multivariate New York analysis.[31]

It is also at least theoretically possible that teachers who are weak on all these measures are nevertheless outstanding teachers. Again, however, considerable research suggests that these factors are related—albeit imperfectly—to effectiveness in producing student learning gains.

Academic Skills and Knowledge

The strongest finding in the research is that a teacher's academic skills matter. Robert P. Strauss and William B. Vogt in their 2002 article "Should Teachers Know, or Know How to Teach?" conclude that "hiring teachers with greater general knowledge has a very large effect on our composite measure of student achievement."[32] Two earlier studies had similar results. Ronald F. Ferguson and Helen F. Ladd's modeling for several metropolitan Alabama districts shows that an increase of one standard deviation in the test scores of teachers who teach black children would produce a decline of about two-thirds in the black-white test score gap in that state.[33] Strauss's study of student achievement in North Carolina suggests that a 1 percent relative increase in teacher scores on the National Teacher's Examination Core Knowledge Test would bring about a 5 percent relative decline in the percentage of students who fail standardized competency exams.[34]

While each study on this topic uses a slightly different measure, the findings are so robust and so consistent that there is broad agreement among both education researchers and the economists who study these issues that teachers' academic skills have considerable impact on student achievement. Both Grover J. Whitehurst's 2002 review of the literature and Linda Darling-Hammond and Peter Young's scathing critique of that review agree that teachers' academic skills have an important effect on student learning.[35]

Mastery of Content

Considerable research shows how important teachers' content knowledge is to their effectiveness with students, especially at the middle and senior high school levels. The data are especially clear in mathematics and science, where teachers with majors in the fields they teach routinely get higher student performance than teachers who majored in something else.[36]

While the data are less clear in English and social studies, other evidence suggests that content knowledge is no less important in these subjects. For example, a recent study of social studies teachers in Hawaii found that students perform best in the domains where teachers indicate the most expertise.[37]

Pedagogical Skill

All of this seems to beg the question: What about pedagogical knowledge and skills? Clearly, content knowledge is not sufficient for effective teaching. One has only to spend a few semesters in higher education to understand that the deep knowledge of subject matter inherent in the Ph.D. does not necessarily translate into effective teaching.

That said, large-scale research is less clear about the value of measurable proxies such as coursework in pedagogy, advanced education degrees, and scores on exams about pedagogy. Some researchers find a relationship (see, for example, Darling-Hammond and Young's overview); others do not.[38]

There is, however, incontrovertible evidence that experience helps. Most available research suggests that teachers are considerably more effective after completing two years on the job. "Those in the first two years of experience do substantially worse," say Stephen G. Rivkin, Eric A. Hanushek, and John F. Kain.[39] But some researchers, including William L. Sanders and June C. Rivers, find growth in effectiveness over as many as the first ten or twelve years of experience.

Regardless of the duration of teacher growth, however, assigning inexperienced teachers disproportionately to high-poverty and high-minority schools clearly deflates student achievement in those schools.

Data from Value-Added Research

Proxies of any sort are unnecessary to understand how much teachers vary in their ability to influence student achievement—or that those variations frequently disadvantage poor and minority students.

The variation in how teachers affect children is probably clearest in the research of the statisticians and economists who are studying the relationship between individual teachers and the growth students achieve in their classrooms during the school year. This approach is called value-added measurement.

William L. Sanders, who founded the Value-Added Research and Assessment Center at the University of Tennessee, Knoxville, has studied teacher and student data extensively. On average, he finds that low-achieving students gain about 14 points each year on the Tennessee test when taught by the least effective teachers, but they gain more than 53 points when taught by the most effective teachers. Teachers make a difference for middle- and high-achieving students as well. On average, high-achieving Tennessee students gain only about 2 points a year when taught by low-effectiveness teachers, but more than 25 points a year when guided by top teachers.[40]

Rivkin, Hanushek, and Kain find similar patterns in their analysis of Texas data. "A one standard deviation increase in teacher quality for a grade raises average student achievement by at least .11 standard deviations of the total test score distribution," an effect considerably larger than reductions in class size.[41] In summarizing available research, Hanushek estimates "the difference in annual achievement growth between having a good and having a bad teacher can be more than one grade level equivalent in test performance."[42]

These teacher effects appear to be cumulative. For example, Tennessee students who had three highly effective teachers in a row scored more than 50 percentile points above their counterparts who had three ineffective teachers in a row—even when they started at the same score.[43] An analysis focusing on Dallas found essentially the same pattern—a difference after three years of about 50 percentile points.[44]

As in the case of annual impact, the cumulative impact of teacher quality is biggest for initially low-achieving students. A recent study in Tennessee suggested that students who failed the state's fourth-grade examination were six times more likely to pass the graduation examination if they had a sequence of highly effective teachers than if they had a sequence of low-effectiveness teachers.[45]

In sum, students whose initial achievement levels are comparable have "vastly different academic outcomes as a result of the sequence of teachers to which they are assigned."[46] Differences of this magnitude—50 percentile points difference in just three years—are stunning. For an individual child, they can represent the difference between a "remedial" label and placement in the accelerated or even gifted track. And the difference between entry into a selective college and a lifetime working at McDonald's.

Sadly, however, data on teacher effectiveness in promoting student learning show much the same maldistribution as data on the teacher characteristics. In Tennessee, for example, African American students are about twice as likely as white students to be assigned to that state's least effective teachers, and they are considerably less likely than white students to be assigned to the most effective teachers.[47] Data in Dallas, one of the few districts outside of Tennessee to have collected such data over multiple years, show much the same pattern.[48]

What Contributes to Uneven Distribution of Teacher Talent?

The patterns are so consistent across measures that they almost look like somebody's diabolical design. But the truth is that the roots of these inequities are varied.

DIFFERENCES IN THE INITIAL PREFERENCES OF NEW TEACHERS AND THE SCHOOLS THAT HIRE THEM. Researchers such as Carnegie Mellon University's Robert Strauss have long called attention to the preferences of many school districts for hiring their own graduates—and the preferences of many teacher education graduates to return to their home school districts (or districts much like them). Similarly, in his work in New York State, Lankford finds distance very important: Nearly 60 percent of new teachers take jobs within fifteen miles of where they went to school; 85 percent take jobs within forty miles.

All things being equal, there is probably nothing wrong with some amount of this behavior. But all things are not equal. In urban areas and other high-poverty communities, this pattern alone often means that graduates of poor-quality schools, who presumably went to college with relatively weak skills, often bring those weaknesses right back to the districts they came from.[49]

DIFFERENCES IN THE CAPACITY AND CONSTRAINTS OF DIFFERENT SCHOOL DISTRICTS. District practices and policies also play a role in shaping the quality of the teacher force in high- and low-poverty schools. One obvious problem in many urban districts is too-late hiring.

This problem has long been blamed on incompetent human resource departments in urban school districts. But data compiled by the New Teacher Project suggest that, even when the initial applicant pool is both large and strong in the spring—more than adequate for a highly selective hiring process—both the size and the caliber of applicants dwindle by the normal end-of-summer hiring.[50]

Bureaucratic snafus in human resource departments and poor customer service contribute to these delays. But there are other structural problems as well. Many districts, for example, have such extensive contractual requirements for internal transfer notification that they cannot even begin to make final new candidate offers until mid- to late summer.[51] By this time, the strongest applicants have often accepted jobs in districts that complete their hiring in the spring. Other factors that contribute to late hiring include the effects of school reconstitutions (which normally mean that the entire teaching population of certain schools must be placed elsewhere) and incentives for retiring teachers to delay notifying their schools until school begins.

DIFFERENCES THAT OCCUR AS A RESULT OF TEACHER TRANSFER OR LEAVING. Teaching is a more stable profession than most people believe. No other profession for which one prepares during an undergraduate program has a higher four-year retention rate for those who enter following their preparation period.[52] Nonetheless, significant numbers of teachers move to another school or district or leave the profession entirely.

This phenomenon affects minority and poor children more than other children. Disproportionately large numbers of teachers—especially white teachers—leave high-minority and high-poverty schools, generally transferring to lower-minority and lower-poverty schools.

In Georgia, for example, teachers who transfer to another school or district typically reduce the number of minority and poor children in their classrooms by about half. Multivariate analyses suggest that student race is the driving factor.[53] Researchers in Texas find a similar pattern, with transferring teachers "systematically favoring higher achieving, non-minority, non-low-income students." However, in Texas, "the most dramatic differences in school transfer rates are related to achievement."[54] In New York, teachers transferring from New York City to another district also end up teaching fewer poor and minority children. On average, they reduce the number of poor children in their classrooms by about two-thirds, the proportion of Limited English Proficient children by about one-half, and the proportion of nonwhite children by a little more than half.[55] California's experiment with quick, across-the board class-size reduction exacerbated a preexisting pattern of this sort in that state.[56]

Virtually all of the researchers who study these patterns find that the teachers who leave high-poverty and high-minority schools to go elsewhere are, on average, stronger than those who stay.

Another pattern bears mentioning here. In the so-called dance of the lemons, underperforming teachers get shoved out of relatively high-performing schools into lower-performing schools. While principals (and some teachers, too) talk about this problem all the time, it is not easy to determine how extensive it is. However, reformers at the Boston Plan for Excellence found the problem of so-called must-place teachers to be interfering so significantly with their school-based improvement efforts that they led a citywide fight to alter the contract.[57]

DIFFERENCES WITHIN SCHOOLS THAT RESULT FROM ASSIGNING VETERAN TEACHERS TO THE EASIER CHILDREN. In many schools, considerable arguing—and maneuvering—surrounds the question of who has to teach whom. Generally, especially in districts where teachers themselves control assignment, the more senior teachers reward themselves with the kids who arguably least need their help. In his analysis of North Carolina data, for example, Charles Clotfelter found that two-thirds of the black-white differences in exposure to novice teachers occurred within, not between, school buildings.[58]

But, especially in secondary schools, principals often seem to have similar preferences—choosing, for example, to assign the one math major to teach the upper-level mathematics courses (typically enrolling fewer poor and minority students), leaving the physical education majors to teach the lower-level courses (typically enrolling more poor and minority students).[59]

Other Factors Affecting Teacher Mobility

In an effort to understand the interaction of these preferences and practices with matters such as salary and regional labor market differences, Lankford and his colleagues sought to sort out some of these forces. In New York State, they found only a small part of the variation in teacher quality between labor markets (about 25 percent), with another 40 percent between districts in the same labor market and 35 percent between schools in the same district. Their analysis of teacher movement—both outside of the New York City region, where few salary differences are evident between districts, and inside the New York City region, where surprisingly little transferring takes place from New York City to the districts with higher salaries—suggests that the desire to teach easier students is typically a stronger motivator than the desire to improve salary.[60]

This same pattern is clear in research conducted in Georgia and Texas, which shows that student race, socioeconomic class, and achievement are strong motivators, especially for white female teachers. "Our analysis," said the Georgia researchers, "identifies the race of the student body as the main factor associated with teacher mobility between schools and teacher mobility out of the Georgia teaching force."[61] Student characteristics are such strong motivators in the leaving behavior of white teachers that researchers in Texas concluded that "a school with 10% more black students would require about 10% higher salaries in order to neutralize the increased probability of leaving. . . . Schools serving a high proportion of students who are academically very disadvantaged and either black or Hispanic may have to pay an additional 20, 30 or even 50% more in salary than those schools serving a predominantly white or Asian, academically well-prepared student body."[62]

Given that the teaching profession is overwhelmingly white and female, these are troubling conclusions.

Changing Current Patterns

Over the past several years, as they have come to understand the ways in which the teacher quality gap contributes to the achievement gap separating poor and minority students from others of their age, some district and state leaders have begun to experiment with strategies to remedy the problem.

The rest will have to begin soon, however, because the federal No Child Left Behind Act requires them to take aggressive steps to close both the achievement gap and the teacher quality gap.

So far, most of the hand-wringing about this law has focused on its dramatically different approach to accountability. But unbeknownst to most educators (at least in part because the U.S. Department of Education has not done much to publicize anything but the accountability and choice provisions), the act also demands big changes in the distribution of teachers. The act's teacher-related provisions include

—A requirement that all teachers be "highly qualified" by 2005–06;

—A requirement that states collect and regularly report information on the number and distribution of less than fully qualified teachers;

—A requirement that principals, superintendents, and chief state school officers develop plans to assure that poor and minority students do not continue to be taught by more than their share of uncertified, inexperienced, or out-of-field teachers;

—A "parent right to know" requirement that schools notify parents in writing when their children are taught by unqualified teachers; and

—Language that allows—and in some cases requires—states and districts to use the teacher quality allocations in both Title I and Title II to provide increased salaries and professional development for teachers in high-poverty schools.

In other words, both districts and states need to make progress on this issue.

To date, most efforts to reduce the inequities in teacher talent fall into seven categories.

1. *Salary Increases or Bonuses.* Some districts and states are providing salary increases or bonuses to fully qualified new teachers and especially talented veterans willing to teach in high-poverty or low-performing schools. These range in size from a few thousand dollars (for example, in Charlotte, North Carolina) to as much as $10,000 per year (in Palm Beach County, Florida, and Chattanooga, Tennessee).

2. *Special Financial Awards for Teachers with Board Certification or Other Advanced Certificates.* While many states and districts are providing bonuses for all teachers with national board certification, some are making those considerably more generous if the person is willing to teach in a hard-to-staff school and mentor other teachers. California is one such example, providing $10,000 to all new board-certified teachers and an additional

$20,000 if the person will teach for four years in schools in the bottom half of the state's distribution. Florida pays an additional $1,000 a year to board-certified teachers who teach in its F-rated schools; New York provides $10,000 for up to three years to board-certified teachers in its low-performing schools.

3. *Rich and Intensive Professional Development.* Because a substantial part of the distribution problem would be solved if high-poverty schools just improved—and held onto—the teachers they have, some districts are betting on high-quality professional development. They are shifting professional development resources out of the mind-numbing drive-by workshops into more intensive, content-rich professional development. They also are putting high-poverty schools at the head of the line, instead of always leaving them at the end.

4. *Subsidized Master's Degree Programs.* The Charlotte school district is one of several offering subsidized master's programs for teachers who teach in hard-to-staff schools. According to district officials, this is the most powerful of the incentives they offer, which also include a salary bonus and a reduced student load.

5. *Housing Assistance.* Help with securing and paying for housing is an increasingly popular incentive at the district and state levels. Mississippi provides such support to teachers willing to teach in its remote rural schools. Chattanooga provides such support, in addition to a salary bonus, for teachers with proven value-added effectiveness who are willing to teach in its high-poverty schools.

6. *Increased Student Support Services and Reduced Student Loads for Teachers.* At least some anecdotal evidence suggests that many teachers leave high-poverty schools not because they do not like the kids, but because they feel overwhelmed by the magnitude of their problems and do not feel they can be effective. By reducing class size or student load and providing other professionals in the school to help with nonacademic problems, some district and school leaders are trying to help teachers feel more effective and encourage them to stay instead of fleeing to easier conditions. The core idea here is to more nearly equalize the load on teachers in different kinds of schools.

7. *Strong and Supportive School Leaders.* Teachers unions have for years argued that schools in even the poorest communities are rarely hard to staff when they have experienced, consistent, and consensual school leaders at the helm. While that charge is often a facile way to avoid confronting the

need to depart from a single salary structure, more than a kernel of truth can be found here. As leaders in Charlotte report, their package of incentives has been marvelously effective in recruiting and retaining high-quality teachers in schools where they also have an effective principal. But the same incentives have been completely ineffective where the district has failed to put such a principal in place.

Combining Strategies

While researchers have not yet evaluated these relatively new efforts, there are clearly troubling signs that they are not having much effect. In Palm Beach County, for example, of the more than ninety highly effective teachers offered $10,000 stipends to transfer to high-needs schools, fewer than ten took up the offer. In view of the research on the complex interaction of factors such as teacher motivation, school preferences, district capacity, contractual requirements, and the like, this outcome is hardly surprising because most of these existing efforts simply layer some combination of small incentives on a system that is still heavily rigged.

In my judgment, existing approaches are likely to fail for at least five reasons. (1) They do not even look at the fundamentally important question of who enters the teaching pipeline. (2) They do not address the serious systemic problems—including contractual obligations—that impede the hiring of high-quality teachers in high-poverty districts. (3) They do not address the problems associated with removing teachers who will not or cannot teach children to state standards. (4) The dollars are typically far too small or insufficiently targeted or both to approach the incentivizing levels suggested in the research. (5) Most rely not on reasonably sound measures of who is a good teacher (for example, value-added), but on relatively weak proxies.

Elements of a More Powerful Alternative

Nobody knows for sure what it will take to secure a distribution of teacher talent that more closely matches the nation's goals. Why? Because nobody has tried. Until recently, anyway, it never seemed worth the inevitable agony that such an effort would entail because the payoff for children was not clear.

But it is clear now. How could anybody who cares about the future of the United States not be inspired to action by Eric A. Hanushek's thumbnail overview of the findings in Texas? He reports, "By our estimates from Texas schools, having an above average teacher for five years running can completely close the average gap between low-income students and others."[63]

What are some of the elements of an approach that might avoid the problems associated with the distribution of teacher talent? As Al Shanker, who served as head of the American Federation of Teachers, suggested, "Unless you start with a very heavy emphasis on accountability, not end with it, you'll never get a system with all the other pieces falling into place." Shanker was clear about the need for consequences, both for students and for teachers. "As long as there are no consequences if kids or adults don't perform, as long as the discussion is not about education and student outcomes, then we're playing a game as to who has the power." Shanker went on to ask, "What would happen if we had a system where we had pay for performance in the sense of a series of graded sets of rewards, depending upon student outcome?" He answers his own question this way:

> What would happen in a faculty meeting if this incentive system were about to happen in the schools? It's very important to imagine what teachers would say to each other. What do you think they would do about colleagues who were likely to drag down the school? What would they say if they didn't have enough math teachers in the school? Do you see how things like protecting teachers who aren't performing and a single salary structure become less desirable?
>
> I'm worried about how to prevent the pay-for-performance issue from becoming dysfunctional, dog-eat-dog. But I'm sure that we can develop such a system and that it would be pretty good. Its flaws would be very small compared to what we have now or compared to what you would have without such a system.[64]

ELEMENT ONE: VALUE-ADDED ASSESSMENT. The first step is value-added assessment. Because No Child Left Behind has removed the last technical obstacle to widespread use of value-added techniques (the absence of grade-by-grade assessment), efforts should move ahead quickly to install such a system to look at the contributions to student learning of both individual teachers and whole schools, at least in the core academic subjects. Tests do not measure everything that teachers do. But if policymakers make them so terribly important to students, they should make these assessments important to teachers as well. Student learning scores perhaps should not be the only criterion for evaluation, but surely a central one.

ELEMENT TWO: A DIFFERENTIATED SALARY STRUCTURE. Teachers who produce unusually big gains in student learning should be rewarded generously. Moreover, to maximize salary, teachers should have to maximize both gains and the level of challenge. In return for the higher salary, teachers should agree to go where they are needed.

ELEMENT THREE: NO CONTRACTUAL BURDENS ON DISTRICTS. Unnecessary contractual constraints—such as lengthy transfer periods or must-hire provisions—on the hiring processes in urban school districts should be removed. Principals and teachers together should choose from all qualified applicants.

ELEMENT FOUR: HELP, FOLLOWED BY DECISIVE ACTION WHEN RESULTS LAG. New teachers need help from veterans with proven track records in getting students to high levels of achievement. However, when value-added analyses suggest that some teachers still simply cannot produce results, they should be terminated. Teachers who produce unusually low growth in student achievement during their first two years on the job should not advance to tenure.

ELEMENT FIVE: MORE RESEARCH, THEN NEW ACCOUNTABILITY SYSTEMS FOR HIGHER EDUCATION. State and local efforts should support aggressive efforts to combine data on teacher choice and mobility patterns with data from value-added analyses to understand more about the teachers who choose more difficult environments (traditional versus alternate route, for example) and which teachers are successful (their attributes, institutions attended, and classroom practices). States and localities should then use that knowledge to reframe the accountability systems for colleges and universities that prepare teachers. Instead of simple licensure exam pass rates, for example, colleges should be judged by the ability of their teachers to produce student achievement gains. Such systems should also discourage the continued overproduction of certain kinds of teachers (elementary education or small town–bound, for example) and provide strong incentives to increase production of the kinds of teachers that schools need.

Over time, I am convinced that a system with some of these features would begin to turn around attitudes, practice, and, most important, student achievement. But none of the pieces gets at the core issue that I worry about in the dark of night: the deeply perverse status hierarchy within the profession, where one's status flows not from how good a teacher one is, but from how elite the kids are that one teaches. This is a problem not just in K–12, but also in higher education, where even the most wretched professor in a research university has more status then the best professor in a community college. This status hierarchy must be turned around—to restore honor to those who are doing the most crucial work.

Restoring Honor

When I think about the role that honor plays in all this, my mind inevitably goes back to a conversation I had more than ten years ago with Sabra Besley, at the time a principal in a high-poverty high school in Southern California. That day we talked about how Besley had landed in that particular school. She told me that her decision was made, forever, during her student teaching experience.

Besley spent her first week teaching her heart out in a wealthy school in Palm Springs. But by Friday, the only response she had prompted from her distracted students was a single question: "Mrs. Besley," asked one girl, "where'd ya get those shoes?"

The following week, a dispirited Besley was assigned to a school on the far side of the county. Her first task was to accompany the teacher on a series of evening home visits. The first visit was to a Hispanic family that lived in an abandoned boxcar. This family, said Besley, had very little. But when the two teachers arrived, the family stopped everything, split their meager dinner into two extra portions, honoring their guests with what little they had. "My decision was made that night," Besley said.

What she realized is what is too often forgotten. There is honor in the boxcar.

Educational researchers and policymakers know that the boxcars are now often dangerous tenements, where mothers sometimes have to shield their kids from ricocheting bullets. And they know, too, that simply saying there is honor in such work, without backing it up with concrete supports, is wrong.

Researchers and policymakers must provide those supports. But they must also change the dialogue. There is honor in the boxcar, in the barrio, in the poorest classroom, and in the blackest classroom. And together, leaders in the profession and in the community must not allow anyone to forget that simple fact.

Comment by Hamilton Lankford

Kati Haycock has written an informative paper that will prove useful to researchers, policy analysts, and practitioners. The paper surveys a wide range of research to document how low-income and minority students are most often taught by the least qualified teachers; it discusses research findings regarding the relationship between teacher qualifications and quality and student outcomes; it examines recent efforts to attract and retain better teachers in difficult-to-staff schools; and it considers policy elements that she believes would characterize a more promising alternative.

The body of research documenting disparities in the distribution of teachers within particular states, metropolitan areas, and districts has greatly expanded in recent years. Readers will find Haycock's paper valuable in terms of its overview of the literature, including references and the paper's synthesis of findings. These findings strongly support Haycock's observation that "students who are most dependent upon their teachers for academic learning are systematically assigned to teachers with the weakest knowledge and skills." Even though it is generally understood that such qualitative differences exist, the synthesis of research findings makes clear that these differences are large in magnitude as well as consistent across both a wide range of measures and schools in many states.

Haycock focuses on the relationship between teacher attributes and the race and poverty status of students. However, similar patterns hold when students and schools are instead grouped by the academic performance of students. For example, grouping elementary schools in New York based on fourth-grade students' performance on the statewide English language arts (ELA) exam, one finds large systematic differences in the qualifications of teachers. In the quartile of schools having more than 20 percent of students failing all sections of the ELA exam, 14 percent of teachers had no prior teaching experience, 22 percent were not certified in any assignment, and 35 percent of the teachers taking the liberal arts teacher certification exam failed on their first attempt. This starkly contrasts with the attributes of teachers in the quartile of schools not having any students failing all sections of the ELA exam. In these schools, 6 percent of teachers had no prior teaching experience, 3 percent were not certified in any assignment, and 9 percent failed the certification exam.

It is important to be clear whether the central issue is one of teacher adequacy or the inequity associated with relative differences in the qualifications of teachers. When considering the typical attributes of those teaching
minority, poor, or low-performing students, a natural tendency exists to
compare these attributes with the qualifications of those individuals teaching other, often more advantaged, students—as I did above and as Haycock
does in her paper. Even though such comparisons may be important in
understanding the corresponding differences in educational outcomes and
issues regarding educational equity more generally, focusing on differences in qualifications can distract from what I view as the most pressing
problem: Those students failing to achieve even minimum educational standards far too often are taught by individuals whose qualifications and skills
are woefully inadequate, even though these students typically are most
dependent upon their teachers for academic learning. With issues of standards and adequacy receiving increased attention in recent years, a focus
on the adequacy of teachers is likely to yield broader public support for
reform than would analyses focusing on relative differences in the qualifications of teachers.

Haycock explains the distribution of teachers as resulting from the preferences of teachers and school officials; differences across schools and districts in their capacities and constraints, especially their collective bargaining
agreements; differences in transfers and quits; and within-school differences. While these factors are all pertinent to the observable outcomes, I find
a somewhat different organizing framework useful. First, the supply of
teachers is affected by a range of factors that make teaching more or less
attractive, both in general and in particular schools and districts. Here
teacher preferences are pertinent, as Haycock discusses. Second, on the
demand side, various factors affect hiring practices and the screening of
prospective and practicing teachers. Factors pertinent here would include the
preferences and objectives of school officials making personnel decisions as
well the constraints they face. The decisions of teacher candidates and
school officials interact in complex ways to determine both the composition
of the teacher work force and the sorting of teachers across jobs. A third set
of factors affecting the quality of the teacher work force relates to teacher
education, professional development, and teacher effort. Together these factors determine who teaches, where they teach, and their qualifications and
skills. Haycock's emphasis on the preferences of teachers and school offi-

cials and differences in capacities and constraints, although different in taxonomy, overlaps with my organizing framework. However, I view the pattern of quits and transfers as well as within-school differences as reflecting choices made by teachers and school officials instead of being an explanation for the underlying problem. Substantial improvements in the average quality of those teaching in schools having large numbers of low-performing, minority, and poor students will require that working in these schools be made substantially more attractive for teachers and that school officials be motivated and given the flexibility to make good personnel decisions. Only then will these schools be able to attract and retain significantly more high-quality teachers.

Even though the importance of teacher preferences in explaining the sorting of teachers is generally recognized, one aspect is not well understood. Teachers have a strong preference to teach close to where they grew up. For example, over 60 percent of first-year public school teachers in New York take jobs within fifteen miles of where they grew up, with 85 percent taking jobs within forty miles. Also, teachers show a strong preference for teaching in areas having characteristics similar to their hometown. This preference for both proximity and similarity of place works to disadvantage urban districts as a result of these districts being net importers of teachers. With the number of teacher recruits who grew up in urban areas falling short of the number of positions being filled in urban districts, these districts must recruit teachers from the suburbs or other regions. Thus urban districts must overcome these preferences with respect to distance and urbanism, in addition to addressing the problems typically identified with respect to recruiting teachers to difficult-to-staff urban schools, such as salary, working conditions, and the characteristics of the student population. In general, urban schools must have a combination of salaries, working conditions, and student body attributes that are more attractive than those of the surrounding suburban districts for the urban districts to attract equally qualified teachers living in the suburbs. To the extent that they do not, teachers with suburban hometowns who take jobs in urban areas are likely to be less qualified than those teaching in the suburbs.

Moreover, urban districts face a second disadvantage. Graduates of urban schools receiving less than an adequate education can result in cities facing a less qualified pool of potential teachers, even if they are not net importers. Preferences for proximity contribute to the perpetuation of inequities in the qualifications of teachers. The general tightness of teacher labor markets is another important factor affecting both the sorting of teachers and the absolute quality of those teaching in difficult-to-staff schools.

As is clear from the consequences of the recent class-size reduction in California, a general shortage of teachers creates expanded opportunities for more qualified teachers to take first jobs, or transfer into positions, in schools that are relatively more attractive. This is true with respect to differences across districts as well as across schools within districts. With respect to the latter, the seniority post and fill system together with an increasing number of job openings allows an increasing number of the most experienced teachers to transfer out of the schools having the greatest needs. The net result is that the problems associated with a general shortage of highly qualified teachers are greatly amplified for the districts and schools having relatively large numbers of low-income, minority, and low-achieving students. This reality is cause for concern when considered in combination with two ongoing trends. First, increasing numbers of teachers are retiring or are approaching retirement age. Second, enrollment growth and class-size reduction across the country have increased the demand for new teachers, trends that likely are to continue in at least certain parts of the country.

The consequence of this general tightening of teacher labor markets in recent years can be illustrated using changes in New York City. Since the mid-1990s, the annual proportion of New York City teachers transferring to suburban schools has increased dramatically. Approximately 0.25 percent of New York City teachers transferred to suburban districts each year in the early 1990s. This increased to a 0.63 percent annual transfer rate in the mid-1990s and to 1.80 percent of all teachers by 2000. The sevenfold increase in the transfer rate over the decade resulted in New York City having to hire approximately nine hundred more teachers in the fall of 2002 than would have been needed had the transfer rate not changed, a 12 percent increase in total hires. This is on top of more than a 50 percent increase in new hires necessitated by the retirement of increasing numbers of New York City teachers.

Even though current trends make it unlikely that significant further tightening of teacher labor markets will be seen, neither is it likely that markets will slacken to any great degree over the next five years. Thus the outflow of teachers from urban districts is likely to continue at meaningful rates, implying that there is cause for concern.

First, as discussed by Haycock, those teachers transferring out of high-poverty and high-minority schools, on average, have stronger qualifications than do those who remain. Second, the changing pattern of transfers almost certainly is mirrored by related changes that relatively disadvantage urban schools seeking to hire large numbers of new teachers. Third, this increased annual outflow of teachers is in part cumulative. Significant numbers of those transferring otherwise would have continued to teach in New York City for many years so that the cumulative effect is larger than the annual flow would indicate. Finally, urban districts are now hiring large numbers of new teachers to fill openings created by retirements, at the same time that the labor market for teachers is tighter than it has been for thirty years.

Given the relatively slow turnover of the teacher work force, hiring large numbers of teachers having qualifications falling short of those desired can have long-lived consequences for generations of students. From a slightly different perspective, the attributes and distribution of the teacher work force documented in the research Haycock discusses in large part do not reflect most of the consequences of the recent increases in enrollments and teacher retirements. Thus market forces in play could result in a further deterioration in the average quality of the teachers in traditionally difficult-to-staff schools.

In her paper, Haycock outlines recent efforts to attract and retain better teachers in difficult-to-staff schools. These include compensation (for example, salary supplements and increases and housing assistance), efforts to reduce the burdens of teaching in these schools (for example, added student support services, reduced student loads, and strong and supportive school leadership), and targeted professional development. She then argues that these approaches will fail for several reasons. First, the dollars are inadequate. Second, the policies do not address serious systematic problems (for example, contractual obligations leading to late hiring in urban districts). Third, the policies do not address issues regarding who enters the teaching pipeline. Fourth, the policies fail to address the problem of removing incompetent teachers. Finally, the policies do not rely on good measures of high-quality teachers.

I view the first three of these as being especially important. In particular, far bolder action will be needed before sufficient numbers of high-quality teachers find teaching in traditionally low-performing schools to be an attractive career alternative. Similarly, far more needs to be done to remove contractual, legal, and administrative constraints that work against urban districts making more timely and effective hiring decisions. From my perspective, existing efforts are dwarfed by the magnitude of the personnel problems faced by difficult-to-staff schools and districts. The actions taken are modest, even if viewed as experiments intended to see what works.

Haycock argues that a more promising approach would emphasize accountability and include the following elements: value-added assessments; a differentiated salary structure that rewards both student educational gains and the level of challenge faced by teachers; the elimination of contractual burdens on schools; assistance, followed by decisive action when results lag; and a new accountability system for higher education.

I agree that getting the incentives right is extremely important, but I am concerned that Haycock's approach is very general in its focus and seems more pertinent to improving educational outcomes generally. Getting the incentives right is key, but these incentives must be both meaningful and targeted to the staffing of schools having relatively large numbers of low-performing, low-income, and minority students. For example, even though many urban districts will need to increase salaries, especially starting salaries, to attract more high-quality teachers, it is extremely important that urban districts use a large part of such funding to introduce intradistrict salary differentials. Here action could be taken quickly and need not wait for the design and implementation of systems for merit-based pay. Financial rewards, working conditions, and leadership support in traditionally difficult-to-staff schools all must be improved substantially so that teaching in these schools is relatively more attractive.

Haycock's emphasis on global solutions related to improved accountability and general incentives raises another issue. I am concerned whether such global solutions will ever be implemented. Recent studies and reports have documented differences in teacher qualifications and student outcomes, and reporting requirements under No Child Left Behind will make inadequacies and disparities even more apparent. However, the political, economic, and social forces that led to the current system will not vanish.

The political forces that brought forward the current distribution of education resources came about not because of ignorance of differential quality. Sure, documenting the nature and extent of these differences has become more sophisticated, but my bookshelves are lined with blue-ribbon commission reports, academic studies, and reports from state and federal agencies showing disparities. Educational researchers can agree that if only urban, low-performing, poor, nonwhite schools could be made as attractive to high-quality teachers as are the schools populated with suburban, upper-middle-class white kids, then the problems would be solved. However, little empirical evidence indicates that this can be accomplished in anything close to the scale needed.

An alternative to focusing on global solutions is to focus on some of the pieces of the puzzle. For example, the importance of job proximity and similarity of place in teachers' preferences suggests a "grow your own" strategy that focuses on recruiting individuals living in the urban districts to enter teacher education programs and employment in urban schools. Given the strong preferences for teaching close to home and that most students attend college close to home, an important part of the solution is likely to be partnerships between urban schools and higher education institutions in close proximity to the district. This then places a premium on teacher preparation and recruitment in urban areas, where the graduates are most likely to become the teachers in difficult-to-staff urban schools. Policies could also create incentives for academically successful urban high school graduates to attend college and choose careers in teaching. There are also important issues regarding induction, professional development, and school leadership.

As noted by Haycock, a second set of reforms is needed so that urban districts make a substantially larger portion of their job offers earlier in the year. Also, substantial bonuses or salary increments for teaching in difficult-to-staff schools can be added to the traditional structure of teacher salary schedules. Such differential pay need not be delayed until more systemic reforms in teacher compensation are carried out. Even though implementing such reforms presents many challenges, doing so does not require completely changing the face of the labor market for teachers, which is undoubtedly desirable, but unlikely to occur. If so, more modest proposals might make more of a difference. Even if more major reforms are carried out, these other pieces would complement more systemic reforms and are good and worthy in their own right.

Comment by Lynn Olson

Kati Haycock provides a good summary of what *Education Week* came to call the teacher gap in its 2003 edition of *Quality Counts*. The report, *"If I Can't Learn from You": Ensuring a Highly Qualified Teacher for Every Classroom,* focused on the fact that students in high-poverty, high-minority, and low-achieving schools typically have the least access to good teachers. The report also examined what states are doing—or not doing—to try to address the issue.

I would like to pick up on a few points Haycock made in her essay as well as one she did not that has implications for how well any potential solution will address the systematic inequity in the distribution of teachers.

Haycock rightly notes that while all of the existing measures are only proxies for teacher quality, no matter which characteristic you choose, children in high-poverty, high-minority, low-achieving schools wind up on the short end of the stick.

Poor and minority children are more likely to be taught by teachers who are uncertified, who are brand-new to the profession, who do not have a major or a minor in the subject they teach, who performed poorly on college admissions tests, and who graduated from less selective colleges and universities.[65]

Haycock mentions that differences in the initial preferences of new teachers and in the schools that hire them contribute to the teacher gap. In particular, she notes that many school districts prefer to hire their own graduates and many teacher education graduates prefer to return to their home school districts. This problem is then compounded by district practices that can constrain their ability to hire well-qualified candidates in a timely fashion. One example is extensive contractual requirements that permit senior teachers to transfer to the plum assignments before school systems can even begin to make final job offers to new candidates.

For *Quality Counts,* reporter Bess Keller followed a dozen job seekers in the Cleveland, Ohio, metropolitan area. Her findings largely confirm Haycock's analysis. In particular, Keller found that many teachers do not even want to go downtown, much less feel prepared to deal with the real problems found there. When teachers with other choices do pick a district where most students are poor and members of minority groups, their preferences are often rooted in a commitment to the local community and the people who live there.[66]

Yet lack of interest in urban teaching is not the only obstacle to filling the ranks with well-qualified instructors. Young, mobile teachers who might be drawn to city schools often face an impersonal or sluggish system that prompts them to go elsewhere. Large districts, in particular, often have trouble moving nimbly when faced with attractive candidates. And their impersonal hiring proceedings can turn off—and turn away—potential teachers.

As Keller chronicled in her article, while urban districts plod through contract provisions that reserve jobs for teachers already in the system, beg veterans to decide early whether they are retiring, and try to keep track of hundreds of job openings, smaller, more nimble districts snap up new hires. The shifting sands of urban districts' budgets further complicate and delay their ability to forecast the number of openings they will have come September.[67]

Haycock also describes how differences in the distribution of teacher quality occur as teachers—especially white teachers—leave high-minority and high-poverty schools, generally transferring to lower-minority and lower-poverty schools. A point she does not discuss is how working conditions contribute to these patterns.

While student characteristics clearly matter, some studies suggest that the poor working conditions often associated with high-poverty, high-minority schools are the primary culprit. Working conditions may influence whether job candidates seek out high-poverty, high-minority schools in the first place, and they appear to influence whether they stay there.

In a study of fifty newly minted teachers in Massachusetts, Susan Moore Johnson and her colleagues at Harvard University found that all the teachers who switched schools voluntarily transferred to sites serving wealthier populations than their original schools did. But the teachers said they were not seeking more affluent students; they were seeking schools where they could be successful.[68]

The respondents reported that they felt their chances for success depended largely on a set of school-site factors, including their teaching assignments and work loads, student behavior, the supportiveness of principals and colleagues, the availability of effective curricula and other resources, and the schools' relationships with parents.[69]

Similarly, a study by Linda Darling-Hammond and her colleagues at Stanford University found that salaries and working conditions, not student characteristics, predicted high turnover in California schools.[70] "Because bad working conditions and relatively noncompetitive salaries are coincident with low-income and minority student populations," Darling-Hammond argues, "we often have been confused about what the major drivers are."[71]

This is an area where more research probably is needed to ferret out what is driving teacher decisions. Most likely it is a mix of factors, as would be true of anyone making a career decision in any other occupation.

So I would argue that Haycock is partly right. Most teachers do have a natural preference to avoid poor and minority students. But school systems make that challenge even greater by systematically depriving the schools that serve such students of strong leaders and better working conditions that would allow teachers to succeed.

Based on an analysis of data from the federal Schools and Staffing Survey, *Education Week* found teachers in high-poverty, high-minority schools typically report much more difficult working conditions across a variety of measures than do teachers in other schools.[72]

For example, teachers in high-poverty schools were more likely than teachers in low-poverty schools to agree that

—Student disrespect is a "moderate" or "serious" problem (56 percent versus 37 percent);

—Students are unprepared to learn (80 percent versus 45 percent); and

—Lack of parent involvement is a moderate or serious problem (75 percent versus 36 percent).

Larger percentages of teachers in high-poverty schools also stated that student and teacher absenteeism and student apathy were moderate or serious problems in their schools.

Teachers in high-poverty or high-minority schools were less likely to agree that they were satisfied with their salaries, received a great deal of support from parents, or possessed the necessary materials to teach. They also were less likely to agree that there was a "great deal of cooperative effort among the staff members."

This suggests that solutions that do not address the working conditions in high-needs sites will not keep teachers there, even if they get them through the door initially, or, worse yet, they will keep only the teachers who lack other choices.

In addition to the combination of strategies that Haycock suggests—and the mix of incentives that states and districts are now trying—public education needs a concerted focus on the working conditions in high-poverty, high-minority schools. And that, in turn, may require addressing much deeper inequities in how schools are funded.

Finally, Haycock asserts that the levers most policymakers have at their disposal are "awfully blunt" and that most of the solutions to date are likely to fail because they simply layer some combination of small incentives on a system that is still heavily rigged. I absolutely agree with both statements. But I would add a third. *Education Week*'s fifty-state survey for *Quality Counts 2003*, as well as a one-time survey of thirty large districts, discovered that most policy levers were not even focused on finding teachers for high-needs sites, even when that was the purported goal.[73]

—While twenty-four states provide college scholarships, loans, and other tuition assistance to prospective teachers, only seven of them target such programs at candidates committed to working in high-poverty, high-minority, or low-achieving schools.

—Five states provide signing bonuses for teachers, but only California and Massachusetts gear such bonuses toward teachers willing to work in high-needs schools or districts.

—Thirty-four states and the District of Columbia offer retention bonuses to veteran or highly qualified teachers, but only five of them target those bonuses at teachers in high-needs schools.

—Of the twenty-four states and the District of Columbia with structured alternate routes into teaching, only three states—Massachusetts, Missouri, and Texas—targeted their efforts on finding candidates for high-needs sites.

And on and on. As with class size, most states have taken a one-size-fits-all approach to a problem that would benefit from a much more fine-tuned solution. That is, in part, because not targeting these approaches is politically easier and more popular. Even when states do target their efforts, they rarely evaluate the results of those policies.

While the No Child Left Behind Act will start to force states to come clean on the disparities in their teaching force, few have done so as of fall 2003. *Education Week* found that while twenty-two states required school or district report cards to include some information about teacher characteristics, just four publicly reported teacher qualifications disaggregated by school type, such as the percent of children from low-income families.

Only California, Indiana, Kentucky, Louisiana, and Tennessee provide parents with information on a website about the credentials of every public school teacher. Kentucky alone barred out-of-field teaching, the practice of assigning teachers to classes for which they are not certified. Ten additional states either limited the number of out-of-field teachers in a school or district or imposed accreditation penalties on districts that hire too many out-of-field teachers.

Until the advent of the new federal law, only New York State banned the hiring of teachers with emergency credentials in its lowest-performing schools.[74]

Finally, I would like to address Haycock's solutions. Value-added techniques that examine how much an individual teacher contributes to the performance growth of his or her students offer a promising strategy for identifying and rewarding good teaching. But, as with various methods for calculating dropout and graduation statistics, value-added measures may not be fully ready for prime time. For example, policymakers would want assurances that the tests used have sufficient stretch to recognize growth for students at the high and low end of the achievement scale. States and districts also would need tests that do not just measure mathematics and reading achievement to capture the performance of all teachers and their students.

But I think the bigger question begged by Haycock's solutions is: Where are the incentives to change the behavior of the system—whether that is the way principals hire, place, and evaluate teachers or the contractual obligations agreed to by district and union officials? Right now, I am not sure where the push is coming from that might lead districts to renegotiate contractual burdens, fire incompetent teachers, place their best teachers in their toughest or lowest-performing schools, and create differentiated pay structures—all of which entail big political fights. Similarly, I am not sure that paying teachers more is enough of an incentive to get good teachers to go where they are needed most unless those jobs are made more attractive. Salary—at least, unless it is a big salary boost—is probably not enough. Sadly, despite considerable rhetoric, I am not convinced that the political will exists to make the changes necessary.

Notes

1. Duke Helfand, "State, U.S. Feud Over Teachers," *Los Angeles Times,* August 6, 2002, p. A1.

2. Peter Simon, "Discontent Widening Over Regents Standards," *Buffalo News,* October 21, 2002.

3. James Coleman and others, *Equality of Educational Opportunity* (Government Printing Office, 1966).

4. Stephen G. Rivkin, Eric A. Hanushek, and John F. Kain, "Teachers, Schools, and Academic Achievement," Working Paper (Cambridge, Mass.: National Bureau of Economic Research, July 2002), p. 31.

5. See, for example, C. Clotfelter, H. F. Ladd, and J. L. Vigdar, "Segregation between and within Schools: Evidence from North Carolina," Working Paper (Duke University, 2002); June C. Rivers-Sanders, "The Impact of Teacher Effect on Student Math Competency Achievement," Ed.D. dissertation, University of Tennessee, August 1999; and Rivkin, Hanushek, and Kain, "Teachers, Schools, and Academic Achievement," p. 10.

6. See, for example, Hamilton Lankford, Susanna Loeb, and James Wyckoff, "Teacher Sorting and the Plight of Urban Schools: A Descriptive Analysis," *Educational Evaluation and Policy Analysis*, vol. 24, no. 1 (Spring 2002), pp. 37–62; and Patrick M. Shields and others, *The Status of the Teaching Profession 2001* (Santa Cruz, Calif.: Center for the Future of Teaching and Learning, California, 2001), pp. 20–26.

7. Editorial Projects in Education, *Quality Counts* (Washington: 2002).

8. Good state-level data are, however, hard to come by. In the most recent federal summary of state statistics on teacher quality, for example, many states did not bother to submit the required data on distribution across different types of schools. And others submitted data so woefully incomplete that conclusions are impossible. For example, South Carolina reports that about 5 percent of the teachers in both its high- and low-poverty districts are uncertified. A close inspection of the footnotes in the state's submission, however, shows that these are voluntary, self-reported data from the districts—and that most of the state's urban school districts did not participate. For more on this problem, see Sandra Huang, Yun Yi, and Kati Haycock, *Interpret with Caution* (Washington: Education Trust, 2002).

9. Department of Education, Office of Postsecondary Education, *Meeting the Highly Qualified Teacher Challenge: The Secretary's Annual Report on Teacher Quality* (Washington: 2002), p. 61.

10. See Shields and others, *The Status of the Teaching Profession 2001*, p. 26, figure 2-12; Thomas C. Dawson and K. Lloyd Billingsly, *Unsatisfactory Performance: How California's K–12 Education System Protects Mediocrity and How Teacher Quality Can Be Improved* (San Francisco: Pacific Research Institute for Public Policy, 2002); and Huang, Yi, and Haycock, *Interpret with Caution*.

11. Christopher Jepsen and Steven Rivkin, *Class-Size Reduction, Teacher Quality, and Academic Achievement in California Public Elementary Schools* (San Francisco: Public Policy Institute of California, 2002).

12. Department of Education, *Meeting the Highly Qualified Teacher Challenge*, p. 60.

13. Lankford, Loeb, and Wyckoff, "Teacher Sorting and the Plight of Urban Schools," p. 13.

14. Department of Education, *Meeting the Highly Qualified Teacher Challenge*, pp. 60–61.

15. Fordham University, Graduate Schools of Education and Social Services, National Center for Schools and Communities (NCSC), *Baltimore City Schools: 2001–2002—A Failing System Riddled with Inequities,* NCSC Public School Analysis Series (New York: 2003).

16. Richard Ingersoll, special analysis of Schools and Staffing Survey (SASS) data prepared for the Education Trust, 2002.

17. Daniel P. Mayer, John E. Mullens, and Mary T. Moore, *Monitoring School Quality: An Indicators Report,* NCES 2001–030 (Department of Education, National Center for Education Statistics, December 2000).

18. Hamilton Lankford, Jim Wyckoff, and Frank Papa, *The Labor Market for Public School Teachers: A Descriptive Analysis of New York State's Teacher Workforce* (University at Albany, 2000), p. 22.

19. Rivkin, Hanushek, and Kain, "Teachers, Schools, and Academic Achievement," table A-3.

20. Jepsen and Rivkin, *Class-Size Reduction, Teacher Quality, and Academic Achievement in California Public Elementary Schools.*

21. Ingersoll, special analysis of SASS data.

22. Craig D. Jerald, *All Talk, No Action: Putting an End to Out-of-Field Teaching* (Washington: Education Trust, 2002).

23. Jerald, *All Talk, No Action.*

24. John F. Kain and Kraig Singleton, "Equality of Educational Opportunity Revisited," *New England Economic Review* (May/June 1996), p. 109.

25. Kate Grossman, Becky Beaupre, and Rosalind Rossi, "Investigative Report: Failing Teacher," *Chicago Sun-Times*, September-October 2001.

26. Kain and Singleton, "Equality of Educational Opportunity Revisited," p. 109.

27. Ronald F. Ferguson and Helen F. Ladd, "How and Why Money Matters: An Analysis of Alabama Schools," in Helen Ladd, *Holding Schools Accountable: Performance-Based Reform in Education* (Brookings, 1996), pp. 265–98.

28. Jianping Shen, *The Distribution of the Quality of the New Teaching Force: Results from the Baccalaureate and Beyond Longitudinal Study 1993–97* (Washington: Education Trust, 2003), p. 8.

29. Andrew J. Wayne, "Teacher Inequality: New Evidence on Teachers' Academic Skills," *Education Policy Analysis Archives,* vol. 10, no. 30 (June 13, 2002), p. 5.

30. Lankford, Loeb, and Wyckoff, "Teacher Sorting and the Plight of Urban Schools," pp. 32, 35.

31. Lankford, Loeb, and Wyckoff, "Teacher Sorting and the Plight of Urban Schools," pp. 10–11.

32. Robert P. Strauss and William B. Vogt, "Should Teachers Know, or Know How to Teach?" Carnegie Mellon University, H. John Heinz III School of Public Policy, April 23, 2002, p. 22.

33. Ferguson and Ladd, "How and Why Money Matters."

34. Robert P. Strauss and Elizabeth A. Sawyer, "Some New Evidence on Teacher and Student Competencies," *Economics of Education Review,* vol. 5, no. 1 (1986), p. 41.

35. Grover J. Whitehurst, "Research on Teacher Preparation and Professional Development," paper prepared for the White House Conference on Preparing Tomorrow's Teachers, Washington, D.C., March 5, 2002; and Linda Darling-Hammond and Peter Youngs, "Defining 'Highly Qualified Teachers': What Does Scientifically Based Research Actually Tell Us?" *Educational Researcher*, vol. 31 no. 9 (December 2002), pp. 13–25.

36. D. D. Goldhaber and D. J. Brewer, "Evaluating the Effect of Teacher Degree Level on Educational Performance," in W. J. Fowler, ed., *Developments in School Finance* (Washington: National Center for Education Statistics, 1996); David H. Monk and Jennifer K. King, "Multilevel Teacher Resource Effects on Pupil Performance in Secondary Mathematics and Science: The Case of Teacher Subject-Matter Preparation," in Ronald G. Ehrenberg, ed., *Choices and Consequence: Contemporary Policy Issues in Education* (Ithaca, N.Y.: ILR Press, 1994), pp. 29–58.

37. Eva Baker, *Report on the Content Area Performance Assessments (CAPA): A Collaboration among Hawaii Dept. of Education, the Center for Research on Evaluation Standards and Student Testing (CRESST), and the Teachers and Children of Hawaii* (University of California at Los Angeles, CRESST, 1996), p. 17.

38. Darling-Hammond and Youngs, "Defining 'Highly Qualified Teachers.'"

39. Rivkin, Hanushek, and Kain, "Teachers, Schools, and Academic Achievement," p. 29.

40. William J. Sanders and June C. Rivers, *Cumulative and Residual Effects of Teachers on Future Students' Academic Achievement* (University of Tennessee, Value-Added Research and Assessment, 1998), p. 9.

41. Rivkin, Hanushek, and Kain, "Defining 'Highly Qualified Teachers,'" p. 29.

42. Eric A. Hanushek, "The Trade-Off between Child Quantity and Quality," *Journal of Political Economy*, vol. 100, no. 1 (February 1992), p. 107.

43. Sanders and Rivers, *Cumulative and Residual Effects of Teachers on Future Students' Academic Achievement.*

44. H. Jordan, R. Mendro, and D. Weerasinghe, "Teacher Effects on Longitudinal Student Achievement," paper presented at the CREATE annual meeting, Indianapolis, Indiana, July 1997, p. 3.

45. Rivers-Sanders, "The Impact of Teacher Effect on Student Math Competency Achievement."

46. Sanders and Rivers, *Cumulative and Residual Effects of Teachers on Future Students' Academic Achievement,* p. 9.

47. Sanders and Rivers, *Cumulative and Residual Effects of Teachers on Future Students' Academic Achievement,* p. 10, table 2.

48. Jordan, Mendro, and Weerasinghe, "Teacher Effects on Longitudinal Student Achievement."

49. Robert P. Strauss, "Who Gets Hired to Teach? The Case of Pennsylvania," in Marci Kanstroom and Chester E. Finn Jr., eds., *Better Teachers, Better Schools* (Washington: Fordham Foundation Press, July 1999), p. 191.

50. Jessica Levin and Meredith Quinn, *Missed Opportunities: How We Keep High-Quality Teachers Out of Urban Classrooms* (Washington: New Teacher Project, 2003).

51. See, for example, John K. DiPaolo, *Towards an Open Teacher Hiring Process: How the Boston Public Schools and the Boston Teachers Union Can Empower Schools to Hire and Keep the Best Teams* (Boston Plan for Excellence in the Public Schools, March 2000); and Howard L. Fuller, George A. Mitchell, and Michael E. Hartman, "The Milwaukee Public Schools' Teacher Union Contract, Its History, Content, and Impact on Education," Marquette University, Institute for the Transformation of Learning, October 1997.

52. Mayer, Mullens, and Moore, *Monitoring School Quality.*

53. Catherine Freeman, Benjamin Scafidi, and David Sjoquist, *Racial Segregation in Georgia Public Schools, 1994–2001: Trends, Causes, and Impact on Teacher Quality* (Georgia State University, Andrew Young School of Policy Studies, 2002), p. 27.

54. Hanushek, Kain, and Rivkin, "Teachers, Schools, and Academic Achievement," p. 17.

55. Lankford, Wyckoff, and Papa, *The Labor Market for Public School Teachers.*

56. Jepsen and Rivkin, *Class-Size Reduction, Teacher Quality, and Academic Achievement in California Public Elementary Schools,* pp. 19–33.

57. DiPaolo, *Towards an Open Teacher Hiring Process.*

58. Clotfelter, Ladd, and Vigdar, "Segregation between and within Schools."

59. See, for example, Marilyn Crawford and Eleanor Dougherty, *Updraft/Downdraft: Secondary Schools in the Crosswinds of Reform* (Lanham, Md.: Scarecrow Press, 2003).

60. Lankford, Wyckoff, and Papa, *The Labor Market for Public School Teachers.*

61. Freeman, Scafidi, and Sjoquist, *Racial Segregation in Georgia Public Schools,* p. 27.

62. Eric A. Hanushek, John F. Kain, and Stephen G. Rivkin, "Why Public Schools Lose Teachers," Working Paper (Cambridge, Mass.: National Bureau of Economic Research, November 2001), p. 23.

63. Eric A. Hanushek, personal communication with author.

64. Albert Shanker, quoted in *Education Week*, May 14, 1997.

65. Education Week, *Quality Counts 2003: "If I Can't Learn from You": Ensuring a Highly Qualified Teacher for Every Classroom* (Bethesda, Md.: January 9, 2003).

66. Bess Keller, "The Job-Seekers," in Education Week, *Quality Counts 2003: "If I Can't Learn from You": Ensuring a Highly Qualified Teacher for Every Classroom* (Bethesda, Md.: January 9, 2003), pp. 41–51.

67. Keller, "The Job-Seekers."

68. Susan Moore Johnson and S. E. Birkeland, "Pursuing a 'Sense of Success': New Teachers Explain Their Career Decisions," October 2002 (revised version forthcoming in *American Educational Research Journal*).

69. Johnson and Birkeland, "Pursuing a 'Sense of Success.'"

70. Susanna Loeb, L. Darling-Hammond, and J. Luczak, *Teacher Turnover: The Role of Working Conditions and Salaries in Recruiting and Retaining Teachers* (Stanford University, School of Education, 2003).

71. Lynn Olson, "The Great Divide," in Education Week, *Quality Counts 2003: "If I Can't Learn from You": Ensuring a Highly Qualified Teacher for Every Classroom* (Bethesda, Md.: January 9, 2003), pp. 9–18.

72. Education Week, *Quality Counts 2003*.

73. Education Week, *Quality Counts 2003*.

74. Education Week, *Quality Counts 2003*.

Panel Discussion on Obstacles to Entering the Teaching Profession

The first day's session of the 2003 Brookings conference on education concluded with a roundtable discussion of the obstacles to recruiting new teachers into the profession, especially for urban schools. The discussion, moderated by Diane Ravitch, began with informal presentations by two people who have been deeply involved in addressing this problem: Michelle Rhee of the New Teacher Project and Vicki Bernstein of the New York City Teaching Fellows Program, which is part of the New York City Department of Education. The commentators were Lewis C. Solmon of the Milken Family Foundation (and former dean of the School of Education at the University of California at Los Angeles) and C. Emily Feistritzer, who directs the National Center for Education Information and has studied alternative certification programs for many years. The other participants in the discussion were Richard Rothstein, Caroline M. Hoxby, Eric A. Hanushek, John T. Wenders, Adam F. Scrupski, Nesa Chapelle, Susan Sclafani, Deborah Meier, Leslie Fritz, Alvin Sanoff, Robert Spillane, Michael Podgursky, and Frederick M. Hess.

Michelle Rhee began by describing the New Teacher Project, a national nonprofit organization that consults with school districts, state departments of education, and colleges and universities across the country to help them more effectively recruit, select, train, place, support, and certify new teachers. The project works primarily on two different types of contracts: those in which school districts set up programs to recruit young and midcareer professionals and folks with strong content knowledge for hard-to-staff urban schools; and those seeking to increase the number and quality of certified teachers.

According to Rhee, the nature of the teacher shortage and recruitment issues over the past few years is usually mischaracterized as a lack of interest on the part of potential teachers. One often hears the complaint that not enough people, whether certified or noncertified, want to teach in hard-to-staff urban schools. Furthermore, finding highly qualified people is difficult. Yet Rhee found through her experience at the New Teacher Project working with school districts across the country that aggressive and targeted recruitment efforts will generate a large supply of people who are willing to teach in urban schools. This pertains to both nontraditionally and traditionally certified candidates. Across the country in the project's alternate route programs, there are about nine applicants for every vacancy. Even with certified cohorts, between five and six applications are submitted for every vacancy in the program.

Rhee said that those recruited by the project are extremely well qualified. The alternate route people have on average a grade point average (GPA) of about 3.2, approximately 40 percent are people of color, and about 35 percent hold advanced degrees. The project has been showing school districts how to develop a larger applicant pool. For example, the New York City Teaching Fellows received 19,930 applications in 2003 and would place about 2,800 new fellows in classrooms. The Los Angeles Unified School District by May 2003 had received about 6,000 applications for about 700 positions.

The project has encountered barriers to entry for new recruits to teaching, both for certified and for alternate route programs. While many of these stem from internal inefficiencies in the human resources division, external policy issues also contribute to the problems of timely teacher hiring. For example, according to a survey the project conducted of six large urban sites, more than 35 percent of the applicants for teaching jobs withdrew their application before the beginning of school. Seventy percent of this group cited poor customer service, inefficient processes, and delayed time lines as the reason for their withdrawal.

Rhee reported that at one site over half of the candidates had been waiting more than a month for some kind of action on their application by the school district. Two-thirds of those who wanted principal interviews waited for two and a half months or more. Presumably these were quality applicants, she said, because the education field loses the highest quality applicants the fastest.

In an ideal hiring process, the pool of applicants gets better and better as time goes on because the worst people are weeded out. But in many urban school districts, the pool gets worse and worse because the best people become so frustrated by the inefficiencies, the time lines, and so on that they opt out of the process and go to work elsewhere. According to Rhee, the project collected data showing that the GPA of the candidates who drop out is higher for those who withdraw in April than those who withdraw in June or July. Those ultimately hired by the district have a GPA that is much lower than the GPA for the original pool of people. The districts are losing the very candidates that they claim to want and need the most. In one district, 69 percent of the withdrawers held standard certification in math, science, or special education. Meanwhile, the district said it could not find these kinds of people.

The project has learned over time, Rhee said, that the withdrawers are very serious applicants. The human resources departments of urban districts often say that their district is a choice of last resort. This is their myth. They believe that people put in their applications just in case they do not get a job offer anywhere else but that they really do not want to take a job in a city district. The human resources people believe that once these candidates get a job in a suburb, they abandon their job search.

Rhee said that this myth is not true. A survey of the withdrawers conducted by the New Teachers Project found that the majority of them said that, if they had received a job offer from the city schools at the same time as the suburban schools, they would have accepted the city offer. Even more astonishing was that 80 percent of the people teaching in suburban schools who withdrew from the process said that they would absolutely consider taking a job in a city school if they could be brought in through a timely, efficient process. Thus a considerable pool of well-qualified people want to teach in these urban centers.

Even the highest functioning human resources departments would have severe problems ensuring that they get the highest quality candidates because of a number of other factors, said Rhee. These include union contracts and the voluntary and involuntary transfer processes that often hold up a district's ability to open a vacancy to a new hire. Vacancy notifications are a problem, because veteran teachers have many incentives to wait until the last moment to announce that they are leaving the district or that they are retiring. Issues also arise at the state level in terms of when budgets are handed down and when a school feels confident that it can afford to bring in a certain number of teachers. And politics is involved with the principals and their relationships with the human resources departments, for example, in hiding vacancies.

As Rhee stated, the project has seen that there is a much larger pool of candidates than most districts think—people who are willing to teach in high-needs urban districts. But the current systems and processes for hiring often discourage the most qualified candidates from matriculating into a district.

Vicki Bernstein began by noting that the New York City Department of Education has worked closely with the New Teacher Project in hiring candidates for the Teaching Fellows Program, as well as implementing a new initiative intended to bring a certified cohort to those areas with shortages.

In New York City, everything is distinguished by scale, Bernstein noted. The city has 1.1 million children, about twelve hundred schools, and about seventy-eight thousand teachers. Perhaps the best proxy for the teacher shortage, she said, is the number of uncertified teachers employed. About 12 percent of the teachers (about ninety-five hundred) do not have state certification. That is progress from recent years when the proportion of uncertified teachers reached about 16 percent.

Reduction in the number of uncertified teachers is the result of an alternative certification program and international recruitment. In each of the last four years, the city hired about nine thousand teachers. About seventy-five hundred to eight thousand of those are hired for the start of the school year. Four years ago, about 60 percent of new hires were not certified, but in 2002 the proportion of uncertified teachers declined to about 30 percent. Considering that the number of teachers coming through the traditional pipeline—about four thousand—is relatively flat, the improvement is really a consequence of the growth of alternatively certified teachers.

According to Bernstein, the situation is exacerbated by a variety of factors. The city has needed more teachers in recent years. The school system today has about fifteen thousand more teachers than it did just ten years ago, mostly because of enrollment growth and class-size reduction. The city in the fall of 2003 must comply with new state regulations requiring that all teachers be certified. It is working hard to meet this challenging goal.

Three obstacles typically face people entering the teaching profession, said Bernstein. First, teaching is not seen as a first-choice profession, particularly for women who have other options. Many men in the school system became teachers because they did not want to be drafted for the Vietnam

War. The same social influences are not at work bringing the best people into teaching today. Some undergraduate students are hesitant to enter teaching and to put it on their résumés because they think it undermines their competitiveness for entering other fields. Undergraduates are encouraged to broaden their possibilities for future careers by majoring in liberal arts and sciences or in fields with greater remuneration, such as business, engineering, or computer science.

Bernstein also believes a general perception exists that people enter teaching to have more flexible time schedules for the sake of their families, but teaching no longer offers that same benefit. Teaching is still mostly a ten-month position, but most teachers work those extra two months in one capacity or another to make ends meet. And teaching is not an 8:00 a.m. to 3:00 p.m. job. It takes up considerably more time in people's lives.

Second, state obstacles make it hard to get certified. New York no longer graduates education majors. For someone to go the undergraduate route to become certified, he or she must have almost the equivalent of a double major, which means in most instances getting a degree takes more time and the individual can take fewer electives. It is even harder to get certified in shortage areas. So, for someone who wants to get certified in special education or bilingual education or even in math and science, even more credits are needed. A typical master's program for special education requires fifty-plus credits compared with a thirty-six-credit degree for other disciplines.

Teachers in New York must obtain a master's degree. They can start teaching without it if they have the other credentials, but they ultimately must obtain a master's degree. This has an additional impact in terms of time and money for aspiring teachers. Furthermore, the process for getting certified is complex—the exams, the application for the certification, just understanding the certification process.

Third, candidates encounter an impenetrable bureaucracy. For many years in New York City, if somebody wanted to become a teacher, he was told, "Great, come to 65 Court Street, bring your fingers [for fingerprints] and bring your transcripts," which is not the normal response of a prospective employer when someone is applying to an agency. Even then, if he passed that basic threshold, he was told, "Okay, here is the list of the 32 districts, you are on your own." A real problem has emerged about placement because there is a central pool of folks and then there are twelve hundred schools. Bernstein asks, How can the people be disbursed in a way that makes sense, engenders good matches, and is timely so as not to lose people?

The three obstacles take on a life of their own. People say the process just seemed too difficult. Many people conclude, "Oh, you want to get a job as a teacher in New York City? Forget it. It is a nightmare. Don't even bother trying."

Internal attitudes are influenced as well. Efforts to streamline the process from within are often seen as subversion—that somehow the city is trying to bring in less qualified candidates, that somehow it is going to bring in potential criminals—not as how to bring in a larger pool so that the process can be more selective.

Hiring administrators, according to Bernstein, also have an attitude that stems from their perceptions about how important their careers are. Most of them come from an era that was marked by a scarcity of jobs. Thus they treat candidates as if the candidates owe them something, as opposed to acting like recruiters. Administrators give candidates the impression that they should be grateful for an interview instead of welcoming the candidates and doing their best to bring the highest quality folks into the system.

Once in the system, people find it hard to obtain the next level of certification. They are on their own to figure out the requirements that they have to meet, which takes time and money.

Three years ago, with the assistance of the New Teacher Project, the Teaching Fellows Program was initiated. Bernstein reported that it offers an alternate route to the teaching profession, bringing people from all walks of life into teaching. It is not specifically targeted to recent college graduates. The average age of recruits is in the early thirties, ranging from twenty-one to about sixty-five. The program provides an intense preservice program, which lasts about seven weeks. Individuals matriculate into a master's program to meet the state criteria for qualifications. They continue in that program for about two years while they are teaching with an alternative credential given by the state.

In developing the program, the department considered two options to increase the supply of certified teachers. First, try to broaden the traditional pipeline, which means going to the eighteen- or nineteen-year-old sophomores and convincing more of them to go into teaching. Second, go to others in the job market and encourage them to make a career change. Ultimately, the New York City Department of Education thought that the idea of recruiting eighteen- and nineteen-year-olds would have limited prospects. At best, it is a long-term proposition because of other social forces; for example, people are not majoring in education and are not going to pursue education from the get-go. So the department went to the job market, taking advantage of the fact that people no longer stay in one career for twenty-five or thirty years. The alternative certification program was designed to address some of the obstacles. The message was changed from "You should feel lucky we are even talking to you" to "We want you, we need you, you can make a difference, but it is a selective program." The application process was modified. Fingerprints are taken and transcripts are obtained, but far down the road. Before all that, a candidate submits a cover letter and résumé, just like a conventional application process for a job. The structure and process around certification also were changed. The city helps pay for the master's degree and helps make arrangements with universities for the admissions of the fellows. The applicants have a clear path, so they do not have to dissect all of the rules and regulations of the state education department. And the placement process has been streamlined so that the candidates do not have to shop themselves around to twelve hundred different schools.

As a result, Bernstein said, a significant number of people have submitted applications. The number grew from two thousand the first year to eight thousand to fifteen thousand, and in 2003 just shy of twenty thousand applications were submitted, which demonstrates that the interest is out there. In 2002, 75 percent of the applicants said that they always wanted to be a teacher. Many folks want to do this but barriers have stood in their way.

Bernstein said that the major continuing challenge is meeting the state requirement for a master's degree, which is very costly. This program is now probably the single largest discretionary expense in the New York City Department of Education. While the goal is to hire people who have a major in the content area, finding people in the sciences and math, special education, and bilingual education is hard.

And then there is the pay, the "elephant in the living room," as Bernstein put it. For the last three years, people were recruited to start at $32,000 a year. That low pay limits the pool of applicants to the youngest folks, who do not have many fixed expenses, or to those who already have resources, because their partner has made some money, they have family money, or they have already made their money.

Another big obstacle is the first-year experience. The attitude "you are lucky to be here" often carries over into the classroom, where some new teachers have encountered a hazing theory of induction, which is not welcoming and does not have a good impact on retention. New teachers need support. Finally, there is the university experience, which some think is ineffectual. Bernstein said that she asks people, "How is it going?" They reply, "Well, I sit in class and I can grade my kids' papers." The city is paying a considerable amount of money for the university experience. Teachers are devoting their time to it. The city and the teachers should be getting more out of the university experience if it is going to be a requirement.

The Department of Education works with fourteen different institutions of higher education in the New York City area. Bernstein reported that, with the exception of only one or two universities, they have not been willing to tailor their programs to the needs of alternate route candidates. They still offer the vanilla master's program designed for preservice students coming right out of an undergraduate program. But Bernstein expressed her hope that this will change as it becomes clear that the city has created a new market for graduate education students.

Moderator Diane Ravitch asked about the kind of master's degree that New York requires of those taking an alternate route to teaching. Bernstein replied that they must be enrolled in a registered teacher education program that will lead to certification. While this does not have to be a master's program, Bernstein noted that it would be foolish not to enroll in one given that the state requires teachers ultimately to obtain a master's. For the purposes of certification, New York will accept any master's. It does not stipulate graduate-level education coursework, just a master's degree.

Emily Feistritzer has been documenting alternative teacher certification in each of the states since 1983. The biggest obstacle the United States faces right now in education, she said, is a marketing one. There is, according to Feistritzer, an information gap. The problems associated with it have existed for a long time and are likely to be around for a long time unless educators can change the way they do business.

The United States has 1,354 schools, colleges, and departments of education that train teachers. They are turning out in excess of a couple of hundred thousand people fully qualified to teach every year. But 60 percent of baccalaureate degree recipients, who are fully qualified to teach, do not go into teaching.

This is a tremendous waste of resources. And it is not new. At the same time, many districts and states have started programs as alternatives to the approved undergraduate college teacher education program route for certifying teachers. Wherever such programs have been established for people who already have at least a bachelor's degree and want to be teachers, many applicants enroll from other careers and some are early retirees from the military. They want to teach; that is, they are not looking for a degree that they may or may not ever use.

Feistritzer asked, Where are the alternate route programs being established? She then answered: where the demand for teachers is greatest—in New York City, Los Angeles, Houston, Dallas, San Antonio, Chicago, Louisville, Kentucky, and so on. The demand for teachers is greatest in large inner-cities and outlying rural areas.

She reports that forty-six states have enacted legislation for some type of alternate route for certifying teachers, especially in the high-demand areas. They are recruiting people and getting an overwhelming response. No alternate route program has trouble getting far more people who already have bachelor's degrees, many of whom come from other walks of life, who want to become teachers.

States have put people through programs that are tailor-made to this market for teaching. They are not designed for undergraduates. They are not designed for people getting general degrees. They are designed for people who already have a bachelor's degree who want to study the subjects that they are going to be teaching. The people are trained in the schools that they are going to be teaching in. These are generally on-the-job training programs. The candidates may or may not be required to take college courses. The most successful alternate route programs around the country are on-the-job training programs that bring people together as cohorts; that assign mentor teachers who are experienced teachers in the school to help them; and that encourage the new teachers to talk about the problems of teaching and the various experiences that they are having and to help them develop competence to teach on the job.

Feistritzer reported on a survey she conducted asking teachers what was most important to them in developing competence to teach. The no. 1 thing listed was just doing it; that is, their own teaching experience. The second most frequently given reason for developing competence to teach was working with other teachers. The good alternate route programs around the country have incorporated both having people get experience as teachers and having experienced mentors helping the new teachers.

As of 2003, there were 144 or so alternate route programs around the country. Many of them are old programs that states have just renamed to make them appear new. Feistritzer said that in a recent book she identified fifty-nine that she considered good programs. They recruit actively, and they have entry-level requirements to ensure that people know the subject matter they will be teaching. Their teachers have a grade point average that is generally higher than that of those who come through more traditional programs. And, the personnel make a commitment to teach in the district. None of these programs produces people who do not intend to teach.

The U.S. education system turns out about twenty-five thousand newly qualified teachers through alternative certification routes annually. Feistritzer disagreed, however, with the prediction that 200,000 new teachers a year will be needed. She said that the figure is derived from the expected number of people moving from one school to another, from one school district to another, or from one state to another. However, taking into consideration those who are entering teaching, brand new to the profession, the figure is more like fifty thousand or seventy-five thousand. The district-based or university-based alternate route programs will supply probably a fourth to a third of the teachers.

Feistritzer concluded by saying that nothing in American education in her lifetime has been more exciting than the changing market for teaching. The only thing holding it back is reallocating resources to respond to a radically new supply for the teaching profession.

Lew Solmon expressed his concern about obstacles to entering the teaching profession experienced by the best and brightest. He believes that the quality crisis is at least as significant as the quantity crisis.

Data on the topic of obstacles to teaching have come from interviewing teachers, but information is also needed from those who decided not to be teachers, to find out why they did not go into teaching.

He also discussed six ways that he would define entry into teaching. First is the decision to prepare to enter teaching; that is, to go into a certification program. Second is the decision to teach, which is affected by experiences in the academic program and in student teaching. Third is what Solmon calls the permanent entry decision—deciding to stay and make a career after working for a few years. Fourth is the decision to remain in teaching but only if a move can be made out of a hard-to-staff school. Fifth is the decision to reenter teaching after changing residency. And sixth is the decision to reenter teaching after dropping out, to raise one's family or for whatever reason.

Solmon pointed out that the decision to enter teaching cannot be separated from the decision to stay in teaching. If things are being done to attract people into education but the profession is undesirable or less desirable than it used to be (as demonstrated by the statistics on turnover rates), then more people will enter teaching but they will leave, thus imposing a great deal of cost on districts for recruiting and induction. The question is, What is it about the profession that causes people to leave? The answer will indicate what needs to change. Solmon outlined eleven factors to consider.

1. The compensation policies are unappealing. There are three parts to the problem: salaries are not competitive, teachers get paid the same, and teachers are altruistic.

Raising the salaries of all teachers would mean that the best and the worst teachers alike would get more money. Furthermore, Solmon asks, could salaries ever be raised enough to compete with law or medicine or those holding a master's of business administration? But teachers claim that they are not in it for the money, and the salaries show that.

Solmon reported that it would cost $6,000 on average to raise teachers' salaries to the national average in the thirty states that are below the national average. That comes out to about $18 billion a year. He believes that that would break the bank, to which some have said, "If they found billions for the war in Iraq, why would it break the bank? Just pretend there wasn't a war in Iraq." His reply is that such an increase is politically unfeasible because people see the ineffectiveness of education and ask, "Why pay more for the same old thing?" When initiatives around the country are proposed that reward teacher performance, such as Proposition 301 in Arizona or a property tax levy in several places in Colorado, they pass by huge margins. However, people usually do not want to put more money into education just to pay all teachers higher salaries. Some say, "If you paid teachers more, they would get better." But the same is not said about civil servants or public interest lawyers. Solmon would say, "If teachers get better, they will get paid more."

According to Solmon, participants in focus groups of the best and the brightest college graduates report that they do not look at average salaries and do not compare the average salaries of lawyers with the average salaries of teachers, for example. They look at variance. The kids who won all the academic and extracurricular awards say, "I want to know what the best in the field make because I am going to be the best in the field and I want to see what I can earn." The variance is very important to the best people. That is the argument for performance pay.

Union leaders told Solmon that they do not oppose performance pay as long as the plan is fair. He offered to coauthor a paper with any union leader who volunteers to define "fair," and then, once they agreed on that, they could go on to set performance pay based on that criterion. However, as Solmon notes, it is not fair to pay the up-to-date teacher who works eighty hours a week the same amount as the one who has not changed his lecture notes in the last thirty-five years. Equal is not necessarily fair.

Some claim that parents do not want their children taught by people who are in it for the money. Do they mind being operated on by a doctor or defended by a lawyer who is making a considerable amount of money? Solmon thinks that parents want teachers to be qualified and are unconcerned about whether they want money or not. And while it could be possible to set up a small foundation or a civic organization, staffed by dedicated people who are willing to work below market rates for altruistic reasons, an industry of three million teachers cannot be established on altruism.

2. Minorities and women now have expanded career opportunities. Women's lib was great for everything but education.

3. Traditional education programs do not adequately prepare teachers for the classroom. Prospective teachers or college students say they would be wasting their time going to an education school. They want to go somewhere that is challenging, somewhere that is going to prepare them for something. And they hear that education schools do not do that. Teachers indicate that their education school training was not among the top factors that prepared them to teach.

4. Certification limits the supply. Licensing prevents people from practicing the profession. Furthermore, those certified in law or medicine know the same thing within some range, but that is not the case in education. Little agreement exists about what education schools should be teaching credential students. The cost of preparation for certification—sometimes requiring a fifth or sixth year in college—lowers the rate of return to the investment in getting the credential by imposing more foregone earnings. And with the low salaries, it is cost-ineffective.

5. Testing does not guarantee effectiveness. Solmon quoted Albert Shanker, who said in 1985: "Most minimum competency tests for teachers would be considered a joke by members of other professions. Such tests are the equivalent of licensing doctors on the basis of an exam in elementary biology." The tests have gotten better since then, but Solmon did not know if they have been validated to show that teaching candidates who pass them are effective teachers.

6. From the first day in the classroom, new teachers are generally left on their own. Unlike other professions, there is little mentoring and little induction. This, however, is beginning to change and must change, according to Solmon.

7. Teaching is not a high-status profession. People who are in it opt for security instead of accomplishment. The occupation garners little respect from the community. Solmon calls it the Groucho Marx effect. Groucho said, "I don't want to belong to any club that will accept me as a member." Standards in the profession are so low that bright people do not consider it. Teachers are not generally involved in decisionmaking. As somebody at the Brookings conference said, "It is the last part-time job in America." Most teachers basically are forced to join a union; most professions do not have a union. There are not star teachers as there are stars in other professions. Even the stars drive the same cars and live in the same neighborhoods as those who are not stars.

8. The school environment is often unpleasant and dangerous, and the teachers are afforded no respect. Teachers are not allowed to discipline students. Lawsuits are lurking behind every decision or nondecision that a teacher makes.

9. The hiring system is convoluted.

10. Schools of education and other elements of the public school system do not promote or sell the profession properly. To maintain the public school monopoly, they pretend that the broad education profession or business does not exist. If people knew the entrepreneurial possibilities that are open to those who go into education, they might decide to teach. Solmon finds it shocking that some education schools in Arizona do not allow student teachers to teach in charter schools. He asks, Wouldn't it be interesting to have a course in an education school on the business of education that discusses preschool, virtual schools, for-profit schools, and after-school programs?

11. There are barriers to mobility. Many people, when they move to another state, find it too onerous to figure out how to become a teacher. They need to take more classes. They cannot be hired at the same step. Pensions are not portable. These things reduce interstate mobility.

Solmon's solution is alternative certification, differential staffing, more mentoring and professional development at the school site, performance pay based on how teachers perform in the classroom, and how much students learn.

Richard Rothstein commented that some of Solmon's suggestions would be enormously expensive. He referred to an earlier discussion about the trade-off between teacher quality and class-size reduction. Rothstein said he does not think of class-size reduction as a policy to improve student performance but as a working condition. When teachers are asked what it would take to attract them to hard-to-staff schools, the first thing they say is smaller classes. Reducing class size is a big expense.

Solmon responded by relating that an educator recently said that the second thing teachers want is higher salaries. He pointed out that radiologists do not get more income by seeing fewer patients. There are trade-offs between expenses and productivity.

Solmon went on to talk about a Milken Family Foundation program, the Teacher Advancement Program, which costs about $400 per student, or 10 percent of the per student budget in some states. He believes that, if state departments or districts want a program, they find the money. If they do not want it, they say there is no money. He said that money is usually an excuse, not a reason.

Rothstein reiterated that Solmon's interventions are very expensive and would affect the working conditions of teachers.

He then brought up the notion of supervision. According to Rothstein, people often say that teachers are not treated like professionals. And the main thing that differentiates teachers from other professionals is that they are undersupervised. Some of the same people who claim that teacher quality needs to be improved also want to eliminate administrative overhead in schools. To improve teacher quality requires mentoring, which is a very expensive proposition. It means having in a school full-time, nonteaching teachers who are going to mentor, evaluate, and supervise. It requires increasing the teacher-pupil ratio in a school to increase the level of supervision to professional levels. In many U.S. schools, one principal supervises twenty teachers. No other profession has that kind of supervisory ratio. A big law firm generally has a one-to-one ratio between a junior lawyer and a partner in a firm; accountants, one-to-five; newspaper reporters, at most one-to-seven or one-to-eight. No place has a one-to-twenty ratio except in education. So, to improve the quality of teachers to professional levels, much more administrative overhead is needed in education.

Ravitch asked Bernstein what the retention rate is for teaching fellows. Speaking in terms of the New York Teaching Fellows program, she said three years. Of those who start teaching, the retention rate through the first year was 85 percent. About 90 percent of those return for a second year. In one group, Bernstein thought that about 65 percent of the original participants returned for a third year, which is a little higher relative to traditional teachers. The New York program's teachers are predominantly in hard-to-staff schools in the Bronx and central Brooklyn, where the rates are comparable.

Bernstein called the situation in many cases good attrition. The people who leave early often do so because teaching is not for them. Their leaving is not surprising because they have other options and opportunities in their lives. The program is not hanging on to people who do not have the right mix with education.

Caroline M. Hoxby wanted to hear more about vacancy rules. For instance, she asked, when schools and districts know that they have a vacancy, how does that affect teacher hiring?

Hoxby went on to discuss what would happen if undergraduate programs in education were eliminated. People, she said, argued that such an action would cause a restriction of the supply because then the standards for becoming a teacher would have to increase. But she did not agree that that necessarily would happen. In the Canadian system, for example, students are expected to get an undergraduate degree in a normal subject area and then apply to a program and become a teacher after having gone through either a one- or two-year program. They attend more years of school in total, and they emerge with an undergraduate degree in something that is respected and is going to be useful outside of teaching. So these students have not sunk a huge amount of their education into a degree that may not be useful if they decide not to remain in teaching for the rest of their lives. No one in Canada who becomes a teacher has a degree that is useful only in teaching.

Hoxby said that she wished the unions had a greater vision of themselves as a profession. She does not understand why they cannot think about what it would be like to be the American Medical Association (AMA) or the American Bar Association instead of the teachers unions, to be like professional organizations whose members make considerably more money. They make more money, she posited, because they allow people to be paid on the basis of merit once they get into the profession. Admittedly, they are credentialing. Not everybody can just be a doctor; a license is required. But once a person is in the profession, he is not constantly supervised. He is expected to be entrepreneurial and is paid based on how well he does. Hoxby said she would rather be the head of the AMA than the head of a union covering people who do not get paid very much and do not have much prestige. So, she said, let people be paid differently and get paid more.

In addressing Hoxby's question about vacancies, Rhee said that, in most large urban school districts, the union contracts do not open a spot to a new hire until the transfer processes are complete. In many districts, the transfer process happens in July and takes upward of four to six weeks. Some cities and some unions have moved that time line up, to shorten it.

Another reason for delaying notice to new hires, Rhee said, is the reconstitution of schools. Often, the reconstitution of schools is not announced until near the opening of school. When school districts and union officials understand that a reconstitution is going to take place, no new teachers can be hired until the teachers in the reconstituted school have been placed elsewhere. In one district, for example, about four thousand people submitted applications, of whom about 75 percent were certified teachers. Six hundred of them were prescreened and ready to go out to principal interviews in the beginning of May. Not a single teacher contract was signed until August 12.

Hoxby then asked, What does a typical unionized suburban district do? Rhee said that the process happens much quicker in suburban districts as compared with urban districts. The transfer process might take place in March or April instead of July. Suburban districts also quicken the process by opening a position available for new hires after five days instead of waiting for weeks or months.

An unfortunate result, Rhee said, was that teachers rarely transfer to hard-to-staff schools. People want to transfer out of those schools and into more well-resourced schools. Few districts even try to direct some of the most highly qualified teachers into the schools that need them the most and within a quick time frame.

Picking up on what Rothstein said about how too little attention is paid to working conditions in schools, Eric A. Hanushek believes the issue has not been approached in a very analytical way. Furthermore, as others have pointed out, there are many unappealing aspects to teaching, which could be changed at little cost.

Hanushek is not convinced that reducing class size is the obvious way to address working conditions because the results from doing so are mixed. Class-size differences, for example, had nothing to do with where teachers in Texas went. Looking across districts at different salaries that are paid after adjusting for salaries in different areas, there is a slightly higher salary paid in districts with larger class size, but the salary differences are small. Teachers' salaries have fallen over time. Teachers apparently have felt that they could not get higher salaries and so they will take it in class-size and teacher-pupil ratio reductions.

John T. Wenders recounted how Ron Ehrenberg, in his book, said that 40 percent of the teaching in higher education is done by nontenure-track teachers. Yet lower education is automatically thought of as a place to have a career or to climb the career ladder. Right now, Wenders said, once people get past the first few years in education, it seems that they just hang on the grid and ride it to the top. But that is not true in higher education. There have always been part-timers, people who come in and teach one class. A whole area outside the career-type could vastly increase the supply of teachers and reduce the cost.

Adam F. Scrupski asked Bernstein if there was any variation in the retention rate by subject taught. She replied that the older teaching fellows tend to have higher dropout rates and men have higher dropout rates. The statistics carry over to math and science at the secondary level, because that is where many of these people are teaching.

Nesa Chapelle sought to explain why teachers unions do not act, for example, like the American Medical Association. The National Education Association (NEA) has 2.7 million members. The members, who are teachers, tell the NEA heads what to do. Furthermore, teachers, according to Chapelle, are a conservative group.

Teachers, she said, fall short in two areas: economics and politics. They are not savvy when it comes to economics. They are not savvy when it comes to politics. When the topic is teaching and money, teachers get uptight.

Solmon expressed great surprise at the notion that the NEA membership is not interested in politics. Chapelle reiterated that she was talking about teacher members. Solmon went on to say that, at an NEA national meeting a couple of years ago, the leadership offered a proposal on performance pay, and it was voted down. He reported that what he had heard most in the field was that the vote was not representative of teachers, many of whom want merit pay. According to Solmon, many teachers favor performance pay, but the union leadership will not allow it.

Susan Sclafani brought up the issue of certification. New York, for example, requires a master's degree because it says that teaching is a learned profession and one has to have a master's degree to be learned. Yet, as economists have pointed out, this is a major disincentive to people coming into the field. They have to think about spending the time and the money to complete a requirement that they do not see as useful or meaningful to them. So, it is clearly not making them more learned. Sclafani said that the state board of education in New York, and in other places, must be convinced that requiring a master's is an inappropriate way to limit the number of people coming into the field. If more people came into education, they would then find out what they needed to know and seek out ways of learning those things, through either a degree program or a nondegree program. She holds that requiring a master's upfront is counterproductive.

Sclafani advocates a change in perspective: Stop thinking only about the people who enter teaching as a career and stop considering it a failure if only 60 percent are still in the profession at year three. Enough must be done to prepare teachers, they need to get the subject matter knowledge that they can impart to the kids, and their training programs should focus on the issues of classroom management that are so critical to their initial success. Teaching strategies that work would increase the number of successful people in their first, second, and third year, even if they do not have a great abundance of charisma.

Houston, Sclafani said, imported Teach for America's training program so that its students in summer school—while learning how to teach—could interact with the program's well-educated, curious, enthusiastic staff. Although Teach for America participants had been in Houston for only two years, Sclafani expressed her belief that the contribution they made was worth having them, despite the short time frame. They inspired children. They encouraged young children whom others had perhaps ignored or had decided could not be successful. And, as a result, the kids had a sense of personal success that they had not had before. What matters is not how long people are there but what they do when they are there. Sclafani advocates using funds to support them, not require them to go through a set of items that somebody has ticked off for them to complete. The result, she said, would be more exciting people in classrooms working with children.

Deborah Meier noted that a school is a collective community of adults. It must have a core of people who see themselves as the center of a scholarly, intellectual community that they are inducting young people into. A school that is a strong community of adults, Meier believes, also holds adults in schools; the school itself is a learning center for the adults. It should be a powerful community of learners. The adults are interested in what they are doing. They are excited by it. It is not just the kids but it is the entire community that draws them in and holds them there. Meier thinks that not enough attention is paid to that aspect of teaching.

In terms of cost, the issue that Rothstein raised, Meier said that making the school site the center of the education of teachers will pay off in many different ways. Furthermore, some resources may become available if the training in the school makes people not want to leave.

Leslie Fritz voiced her opinion that one of the biggest concerns about alternative route programs is that often people without any real classroom time begin serving as the teacher of record while they are receiving on-the-job training. She asks whether this situation is all right, especially considering the ongoing conversations about the importance of content knowledge and content education. However, what makes these alternative route programs so successful is the emphasis on process and pedagogy, within the school and with the support of the professionals themselves.

Alvin Sanoff then offered a few comments. He said that a certain amount of turnover in teaching is clearly good. However, constantly training new people to come into the profession is costly. A debate is ongoing about whether teaching is a profession or not. Even if teaching is not a career, is it all right that people come and go for two or three years? On a case-by-case basis, it is fine, but, on a macro basis, real and substantial costs accrue.

In response to Bernstein's comment that the people who are leaving are those with choices, Sanoff suggested that the implicit message is that the best people have options so they bail out and the system is left with the rest. Sanoff also weighed in on the comparison between the NEA and the AMA. He noted that lawyers and doctors are not civil servants or public employees, while teachers are. He indicated that a more appropriate comparison may be with doctors who work for the federal government. According to Sanoff, they are locked into the same kind of structured pay scale as schoolteachers are.

Robert Spillane sought to inject some political reality into the discussion. Data can be analyzed and plans researched, he said, but the general consensus is that merit pay throughout the nation is a failure. As a policy, it just does not work.

Spillane then related a personal experience. Teachers in Fairfax County, Virginia, approved a merit pay plan that gave teachers up to a $5,000 bonus each year for three years. The plan put principals back into the classroom as educational leaders instead of building managers. A side effect of rewarding teachers is that positions need to be eliminated. The county, with a staff of around twelve thousand teachers, had never let a teacher go for lack of competence in the classroom. Over an eight-year period when the plan was being implemented, one hundred teachers a year on average were dismissed. Then, the members of the board of education were elected, no longer appointed. With the electoral process comes extremists from different ends of the political spectrum. With teacher morale down, the unions decided that teachers should be treated the same and pushed to end the program. The merit pay component of the $1.3 billion budget cost about $10 million a year. It became too expensive, so the rug got pulled. The program was a total failure but a great experiment.

The public, Spillane believes, is willing to pay for great teachers and wants to get rid of those who are not. However, when the going gets tough, the first thing to go is merit pay because of the politics of the issue. When fifteen hundred people in a meeting say that the budget is too high and they are going after merit pay, the elected officials tend to get a little nervous.

Michael Podgursky made an observation about hiring practices. He said that hiring is much simpler at charter schools and private schools. Dysfunctional hiring structures should be decentralized.

Frederick M. Hess spoke about how absolutely miserable the information technology and the infrastructures and the processes of hiring are in large urban districts. One of the problems is that many of those running human resources departments were once seventh-grade English teachers, have no background in human resources, and have no technology at their disposal.

He expressed his surprise that the attrition rates are not higher than they are. The compensation and promotion system in place rewards mediocrity. An entrepreneurial or ambitious twenty-five-year-old probably will not look for a career in K–12 teaching. There are not many rewards there. So the fact that they are sticking around is somewhat surprising to Hess. Furthermore, he said, the real test of alternative models of recruitment is how many teachers are kept in systems that create incentives and offer rewards for hard work, for effectiveness, for doing a good job with the kids. Determining that would lead to a much firmer understanding of how many people are likely to stay around for five or ten years. If high achievers are brought into a system that accepts low achievement, they are likely to depart at a high rate.

Regarding bonus pay and career ladders, Hess noted how tepid and timid the experiments in K–12 education have been. Five thousand dollars is an 8 or 10 percent bonus for many teachers and does not create large changes in behavior. However, that does not mean the educators are not responsive to incentives. Instead, it means that the incentives have to be large, ongoing, and built into the fabric of the profession.